GEORGIA

OPEN
LOCAL
GOVERNMENT 2

How crucial legislative changes impact the way municipalities do business in Canada

M. RICK O'CONNOR

from the publishers of
Municipal World

GEORGIAN COLLEGE
ORILLIA CAMPUS LRC
825 MEMORIAL AVE.
P.O. BOX 2316,
ORILLIA, ONTARIO
L3V 6S2

©Municipal World Inc., 2004

All rights reserved. No part of this publication may be reproduced, stored in a retrieval system, or transmitted, in any form or by any means, electronic, mechanical, photocopying, recording, or otherwise, without the prior written permission of Municipal World Inc.

Canadian Cataloguing in Publication Data

The National Library of Canada has catalogued this publication as follows:

O'Connor, Michael Richard, 1959 —
Open local government 2: how crucial legislative changes impact the way municipalities do business in Canada / M. Rick O'Connor

Includes bibliographical references and index.
ISBN 0-919779-71-9

1. Municipal corporations – Canada. I. Title. II. Title: Open local government two.

KEO869.O36 2004   342.71'09   C2003-907179-0

KF5305.O36 2004

Published in Canada by
Municipal World Inc.
Box 399, Station Main
St. Thomas, Ontario N5P 3V3
(Union, Ontario N0L 2L0)

mwadmin@municipalworld.com
www.municipalworld.com
ITEM 0030

Municipal World — Reg. T.M. in Canada, Municipal World Inc.

This book represents the personal opinions of the author and is intended to be used as a guide. Legislation is subject to change and caution should be exercised to ensure that a check is made for amendments to the statutes. The services of a lawyer should be retained in all circumstances where legal advice is considered necessary.

Dedicated to Kyara and Brayden

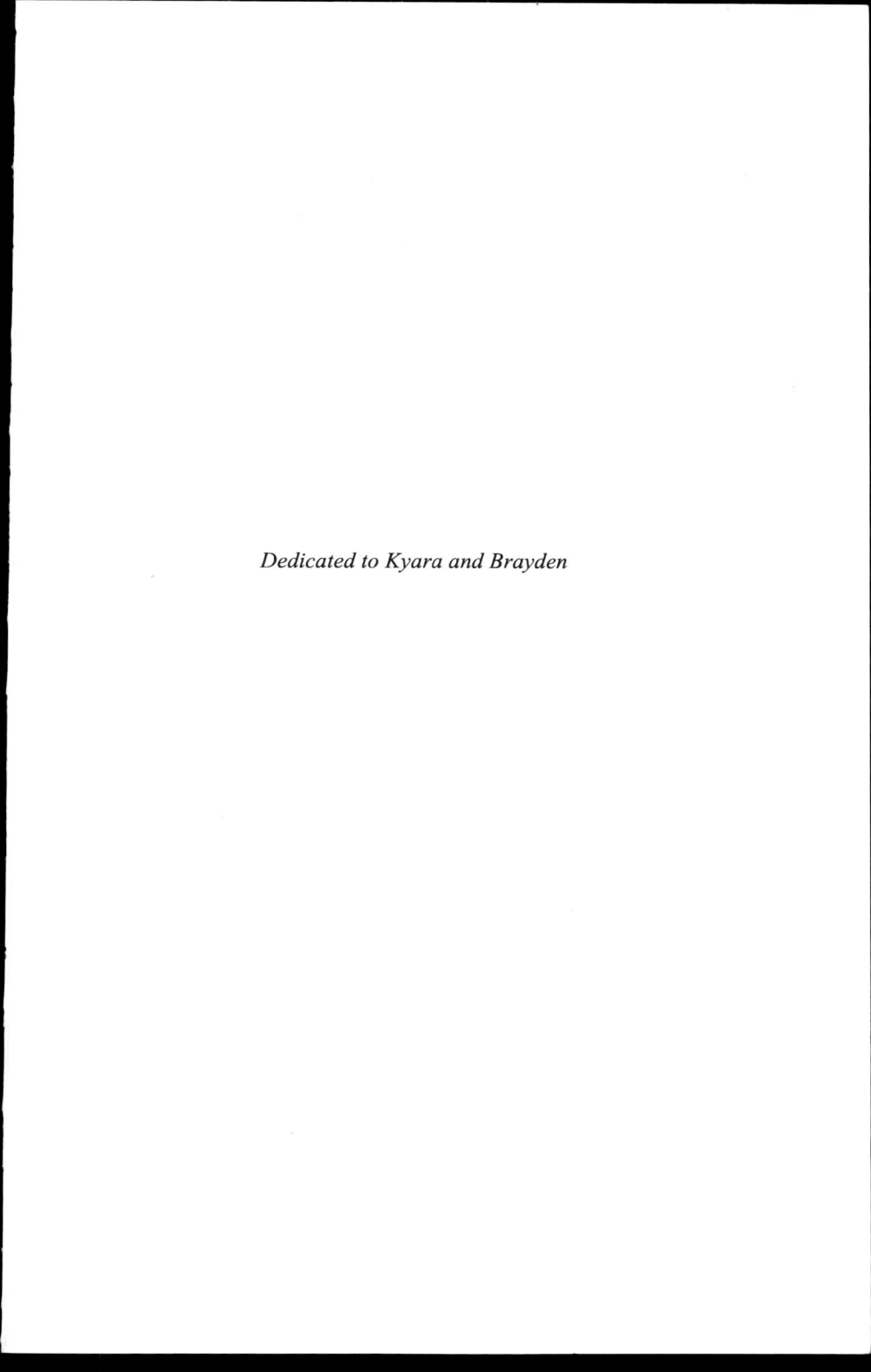

PREFACE TO SECOND EDITION

In revising and updating the text from the first edition of *Open Local Government*, I could not help but acknowledge the numerous and significant changes that had occurred in both my personal life and professional life over the past eight years.

On the one hand, I became a grandfather for the first time, an invigorating and joyous experience to be sure. At the opposite end of the personal spectrum, I joined the entire municipal community in mourning the loss of Michael J. Smither. More than just a publisher or co-author, Michael was not only a friend but also a mentor to me, and he will be greatly missed.

On the professional side, the amalgamation of the City of Ottawa in 2001 resulted in my becoming the Deputy City Clerk and Legal Counsel for the fourth largest municipality in Canada. This change increased my appreciation for those dedicated public administrators who have long endeavoured to achieve the best form of open and accountable local government for their respective municipal councils or local boards.

More significantly, the Ontario Government passed Bill 111, the *Municipal Act, 2001*. This legislation came into force on January 1, 2003, replacing the century-and-a-half old *Municipal Act*. This new statute was a prime motivator for preparing this second edition – not only because it repealed so many provincial statutes, including the never-enacted *Local Government Disclosure of Interest Act, 1994*, but also for its introduction of various new legal concepts to municipalities, including "natural person powers" and the 10 "spheres of jurisdiction."

Therefore, all of the primary statutory citations in the second edition with respect to Ontario will be to the *Municipal Act, 2001*. In addition, reference will also be made to corresponding municipal legislation in other Canadian provinces and territories. As always, for legal opinions, reference should be had to the official statute in question and to your lawyer.

Of similar importance have been the numerous rulings of various courts and administrative tribunals involving local governments across Canada. These decisions have helped demonstrate some of the legal principles set out in the first edition of *Open Local Government*, and are useful tools in measuring the growing liability that can affect municipalities and local boards. A case in point is the June 10, 2003 decision of the Ontario Court of Appeal in *Halpern et al. v. Attorney General of Canada et al.*, which concerned a *Charter* challenge to the common law definition of marriage.[1] Briefly, a three-member panel of the appellate court upheld an earlier decision of the Divisional Court, which determined that the common law definition of "marriage" (requiring it to be between one man and one woman) offended the applicants' (eight same-sex couples) right to equality under subsection 15 (1) of the *Canadian Charter of Rights and Freedoms*, on the basis of sexual orientation. The Court of Appeal declared the traditional definition of marriage to be invalid, and reformulated it to be "the voluntary union for life of two persons to the exclusion of all others." In the absence of a further appeal on this or other similar judicial rulings,[2] as well as the July 2003 reference of the draft Bill on marriage to legally recognize same-sex unions to the Supreme Court of Canada in order to ensure its constitutionality,[3] readers should assess the effects of this evolving area of the law when considering any rules for married couples like those discussed in Chapter 10, Members' Code of Conduct.

As with most worthwhile endeavours in life, writing a book is really a collaborative process involving many family members, friends and colleagues. As such, I wish to express my sincere appreciation to the following people for their tireless efforts on various drafts of this edition: to my Administrative Assistant, Sharon Pagé; Tim Marc and Meg Steele of the City of Ottawa's Legal Services Branch; Peter-John Sidebottom, Manager, Municipal Governance and Structures Branch, Ontario Ministry of Municipal Affairs and Housing; as well as Susan Gardner and Mary Tully, the editors of Municipal World. Most of all, I would like to thank my wife, Claire, whose limitless patience and unbridled support enable me to undertake such challenges.

M. Rick O'Connor

---

1 [2003] O.J. No. 2268.

2 Similar decisions were reached in Quebec, *Hendricks v. Quebec (Attorney General)*, [2002] J.Q. No. 3816, and British Columbia, *EGALE Canada Inc. v. British Columbia (Attorney General)*, [2003] B.C.J. No. 994.

3 See Ministry of Justice Press Release, "Minister of Justice Announces Referral to the Supreme Court of Canada" (July 17, 2003), concerning the draft Bill known as *The Act Respecting Certain Aspects of Legal Capacity for Marriage*.

Contents

Preface to second edition v

Chapter 1
ONTARIO'S MUNICIPAL ACT, 2001 1
   Municipal Act Origins 2
   Recent Reform Attempts 4
   Municipal Act, 2001 6
   Strange New Powers 7
   Purpose Clause 7
   Consultation 8
   Natural Person Powers 9
   Ten Spheres of Jurisdiction 12
   Same Old Restrictions 13
   General Restrictions 14
   Specific Restrictions 14
   General Observations 16
   Regulations 17
   Judicial Interpretation 19

Chapter 2
OPEN VS. CLOSED MEETINGS 23
   Common Law 23
   Municipal Initiatives 25
   Municipal Act, 2001 29
   Mandatory Closing 31
   Discretionary Closings 31
   Procedure 34
   Meeting Closed Under Another Act 34
   Meetings Case Law 39
   Private Briefings = Meetings 39
   Closed Meetings = Bad Faith 40
   Closed Meetings = Cost$ 42
   The Future 43

Chapter 3
LOCAL BOARD MEETINGS 47
   Police Services Board 48
   Public Library Board 50

  School Board. 52
  Conservation Authorities 54
  Conclusions 55

Chapter 4
STATUTORY PROCEDURES. 59
  Inaugural Meeting of Council 59
  Special Meetings of Council 60
  Head of Council 60
  Explusion for Improper Conduct 61
  Members of Council 64
  Quorum 65
  Public Notice and Consultation 66
  Open Voting 67
  Closed Voting 69
  Case Study. 70
  Appeal of a Vote – Abuse of Process 71
  Ultra Vires. 73
  Other Relevant Statutes 75

Chapter 5
PROCEDURE BY-LAW 77
  Parliamentary Procedure 78
  Mandatory Procedure By-laws. 79
  Inclusion of Statutory Procedures 80
  Procedure By-law Structure 82
  Conduct of Members 84
  Waiver Clause 84
  Special Meetings 85
  Violations 85
  Prayer 87
  Revisions 89
  Conclusions 89

Chapter 6
SALE OF SURPLUS LAND. 91
  Background 91
  Application of the Municipal Act, 2001 93
  Property Disposal By-law 94
  Appraisals 95

Exemptions from Appraisals 97
Public Register 98
Compliance Certificates 99
Judicial Review 101
Conclusions. 103

Chapter 7
BIAS: OPEN VS. CLOSED MINDS 105
Pre-1990: Reasonable Apprehension of Bias Test 106
Post-1990: Amenable-to-Persuasion Test 109
Recent Case Law. 112
Other Administrative Boards 118
Conclusions. 119

Chapter 8
LIBEL, SLANDER & DEFAMATION 121
Double-edged Sword 122
Categories of Defamation 122
Elements of Proof 124
Exceptions - Exclusions 125
Defences 127
Justification 127
Fair Comment 129
Consent 130
Privilege 131
Absolute Privilege 131
Qualified Privilege 133
Retraction 138
Malice 138
Municipal Corporations 139
Charter of Rights and Freedoms 141
Conclusions. 141

Chapter 9
NEGLIGENT MISREPRESENTATION 145
Common Law 146
Hercules Management Ltd. v. Ernst & Young 147
Lakefield (Village) v. Black 148
Moin v. Blue Mountains (Town) 150
Wozniak v. Erin (Town) 152

David v. Halifax (Regional Municipality). 152
Conclusions. 154

Chapter 10
MEMBERS' CODE OF CONDUCT 155
Ontario's Legislative Experience 156
Conflict of Interest. 156
Nepotism. 158
Municipal Initiatives 160
Members' Code of Conduct 162
Developing a Code 162
Elements of a Code. 164
Gifts and Benefits 166
Nepotism. 173
Insider/Confidential Information 177
Use of Local Government Property 180
Implementation/Enforcement. 182
Conclusions. 183

Chapter 11
CRIMINAL CODE 185
Breach of Trust 186
Municipal Corruption 190
Selling or Purchasing Office 194
Influencing or Negotiating Appointments. 195
Secret Commissions 197
Theft and Fraud 200
Penalties 200
Criminal Conviction 201
Related Offences. 203
Conclusions. 204

Chapter 12
FREEDOM OF INFORMATION 205
Ontario's Legislation 206
Purposes of the Act - An Interesting Balancing Routine . . . 209
Designation of Head 210
Delegation of Powers 212
Access to Records 213
Obligation to Disclose 216

    Compelling Public Interest. 218
    Access Procedure 221
    Duty of the Head. 223
    Frivolous or Vexatious Requests 223
    Appeal Procedure 227
    Conclusions. 228

Chapter 13
PROTECTION OF PRIVACY 229
    Case Law Review 230
    Mandatory Exemptions 231
    Relations with Governments – ss. 9 (1) and 9 (2) 231
    Third Party Information – ss. 10 (1) and 10 (2) 233
    Discretionary Exemptions 236
    Draft By-laws or Draft Private Bills –
    ss. 6 (1) (a) and 6 (2) (a). 238
    Record that Reveals Substance
    of Closed Meeting – ss. 6 (1) (b) and 6 (2) (b) 240
    Advice/Recommendations of Officer,
    Employee or Consultant – s. 7 248
    Law Enforcement – s. 8 250
    Economic and Other Interests – s. 11 253
    Solicitor-Client Privilege – s. 12 255
    Danger to Safety or Health – s. 13 256
    Information Soon to be Published – s. 15 258
    Personal Privacy Exemption – s. 14 259
    General Exceptions to Exemptions – ss. 5 and 16 266
    Labour Relations Exemption – s. 52 266
    Privacy on the Defensive 270

Chapter 14
ACCESS & PRIVACY 275
    Protection of Privacy 276
    Disclosure of Personal Information 277
    Records of Member 285
    Custody and/or Control 286
    Officer or Employee 290
    Personal/Constituency Records 292
    Physical Location of Records 293

Head of Council – Chair of Local Board 297
Policy of the Institution 299
Custody and Control Case Law 299
Appendix A – City Of Mississauga
Elected Officials Records Policy 306

Chapter 15
PUBLIC ACCOUNTABILITY PUZZLE 309
Putting the Pieces Together 309
Toronto Board of Trade Report 310
Open vs. Closed Meetings 312
Members' Conduct 316
FOI vs. Privacy 317
Some Final Thoughts 318

ABOUT THE AUTHOR 321

Chapter 1
ONTARIO'S MUNICIPAL ACT, 2001[1]

> *I am thy creature, and I will be even mild and docile to my natural lord and king, if thou wilt also perform thy part, which thou owest me. Oh Frankenstein, be not equitable to every other and trample upon me alone, to whom thy justice and even thy clemency and affection, is most due. Remember, that I am thy creature; I ought to be thy Adam, but I am rather the fallen angel, whom thou drivest from joy for no misdeed. Everywhere I see bliss, from which I alone have been irrevocably excluded. I was benevolent and good; misery made me a fiend. Make me happy and I shall again be virtuous.*
>
> Frankenstein by Mary Wollstonecraft Shelley (1816)

In the judicial realm, Canadian municipalities have traditionally been described as "creatures of statute" due to their dependence upon provincial legislation, not only to perform specific functions, but to exist at all. In light of this fact, Mary Wollstonecraft Shelley's first novel, *Frankenstein*, which depicts the unbridled desire of Dr. Frankenstein to create life from the dead, constitutes an appropriate metaphor when discussing the traditional, prescriptive legislation that gave life to local governments across Canada. However, the 1990s bore witness to a number of legislative reforms that sought to assist municipal councils and local boards to develop into more mature, more responsible and accountable governments. The first of these innovations occurred in Alberta with the passage of the *Municipal Government Act, 1994*.[2] This unique statute sought to modernize local government by shedding the prescriptive and paternalistic legislative approach that most provinces had applied to regulate municipal councils and local boards in favour of a more flexible methodology.

---

[1] This chapter was derived from "Frankenstein Redux: Ontario's New Municipal Act, 2001," presented on January 25, 2002 at the Ontario Bar Association 2002 Institute of Continuing Legal Education conference in Toronto, Ontario.

[2] S.A. 1994, c. M-26.1.

In Alberta, this new approach included granting municipalities the powers of a natural person and enabling councils to enact by-laws within broad areas of jurisdiction. In the years that followed, other provinces introduced legislative reforms of varying degrees: Manitoba, *Municipal Act*, S.M. 1996, c. 58; British Columbia, *Local Government Act*, R.S.B.C. 1996, c. 323; Nova Scotia, *Municipal Government Act*, S.N.S. 1998, c. 18; Yukon Territory, *Municipal Act*, S.Y. 1998, c. 19; and Newfoundland, *Municipalities Act*, S.N. 1999, c. M.24.

Finally, on January 1, 2003, those statutory creatures in Ontario were, for the first time, endowed with certain "natural person" powers, thus duplicating the feat of Shelley's hero, Victor Frankenstein. It remains to be seen, however, whether municipal governments will gain happiness and virtue as a result of this metamorphosis.

On December 12, 2001, Royal Assent was granted to Bill 111, better known as the *Municipal Act, 2001*, c. 25. This first chapter will provide an overview of the new legislation, focusing on a number of specific issues, including the much-heralded new natural person powers, as well as the various governmental powers entrusted to municipalities, and examine whether or not these truly are "the tools ... need[ed] to tackle the challenges of governing in the 21st century."[3]

Municipal Act Origins

In order to better appreciate the effect that the *Municipal Act, 2001* may ultimately have on the system of local government in Ontario, it is necessary, however briefly, to examine the origins and evolution of the political system that produced the first comprehensive *Municipal Act* in Canada over 150 years ago.

Although a historical perspective is often illuminating, the emphasis in this section is not on the history *per se*, but rather on the lessons that we can learn about the evolution of municipal government and thereby

---

[3] Remarks by the Honourable Chris Hodgson, Minister of Municipal Affairs and Housing, in the Ontario Legislature.Legislative Assembly of Ontario, *Official Report of Debates (Hansard)*, October 18, 2001.

better understand not only the present situation in Ontario, but most other provinces, as well.[4]

The enabling legislation that governs Ontario's municipalities was first enacted almost 20 years before the Confederation of Canada in 1867. The development of the local government system in 18th century Ontario (or Upper Canada) evolved slowly over many decades, but some obvious and significant influences should be mentioned.

In the years before, during and after the American War of Independence (1775-1783), many of those loyal to Great Britain formed a steady flow of immigrants who moved from the American colonies to British North America. This continuous migration of United Empire Loyalists and the resultant increase in population was accompanied by growing service demands, which exacerbated the need for some form of local government.

Loyalists brought with them their prior political experience in colonial municipal affairs, being the so-called "town meeting," a form of local autonomy they sought to introduce to their new homeland. In the decades that followed, the British response to such demands for municipal government reforms was to provide extremely limited advancements. These included the introduction of the Courts of Quarter Sessions in 1788, the *Constitution Act of 1791*, and the *Parish and Town Officers Act of 1793*. Further legislative reforms in the decades that followed included the first election of school trustees in 1816, and the first board of police established in Brockville in 1832. In response to such gradual changes, the more radical reformers rose up in rebellion against the Crown in 1837.

Originally introduced into the legislature in 1843, the first comprehensive municipal legislation was only enacted in 1849 when the second reform coalition of Robert Baldwin and Louis-Hippolyte Lafontaine was successfully re-elected. Formally called *An Act To Provide One General Law For The Erection Of Municipal Councils And The Establishment and Regulation of Police in and for the Several Counties, Cities, Towns*

---

[4] For more detailed information on the historical origins of Ontario's local government, see: C. Richard Tindal and Susan Nobes Tindal, *Local Government in Canada*, 5th ed. (Nelson: Canada, 2000) at pp. 18-24; Romaine K. Ross, *Local Government in Ontario*, 2nd ed. (Canada Law Book Co: Toronto, 1962) at pp. 1-13; and Ian MacF. Rogers, *The Law of Canadian Municipal Corporations*, 2nd ed. (Carswell: Toronto, 2002) at pp. 34.36.2.

and Townships and Villages In Upper Canada, it has come to be known as the *Baldwin Act*.[5]

This legislation radically altered the system of local government in Ontario by repealing approximately 55 Acts related to various government functions in favour of a single, consolidated municipal statute. Whereas many municipalities had little or no authority prior to 1849, the *Baldwin Act* endowed them with a considerable range of legislative powers, formerly held by either the Courts of Quarter Sessions and/or the District Councils. Occasionally described as the *Magna Carta* of municipal government in Ontario, this statute also increased the legislative powers of most municipal councils to encompass various matters, including:

- provision for municipal officials and officers to be appointed by council;
- an increase in local powers of taxation and licensing; and
- an extension of the electoral franchise, while lowering the property qualifications for potential office-holders.

Recent Reform Attempts

Over the course of the last 150 years, Ontario's *Municipal Act* was often amended. Unfortunately, the various deletions, revisions and additions to the statute were often made in a piece-meal fashion to address the "issue of the day." The end result was a body of legislation that was lengthy, complex, and in the minds of many municipal observers, far too prescriptive to operate effectively in the new millennium.

In 1994, the enactment of Alberta's *Municipal Government Act* coincided with the Association of Municipalities of Ontario (AMO) release of its *Ontario Charter: A Proposed Bill of Rights for Local Government*. At its annual general meeting in August of that year, an AMO representative described the legislative situation in relatively bleak terms:

> The present legislation is too prescriptive. It does not express a purpose, a goal or objective. It describes the responsibilities as a series of tasks. We need new and innovative ways to meet political and financial demands in governance and service delivery.[6]

---

5 S.U.C. 1849, c. 81.

6 Cited in "The Ontario Charter: Beyond the Debate," *Municipal World*, October 1994, p. 14.

In response, the Throne Speech for the newly-elected Progressive Conservative Government on September 27, 1995, stated that the "government is committed to introducing a new *Municipal Act*, and this session will launch consultations with municipalities."[7] Some of those consultations took the form of a massive review in 1996 undertaken by the "Who Does What Panel," chaired by David Crombie. On December 6, 1996, the minister received the panel's general recommendations on governance across Ontario. That same date also saw the release of numerous recommendations by the municipal administration sub-panel, chaired by Dr. Peter Meyboom, in a report simply called "Stage 2 of the Municipal Reform Initiative." Primary among the sub-panel's recommendations was a proposal to overhaul the entire *Municipal Act*. In fact, the recommendations went so far as to propose a "new legislative framework" that would give municipalities two new types of powers:

1. the powers of a natural person to enable them to carry out their corporate and administrative activities; and

2. governmental powers to allow them to make and enforce by-laws and to raise revenues within [13] broad areas of responsibility.[8]

By March 1997, the Ontario government had issued "A Proposed Legislative Framework," a consultation paper that included a new, draft *Municipal Act*, granting municipalities broad powers with respect to service delivery, regulatory activities and various administrative arrangements.[9] However, these powers would be subject to express limitations set out in the new legislation. In February 1998, the Ministry of Municipal Affairs and Housing released a draft statute entitled "A Proposed New Municipal Act" for consultation purposes.[10] This version of the legislation proposed a more streamlined statute, emphasizing flexibility for municipalities accompanied by various checks and balances. The document also introduced the concept of municipal "spheres of ju-

---

7   Speech from the Throne by the Honourable Henry N.R. Jackman, Lieutenant Governor of the Province of Ontario, Legislative Assembly of Ontario, *Official Report of Debates (Hansard)*, September 27 1995.

8   "Stage 2 of the Municipal Reform Initiative," correspondence from Dr. Peter Meyboom to the Honourable Al Leach, Minister of Municipal Affairs and Housing, (December 6, 1996).

9   "A Proposed Legislative Framework, White Paper," Minister of Municipal Affairs and Housing (March 1997).

10 "A Proposed New Municipal Act," Ministry of Municipal Affairs and Housing (February 1998).

risdiction." These 13 spheres were set out in a general format to enable municipal councils to deal with unique circumstances and to avoid amendments to the general enabling legislation every time a new local issue arose. In addition, the draft legislation also proposed that Ontario municipalities be given the powers of a "natural person." Although this particular proposal would not allow municipalities to provide a service for which they did not have the necessary legislative authority, it would enable councils to conduct their day-to-day business without the need for specific legislative authority. The natural person powers included the ability to enter into agreements, to purchase land and equipment, to hire municipal employees, and to delegate administrative responsibilities to various committees, staff members or other bodies such as boards of management. The lengthy consultation process resulted in the provincial government receiving over 300 written comments and submissions on the legislative proposals.

Towards the end of 2000, the ministry initiated further discussions with the various municipal and business stakeholders regarding the new *Municipal Act*. In fact, facilitated consultations arose with respect to a number of specific issues including licensing, user fees and a municipality's authority to establish corporations.

On August 20, 2001, the Honourable Chris Hodgson, Minister of Municipal Affairs and Housing, addressed AMO members at their annual general meeting in Toronto. It was there that the minister released "New Directions: A New Municipal Act For Ontario."[11] The minister assured those in attendance that this was not another consultation paper, but rather a document that set out the framework and key principles of the new legislation.[12]

Municipal Act, 2001

On October 18, 2001, the minister moved First Reading of Bill 111, the *Municipal Act, 2001*, in the provincial legislature. Before Christmas that year, the Act had received Royal Assent, to come into full force on January 1, 2003.

---

[11] "New Directions: A New Municipal Act for Ontario," Ministry of Municipal Affairs and Housing (August 2001).

[12] Remarks by the Honourable Chris Hodgson, Minister of Municipal Affairs and Housing, to the Association of Municipalities of Ontario annual conference, Toronto, Ontario (August 20, 2001).

Chapter 1
ONTARIO'S MUNICIPAL ACT, 2001

As a framework statute, the *Municipal Act, 2001* is meant to provide the appropriate structure, governance and powers for municipalities to function in Ontario. More than 300 pages in length and comprised of almost 500 sections, the Act is subdivided into 18 distinct parts. Perhaps most significantly, the legislation encompasses the following five main policy directions of the Ministry of Municipal Affairs and Housing:

1. enhanced flexibility for innovative municipal service delivery;
2. improved accountability to the public;
3. promotion of well-administered, economically-healthy municipalities;
4. a more comprehensive, understandable, better organized statute; and
5. proposals that address key concerns raised during consultations.

All of that prompts the crucial question: "What's really new in the *Municipal Act, 2001*?"

STRANGE NEW POWERS

During the last few years, a certain amount of rhetoric regarding the ongoing need to improve the ailing municipal-provincial relationship has emanated from various quarters.[13] Therefore, it is worth noting that Part I (sections 1-7) of the *Municipal Act, 2001* brings this relationship issue to the forefront. The definitions set out in section 1 are followed by two key provisions that are, no doubt, intended to improve the municipal-provincial relationship.

Purpose Clause

Firstly, section 2 provides an express recognition that municipalities "are created by the Province of Ontario to be responsible and accountable governments with respect to matters within their jurisdiction." Still creatures of statute, the provision goes on to identify that each municipality is given powers and duties to undertake purposes that include:

---

13 For example, see the AMO News Release "Queen's Park on Wrong Track" (April 27, 2001), which stated that 75% of respondent members surveyed found the municipal-provincial relationship unsatisfactory.

(a) providing the services and other things that the municipality considers are necessary or desirable for the municipality;

(b) managing and preserving the public assets of the municipality;

(c) fostering the current and future economic, social and environmental well-being of the municipality; and

(d) delivering and participating in provincial programs and initiatives.

It is difficult to predict the substantive effect that this "purpose" provision may ultimately have on municipalities. Similar in nature to a legislative preamble, it is also unclear what sanctions would arise should an alleged breach of this section occur. For example, while one of the express purposes of municipalities is "delivering and participating in provincial programs and initiatives," it is unknown, from this section, what will transpire if a municipality fails to meet this statutory objective.

Careful note should also be taken of the precise wording of this provision. The express statement is that the powers and duties of a municipality are those given under this statute "and many other Acts." This is an early and important sign that municipalities must continue to be vigilant of and comply with other provincial statutes. Section 2 will be revisited during a review of the restrictions contained within and external to the *Municipal Act, 2001* as discussed in the General Observations section below.

Consultation

Subsection 3 (1) of the legislation provides that the "Province of Ontario endorses the principle of ongoing consultation between the Province and municipalities in relation to matters of mutual interest." In addition, subsection 3 (2) states that the ministry "shall initiate a review of this Act before the end of 2007 and thereafter within five years of the end of the previous review." This express endorsement of the principle of consultation did not exist in the former *Municipal Act*. Ultimately, the statutory requirement to review this Act in five-year cycles may be one of the most significant provisions in this entire legislative exercise. If undertaken in earnest, it could provide a reasonable timetable within which to resolve outstanding statutory problems in a manner mindful of the entire Act.

On December 19, 2001, a Memorandum of Understanding (MOU) on provincial-municipal consultation was signed by the Minister of Municipal Affairs and Housing and the president of AMO.[14] Describing the document as "much more than a symbolic agreement," the minister said the MOU was a "key element in a new, more mature, more productive and cooperative relationship between municipalities and the province." The MOU establishes the protocols and procedures that will satisfy the principle of ongoing consultation as required by section 3. The MOU took effect on January 1, 2002 and is scheduled to expire on December 31, 2004, but contains a three-year renewal clause, as well as a review provision. The scheduling of meetings will be mutually agreed upon by the parties, as will the agendas. Finally, consultation with AMO under the terms of MOU "does not preclude the province from conducting other consultations directly with the municipal sector."

There is a precedent established elsewhere in Canada for such an agreement. In British Columbia, a Protocol of Recognition was executed between the province and the Union of British Columbia Municipalities in 1996.[15] The principles of recognition and consultation set out therein appear to have been influential in guiding the development of subsequent municipal legislation in that province.[16]

Natural Person Powers

In accordance with the former *Municipal Act*, municipalities were statutory creatures functionally limited by the express terms of their enabling legislation. In general, if the right to undertake a particular course of action was not expressly permitted by the statute, then it was not within the municipality's authority to act. Although this fundamental principle has been re-stated in numerous judicial decisions, Mr. Justice Iacobucci's comments in the Supreme Court of Canada's 1993 decision in *R. v. Greenbaum*, were succinct and to the point: "Municipalities are entirely the creatures of provincial statutes. Accordingly, they can only exercise those powers which are explicitly conferred upon them by a provincial statute."[17]

---

14 Memorandum of Understanding between the Association of Municipalities of Ontario and the Province of Ontario as represented by the Minister of Municipal Affairs and Housing (December 19, 2001).

15 Protocol of Recognition Amongst: Government of British Columbia and Union of British Columbia Municipalities (September 18, 1996).

16 For example, see "Municipalities and the New Local Government Act - Making the Most of Municipal Act Reform," British Columbia, Ministry of Municipal Affairs (2001).

17 [1993] 1 S.C.R. 674 at 687.

In commenting on the nature of municipal governments, the Supreme Court recently reiterated this principle in the 2000 decision, *Pacific National Investments Ltd. v. Victoria (City)*:

> Municipal governments are democratic institutions through which the people of a community embark upon and structure a life together. Even in this context, however, nobody can challenge the proposition that municipal governments are creatures of the legislature – a municipal government has only those powers granted to it by provincial legislation:
>
>> [TRANSLATION] A municipality is a creature of statute and has only those powers that have been expressly delegated to it or that are directly derived from the powers so delegated ...
>>
>> (J. Hétu, Y. Duplessis and D. Pakenham, Droit municipal: Principles généraux et contentieux (1998), at p. 13; *Immeubles Port Louis Ltée v. Lafontaine (Village)*, [1991] 1 S.C.R. 326 at 346).[18]

Furthermore, in the 1992 case of *Magical Waters Fountains Ltd. v. Sarnia (City)*, the Ontario Divisional Court confirmed the distinction that existed between such creatures of statute and natural persons or incorporated bodies in the following fashion:

> The city is subject to the *Municipal Act*, R.S.O. 1980, c. 302 (subsequently R.S.O. 1990, c. M.45), and is in a different position at law from a natural person or limited company. The residents of the city constitute the corporation. The purpose of the *Municipal Act* is to protect the ratepayers of the corporation. The powers conferred on a municipal corporation by the legislature are required to be exercised by council and council must exercise its power by by-law (ss. 9 and 109 of the *Municipal Act*).[19]

In an effort to give local governments increased flexibility in order to discharge their duties, section 8 of the *Municipal Act, 2001* provides that a municipality has "the capacity, rights, powers and privileges of a natural person for the purpose of exercising its authority under this or any other Act." Subject to certain conditions, this provision would per-

---

18 (2000), 193 D.L.R. (4th) 385 at 402.
19 (1992), 8 O.R. (3d) 689 at 691.

mit Ontario municipalities to conduct their daily corporate and administrative operations without the need to rely upon specific legislative authority. In essence, municipalities could enter into contracts or agreements, hire and dismiss employees, purchase and sell property, and delegate administrative responsibilities as they see fit.

Assuming that the difference between a natural person and an unnatural person is that the latter is a statutorily incorporated body like those under the *Business Corporations Act*, then what exactly is this new and wondrous gift, and what does it mean for municipal councils? In answering these questions, section 1 of the Act is of little assistance, as it only defines the term "person" (not "natural person") to include "a municipality unless the context otherwise requires." Similarly, one legal dictionary simply defines "natural person" as "a human being."[20] Clearly, that description is not relevant, because most natural persons in Ontario can vote, but not levy taxes. It is suggested that more can be learned about these natural person powers by examining the restrictions imposed on them in the Act.

To begin with, subsection 5 (3) of the *Municipal Act, 2001* states that a "municipal power, including a municipality's capacity, rights, powers and privileges under section 8, shall be exercised by by-law unless the municipality is specifically authorized to do otherwise." So much for thinking that such natural person powers could provide more flexible and innovative decision making by council. Section 8 of the *Municipal Act, 2001* goes on to expressly limit the natural person powers of a municipality "for the purpose of exercising its authority under this or any other Act." This provision appears to restrict the natural person powers to acting within the spheres of jurisdiction or the specific powers provided by the *Municipal Act, 2001* or "any other" legislation. Furthermore, the new natural person powers would not allow municipalities to provide a service for which they do not have the legislative authority. Finally, section 17, among other provisions, clarifies that natural person powers do not apply to those parts of the *Municipal Act, 2001* that address various financial matters.

Perhaps the most apt characterization of the new natural person powers was the one originally issued by the ministry in 1997, upon its release of the potential policy changes to the *Municipal Act*. In commenting on

---

[20] D.A. Dubelow and Betsy Nuse, *The Dictionary of Canadian Law,* 2nd ed. (Toronto: Thomson Canada Ltd., 1993).

this new, unique feature, the ministry paper humbly concluded that "these natural person powers would not be very different from powers currently available to municipalities."[21]

Ten Spheres of Jurisdiction

Section 11 of the *Municipal Act, 2001* provides municipalities with the power to pass by-laws respecting matters within 10 specified spheres of jurisdiction. Set out below are the spheres, a brief description of them, and the relevant provisions that should be reviewed when seeking to act:

1. Highways, including parking and traffic on highways (eg. regulate traffic and parking). Refer to sections 11 and 24-68.

2. Transportation systems, other than highways (eg. transit, ferries and airports). Refer to sections 11 and 69-73.

3. Waste management (eg. collection, recycling, composting and disposal). Refer to sections 11 and 74-77.

4. Public utilities (eg. sewage treatment facilities). Refer to sections 11, 78-93 and 194-202;

5. Culture, parks, recreation and heritage (eg. parks, arenas, museums and art galleries). Refer to sections 11, 94-95 and 194 - 202.

6. Drainage and flood control, except storm sewers (eg. floodways and purchase of wetlands). Refer to sections 11, 96 and 97.

7. Structures, including fences and signs (eg. requiring fences around swimming pools). Refer to sections 11, 15 (4), 98 and 99.

8. Parking, except on highways (eg. parking lots and garages). Refer to sections 11 and 100-102.

9. Animals (eg. licensing, spaying clinics and limits on exotic animals). Refer to sections 11 and 103-105.

10. Economic development services (eg. industrial parks and economic and tourism promotion). Refer to sections 1, 11 and 106-114.

---

21 "A Proposed Legislative Framework, White Paper," Ministry of Municipal Affairs and Housing (March 1997).

It should be noted that the draft legislation in 1998 provided for 13 spheres of jurisdiction. The three spheres that were moved elsewhere are as follows:

1. Health, safety, protection and well-being of people and the protection of property. Refer to section 130.
2. Natural environment. Refer to sections 135-147.
3. Nuisance, noise, odour, vibration, illumination and dust. Refer to sections 128-129.

Subsection 11 (2) sets out the inter-relationships that will exist between upper- and lower-tier municipalities and these spheres. In general terms, single-tier municipalities like the cities of London or Ottawa would be able to pass by-laws within all 10 spheres of jurisdiction. Conversely, in two-tier municipal systems, the basic rule would be that a lower-tier municipality would have exclusive authority to pass by-laws under a particular sphere unless all or part of the sphere had been assigned to its upper-tier municipality. If all or part of a sphere is assigned exclusively to the upper-tier municipality, then only the upper-tier municipality could pass a by-law under that sphere or part of the sphere. Furthermore, if all or part of a sphere of jurisdiction is assigned non-exclusively to an upper-tier municipality, then both the lower- and upper-tier municipalities may pass by-laws under that sphere. The overall intent would appear to continue the existing division of responsibilities between the two tiers as established in the former *Municipal Act.*

Same Old Restrictions

The fanfare in the municipal sector and the ministry press releases that accompanied the introduction and subsequent passage of the *Municipal Act, 2001*, focused on the new natural person powers and the 10 spheres of jurisdiction that were to give municipalities broader authority and greater flexibility to deliver local government services without the need to rely upon express statutory language. Despite such rhetoric, in practice, the *Municipal Act, 2001* will likely impose limitations on these very powers that closely resemble those under the former statute. In effect, the jubilation surrounding the endowment of natural person powers (section 8) and the spheres of jurisdiction (section 11) to municipalities will likely become much more subdued when municipalities begin to appreciate the number and magnitude of the restrictions that apply to those very provisions.

General Restrictions

It is not surprising, perhaps, that Part II (sections 8-23) of the legislation sets out a number of fundamental restrictions on the powers of municipalities to act. For example, section 14 of the statute broadly states that a municipal by-law is without effect to the extent that it may conflict with a provincial or federal Act (including a regulation made under such an Act), or "an instrument of a legislative nature" including an order, licence or approval, made or issued under a provincial or federal Act or regulation. In a related fashion, section 15 requires that the power to enact a by-law under section 8 or 11 and under a specific provision of the *Municipal Act, 2001* or any other statute "is subject to any procedural requirements, including conditions, approvals and appeals, that apply to the power and any limits on the power contained in that specific provision." Furthermore, section 16 prohibits upper- and lower-tier municipalities from exercising their respective spherical powers over "systems" other than their own, unless otherwise provided. Finally, section 19 restricts municipalities to using their powers within the geographic limits of the municipal boundaries, but then goes on to establish a number of exceptions to this rule in subsection 19 (2).

Specific Restrictions

Should a municipality overcome all of the general restrictions cited above, it would then face the numerous specific restrictions found in subsection 17 (1). Due to the significance of this provision, it is reproduced in full:

17 (1)   Restrictions - ss. 8 and 11 - corporate - financial matters

Sections 8 and 11 do not authorize a municipality to,

(a) incorporate a corporation or nominate or authorize a person to act as an incorporator, director, officer or member of a corporation;

(b) exercise any power as a member of a corporation;

(c) acquire any interest in, or guarantee or exercise any power as a holder of, a security of a corporation;

(d) impose taxes, fees or charges;

(e) borrow or invest money or sell debt;

(e.1) incur debt without borrowing money for the purpose of obtaining long-term financing of any capital undertaking;

(f) enter into agreements for the purpose of minimizing costs or financial risk associated with the incurring of debt;

(g) make a grant or a loan;

(h) provide or make contributions for pensions;

(h.1) delegate to any person the powers and duties with respect to the matters described in clauses (d), (e), (e.1) and (f) and any other prescribed powers and duties;

(h.2) take any other prescribed financial action;

(i) become a bankrupt under the *Bankruptcy and Insolvency Act* (Canada); or

(j) as an insolvent person, make an assignment for the general benefit of creditors under section 49 of the *Bankruptcy and Insolvency Act* (Canada) or make a proposal under section 50 of that Act. 2001, c. 25, s. 17 (1); 2002, c. 17, Sch. A, ss. 6 (1,2).

Although it is arguable that specific provisions elsewhere in the statute may provide municipalities with authority to act in a number of these specific areas, this merely reinforces the notion that Ontario municipalities, despite the new powers granted under the *Municipal Act, 2001*, remain creatures of provincial statute. For example, with respect to clauses (a) to (c) above, subsection 17 (2) refers the reader to section 203 of the Act. Section 203 empowers the Lieutenant-Governor in Council to pass regulations with respect to the establishment of corporations. In effect, such regulations would govern activities by a municipality in this area, including:

- the incorporation of prescribed corporations;
- the nomination or authorization of a person to act as an incorporator, director, officer or member of a prescribed corporation;
- the exercise of any power as a member of a prescribed corporation; and

- the acquisition of an interest in, or guarantee or exercise of any power as a holder of, a prescribed security of a prescribed corporation.

On May 17, 2003, the first regulation entitled "Municipal Business Corporations" was filed pursuant to section 203.[22] Described as "a first step in providing municipalities with authority to create corporations," the regulation provides that a municipality seeking to establish a corporation "will be required to undertake a rigorous up-front process – including at least one public meeting (to present a detailed business case) – to provide a full opportunity for public input."[23]

With respect to those other matters listed under clauses (d) to (h), the *Municipal Act, 2001* is rife with various specific provisions concerning them. Unfortunately, these matters are not governed by a municipality's broad powers found within a particular sphere of jurisdiction. Rather, they are governed by those express powers provided to municipalities by the specific provisions in the Act or, indeed, in other statutes.

General Observations

In addition to adhering to all of the statutory requirements noted above, a similar observation can also be made with respect to many of the detailed provisions set out in Part III and, to a similar extent Part IV (sections 24-149) of the Act. Part III – Specific Municipal Powers – provides municipalities with express authority to act with respect to certain matters that would arguably fall outside the 10 spheres of jurisdiction. These powers, with few exceptions, mirror ones found in the former *Municipal Act*. The correlation between the Part II – General Municipal Powers and Part III – Specific Municipal Powers lends credence to the potential problem of defining the limits in a given sphere. However, the specific municipal powers, while being supplementary to those found in the spheres of jurisdiction, also establish various detailed procedures and other requirements that municipalities must follow when exercising the power under a particular sphere.

Try to appreciate how this new process is likely to work based on the following hypothetical scenario. Assume that a city council would like to undertake some action with respect to one of its highways. Turning first to the new spheres of jurisdiction, it is noted that paragraph 1 of subsec-

---

22 O.Reg. 168/03.
23 See Ministry of Municipal Affairs and Housing Press Release, "Municipal Corporations Could Mean Tax Savings" (May 20, 2003).

tion 11 (1) provides that a single-tier municipality may pass by-laws respecting "highways, including parking and traffic on highways." Standing alone, this clause could give the local government's council or administration the initial impression of "autonomy" within that specific sphere.

However, a further detailed review of the Act will show that nothing could be further from reality. To begin with, municipal solicitors and administrators will have to refer back to section 2, and ensure that any highway-related actions taken by the city council are in compliance with the "many other Acts" for which the municipality received "powers and duties." Afterward, one must examine in detail sections 24 to 68, which establish a host of legislated restrictions regarding highways. For example, if the municipality wanted to close a highway, then section 34 of the Act sets out a series of detailed requirements for closing particular highways.

Furthermore, if the city is interested in implementing a toll highway, then close attention must be paid to section 40. This provision allows a municipality to designate a highway as a toll highway and operate and maintain the designated highway in that fashion. Despite this apparent authority, subsection 40 (2) then states that "a municipality does not have the power to designate, operate and maintain a highway as a toll highway until a regulation is made under this section." Although the provincial government has indicated that it does not expect to permit existing highways to become toll highways, this clause leads to an entirely new set of potential restrictions – provincial regulations.

Regulations

The content of subsection 40 (2) merely serves to emphasize that the recurring trend towards provincial governance by ministerial regulation thrives throughout a variety of provisions in the *Municipal Act, 2001*. To continue with the hypothetical scenario above regarding a proposed toll highway, subsection 40 (3) provides the Lieutenant-Governor in Council (LGIC) with the ability to make regulations that, in its opinion, "are necessary or desirable for the purposes of this section." The provision then sets out the following seven clauses that detail the regulatory parameters in this particular instance:

(a) requiring a municipality to obtain the approval of any person or body before designating, operating or maintaining a highway as a toll highway;

(b) providing for criteria which must be met before a municipality can designate, operate or maintain a highway as a toll highway;

(c) imposing conditions and limitations on the powers of the municipality to designate, operate or maintain a highway as a toll highway;

(d) granting municipalities powers with respect to the operation and maintenance of a toll highway, including powers with respect to the collection and enforcement of tolls imposed for the use of a toll highway;

(e) without limiting clause (d), providing that the provisions of the *Capital Investment Plan Act, 1993*, and the regulations under that Act which relate to toll highways apply to municipalities with such changes as are prescribed;

(f) establishing process requirements with respect to the designation, operation and maintenance of a highway as a toll highway, including requiring a municipality to provide notice to the Minister or any other person or body of its intention to designate a highway as a toll highway;

(g) providing that the Minister or any other person or body who receives notice under clause (f) may prohibit the municipality from making the designation even though the designation is otherwise authorized under the regulation.

In addition to these clauses, subsection 40 (4) states that, if such a toll highway regulation conflicts with "a provision of any Act or regulation, the regulation under this section prevails." Perhaps the ultimate in regulatory governance is found in sections 452 and 453. The former provision empowers the LGIC to "make regulations authorizing municipalities to exercise a power that they had on December 31, 2002." The latter one permits the minister to make regulations for "transitional matters" that in the minister's opinion are "necessary or desirable" to facilitate the implementation of this Act and to "deal with problems or issues arising as a result of the repeal of the old Act and the enactment of this Act."

Finally, an inexhaustive list of the direct and indirect regulatory powers found between Part I and Part XII of the *Municipal Act, 2001* is set out in Appendix A to this chapter.

Judicial Interpretation

Just how will an Ontario court interpret a municipality's natural person powers or its spheres of jurisdiction? The ancient art of prognostication is difficult to interpret and unreliable at the best of times. However, the degree of "difficulty" becomes "impossible" when an oracle seeks to predict how the judiciary will respond to a particular legal issue. In making such a prediction, reference should first be made to section 9 of the legislation. This provision states that "sections 8 and 11 shall be interpreted broadly so as to confer broad authority on municipalities." The express intent of this broad authority is "to enable [municipalities] to govern their affairs as they consider appropriate and to enhance their ability to respond to municipal issues." Furthermore, should there be any ambiguity in either section 8 or 11, the courts, and presumably other administrative tribunals like the Ontario Municipal Board, will be mandated to interpret these provisions "broadly to include, rather than exclude, municipal powers" that existed prior to the coming into force of the *Municipal Act, 2001*. Finally, the purpose clause found in section 2 may be used to support broader interpretations of the spheres.

In at least one other provision, the legislation specifically ousts the court's authority to review the decision of a municipal council. Section 128 gives a local municipality the discretion to "prohibit and regulate" matters that "in the opinion of council" are or could become or cause public nuisances. Furthermore, subsection 128 (2) states that, if council's opinion is arrived at in good faith, it is "not subject to review by any court." Despite the relative clarity in section 128, and in light of the express statutory restrictions imposed on both the natural person powers and the spheres of jurisdiction, it remains to be seen what effect the "broad" interpretation provisions of section 9 will have on future court cases.

APPENDIX A
Provincial Governance by Regulation

Section	Activity	Restriction or Prohibition
44 (4)	Bridge and Highway Maintenance	Minister of Transportation may establish minimum standards of repair
108 (10)	Small Business Counselling	LGIC may limit amount municipalities can spend
109 (11)	Community Development Corporations	Minister may prohibit/restrict assistance by municipalities
110 (20)	Municipal Capital Facilities	LGIC may prohibit/restrict various matters
156 (5)	Reciprocal Licensing Arrangements	Minister may impose conditions/limits on such arrangements
160 (1)	Licensing	Minister may exempt business or class of business from licensing or place limits on municipality's authority
173 (14)	Restructuring	Minister may impose criteria for a restructuring proposal and to prohibit a municipality from exercising a specified power
173 (17)	Restructuring	LGIC may establish powers for minister/commission in implementing a restructuring proposal
176	Restructuring	Minister may establish a commission, and the type of restructuring
179	Restructuring	Minister may establish restructuring principles and standards
193	Transfer Powers Between Tiers	Minister may place conditions/limits on powers transferred
194 (2)	Municipal Service Boards	Minister may prescribe other systems as municipal services
203 (1)	Powers to Establish Corporations	LGIC may prescribe/define and impose conditions on municipal corporations
215	Business Improvement Areas	Minister may establish business property classes and real property classes
216 (7)	Dissolution of Local Boards	Minister may limit/prohibit a municipality from dissolving a local board
218 (6)	Changes to Council	LGIC may authorize a region to exercise this power

Chapter 1
ONTARIO'S MUNICIPAL ACT, 2001

222 (10)	Wards	Minister may prescribe criteria for establishing ward boundaries
268 (13)	Sale of Land	Minister may exempt classes from all or any of the requirements in this section
269 (2)	Policies	Minister can define "local board"
270 (2)	Policies	Minister may prescribe matters and when hiring policies must be adopted
271 (2)	Policies	Minister may establish procurement of goods and services policies and require a municipality to comply
276 (6)	Pensions and Retirement Benefits	LGIC may restrict/limit pensions by municipalities
277 (2)	Pensions and Retirement Benefits	LGIC may restrict/limit retirement incentives and severance payments to municipal employees
292 (1)	Financial Reporting	Minister may make regulations to phase-in changes in the financial reporting requirements
293	Reserve Funds	Minister may limit/prohibit use of reserve funds for specified purposes
301	Financial Information	Minister may prescribe the times, manner and form for copies of by-laws made under Parts VIII and IX
302 (3)	Financial Assistance	Minister may deem other bodies a municipality for this section
303 (1)	Provincial Significance	LGIC may establish standards for activities of municipalities on matters of provincial significance
305 (3)	Sale of Debt	Minister may prescribe a debt or classes of debt

Chapter 2
OPEN VS. CLOSED MEETINGS

> *Our courts have held that openness is the rule,*
> *covertness the exception.*
>
> District Court Judge D.T. Hogg (1986)

The subject of open versus closed meetings of municipal councils and local boards is one upon which there are an infinite number of authoritative opinions, expressed by elected representatives, public officials, lawyers, the media, as well as the general public. Not surprisingly, these opinions are often based upon the least amount of factual information.

The debate of whether a particular meeting should be open or closed to the public is often exacerbated at a moment of significant legislative change, as it was in Ontario with the 1995 revisions to the *Municipal Act*. At such times, it may be difficult to distinguish the nature of such statutory changes from past or current practices. A brief historical overview of the Ontario experience should aid in placing the existing rules for open versus closed meetings in the proper context.

Common Law

In legal circles, the Latin phrase *in camera* generally translates to mean *in chambers*. Legal proceedings were often said to be *in camera* when they were either held in the private chambers of a judge or in the courtroom after all of the spectators had been excluded. English and Canadian common law evolved in accordance with that definition, which was subsequently applied to the closed or private meetings of municipal councils. In the 1908 English case of *Tenby Corporation v. Mason*,[1] the Court of Appeal considered an action regarding the right of the municipality to bar the media and other persons from meetings of the council. Ruling in favour of the municipality, the court confirmed the common law as follows:

---

1 [1908] 1 Ch. 457.

> In a municipal borough, neither the public, nor the burgesses, nor reporters for newspapers, have the right to attend the meetings of the borough council without the consent of the council expressed or implied.

This legal principle was also clearly enunciated in the 1915 Ontario case of *Journal Printing Co. v. McVeity*.[2] In that landmark decision, Chief Justice Falconbridge, addressing the question of the common law rights of a journalist to attend a municipal council meeting, stated that the four members of the court were "of the opinion that no rights exist except such as are expressly or by implication given by the statute."

Sixty years later, in the case of *Re McAuliffe and Metro Board of Commissioners of Police*,[3] the Ontario Divisional Court followed this early precedent. The court held that, as all local authorities in the province had been established by statute, any general requirement to disclose information or any right to attend meetings concerning such authorities must be found within the provisions of the relevant statute. In the same year, the British Columbia Court of Appeal, in the case of *Regina ex rel. Cedar Crescent Developments Ltd. v. Kelly et al.*,[4] focused upon the right of a municipal council to hold special meetings *in camera*. The applicant alleged bad faith where a particular by-law had been passed *in camera*. The court dismissed this contention, expressing the view that "the passing of By-law 165 *in camera* was not objectionable procedure" and that there was no evidence of bad faith. This decision was subsequently affirmed by the Supreme Court of Canada.

Based on these decisions, Ian MacF. Rogers, in *The Law of Canadian Municipal Corporations*, summarized the general state of the law in the following fashion:

> It appears that, where the statute is silent, council meetings are not open to the public or to ratepayers or reporters. At common law there is no right to access on the part of the inhabitants or the press to hear a council's deliberations, and council may have *in camera*

---

2 (1915), 33 O.R. 166.

3 (1975), 61 D.L.R. (3d) 223.

4 [1976] W.W.D. 59 (sub nom *R. v. Kelly*) 9 L.C.R. 256, 63 D.L.R. (3d) 719, affirmed [1977] 2 S.C.C.R. 620, [1976] W.W.D. 188, 11 L.C.R. 96, 80 D.L.R. (3d) 448, 14 N.R. 523.

meetings whenever it thinks it proper to do so ...[5]

In addition to the general rules for council meetings set out in various provincial statutes,[6] other specific Acts also contained stipulations for the conduct of certain meetings and hearings required as part of a particular municipal process. Historically, these statutory requirements, as applied to a meeting of a municipal council, a committee, a public meeting or a hearing, in general terms often stipulated that:

- regular meetings of council were open to the public;

- special meetings of council were either open or closed according to the opinion of the council, expressed by resolution in writing, as the public interest required;

- committee and all other meetings were closed unless opened at the discretion of the council;

- public meetings required by specific legislation were subject to the rules specified in the particular statute; and

- hearings of a quasi-judicial nature were required to meet certain of the higher standards established by such procedure-oriented statutes as Ontario's *Statutory Powers Procedure Act*.[7]

It seems clear that, in the past, it was the type of meeting – not the subject-matter – that determined whether or not the meeting was open or closed to the public.

Municipal Initiatives

The secretive actions of some councils negatively coloured ratepayers' perception of local government as a whole. In April 1983, Ontario's Minister of Municipal Affairs established the Provincial/Municipal Working Committee on Open Meetings and Access to Information to

---

5 Ian MacF. Rogers, *The Law of Canadian Municipal Corporations*, 2nd ed. (Toronto: Carswell, 2002), para 47.2

6 See, for example: Alberta's *Municipal Government Act*, S.A. 1994, c. M-26.1, s. 197; British Columbia's *Local Government Act*, R.S.B.C. 1996, c. 323, ss. 242.1 and 242.2; Manitoba's *Municipal Act*, S.M. 1996, c. M225, s. 152; New Brunswick's *Municipalities Act*, R.S.N.B. 1973, c. M-22, s. 102; Newfoundland's *Municipalities Act*, S.N. 1999, c. M-24, s. 213; Northwest Territories' *Cities, Towns and Villages Act*, R.S.N.W.T. 1988, c. C-8, s. 21; Nova Scotia's *Municipal Government Act*, S.N.S. 1998, c. 18, s. 22; Prince Edward Island's *Municipalities Act*, R.S.P.E.I. 1988, c. M-13, s. 21; and Saskatchewan's *Urban Municipality Act*, S.S. 1983-84, c. U-11, s. 45, as well as its *Rural Municipality Act*, S.S. 1989-90, c. R-26.1, s. 37 and the *Cities Act*, S.S. 2002, c. C-11.1, s. 94.

7 R.S.O. 1990, c. S.22.

"study the subject of municipal procedural by-laws containing provisions with respect to open/closed meetings and information access within Ontario." This intergovernmental group succeeded the Commission on Freedom of Information and Individual Privacy (Williams Commission) that, in 1980, not only recommended freedom of information legislation to apply to both provincial and municipal governments, but had proposed that a "sunshine" law be passed that would require municipal councils and other local bodies to have open meetings with a limited number of express exceptions for holding closed sessions.[8] The Provincial/Municipal Working Committee summarized the situation as follows:

> The [Williams] Commission's recommendations with regard to local government followed a good deal of public commentary and criticism concerning the alleged lack of openness of some municipal councils in the province. It appears that some municipal councils employ lengthy *in camera*, special and committee meetings to discuss matters under debate, and then ratify their decision in full council in a few minutes, with minimal discussion.
>
> This practice prevents the public from knowing the real reasons for decisions, possible alternative courses of action, and the report or reports upon which decisions are based. While this practice complies with the letter of the *Municipal Act*, it certainly is not in accord with the growing demand for public knowledge of and input into municipal decisions.[9]

The committee's report went on to identify three reasons for "creating a presumption in favour of openness and access" at the local government level:

- the need to foster essential democratic values;
- the existence of statutory provisions and legal precedents which favour secrecy or at least work against the development of more open practices; and
- an apparent desire on the part of the electors for more responsive government at all levels.

---

8 Report of the Commission on Freedom of Information and Individual Privacy (1980).

9 Report of the Provincial/Municipal Working Committee on Open Meetings and Access to Information (July 1984) at p. 2.

In its deliberations, the committee "concluded quickly that the provisions requiring open meetings should be contained within the by-law governing the procedure of each municipality." The specific recommendation with respect to open meetings is set out as follows:

> All council meetings, regular or special, shall be open to the public. All meetings of committees of council shall be open to the public, except meetings which are called to consider those special circumstances, which as expressly permitted by the statute, may be considered at a closed meeting.

Recognizing that there were "certain situations in which open meetings would not serve the public interest or the interest of the municipal corporation," the report also provided for 10 specific exemptions, to be included in the *Municipal Act*, which would enable committees of council to meet *in camera*.

Despite such provincial reports, the move toward more openness in local government meetings throughout the 1980s evolved primarily from municipal initiatives, rather than statutory direction. Recognizing changing public attitudes and the demand for greater access, many municipal councils enacted procedural by-laws that set aside the shroud of secrecy cast by the common law and the *Municipal Act*. As a general principle, these by-laws specified that all committee meetings would be open, subject to specific exceptions.[10] While such exceptions would vary depending on the particular by-law, those meetings that were closed to the public were usually restricted to circumstances where the subject-matter met the so-called PLP criteria: matters concerning "property, legal or personnel."

Despite these progressive municipal initiatives, the air of secrecy lingered as other councils chose silence rather than public scrutiny. Even amongst those municipalities that had sought greater openness, unintended circumstances intruded. Two such instances led to landmark court decisions involving access to municipal council or committee meetings.

---

10 For example, see Town of Richmond Hill Municipal Code, Section 38.5.9.

In the 1988 case of *Southam Inc. v. Economic Development Committee of the Regional Municipality of Hamilton-Wentworth*,[11] an *in-camera* "workshop" was held, from which a newspaper reporter was denied entry. The workshop occurred in a lounge, as opposed to the regular committee room, and no report was ever made to council of the proceedings. The workshop was apparently convened to review the committee's terms of reference and to consider its directions for the future. All members of this standing committee, except the chair, were in attendance.

In the judicial review before the Divisional Court, the applicant newspaper argued that the "workshop" was in fact a "meeting," and could not be held *in camera* contrary to the regional municipality's own procedural by-law. That by-law provided that "the public shall not be excluded from any meeting of a standing committee" unless pursuant to the express exclusions contained in the by-law. The court dismissed the application.

However, the newspaper successfully appealed the decision to the Ontario Court of Appeal. Speaking on behalf of the majority of the court, Mr. Justice Grange professed no difficulty in finding that what had occurred was in fact a meeting: "In the context of a statutory committee, 'meeting' should be interpreted as any gathering to which all members of the committee are invited to discuss matters within their jurisdiction." The municipality applied for leave to appeal this decision to the Supreme Court of Canada. Although the application was subsequently granted, the final appeal was dismissed without reasons.

In the case of *Southam Inc. et al. v. Ottawa (City) and the Attorney General of Ontario*,[12] the applicant newspaper sought a judicial review in 1991 of Ottawa city council's decision to hold an *in camera* "retreat" at a ski resort. The newspaper took the position that this was a meeting of council that ought to have been open to the public, their request to attend having been refused. All members of council were invited to the retreat and staff were also in attendance. The topics discussed were unspecified, but apparently included the presence of councillors at official functions, decorum at council meetings, relations with city staff, the performance of the then chief administrative officer and the question of additional salaries to be paid to councillors who were committee chairs.

---

11 (1988), 40 M.P.L.R. 1, 33 Admin. L.R. 125, 30 O.A.C. 39 (C.A.). See also "Candid in-camera: the judicial retreat from Vanderkloet," by M. Rick O'Connor, *Municipal World*, December 1989, p. 330 at 332.

12 (1991), 5 O.R. (3d) 726 (Div.Ct.).

Certain recommendations were made to improve the infrastructure management strategy, the sewage service rate report and to table the subdivision and redevelopment charges reports in order to obtain public consultation.

The Divisional Court held that the "retreat" was in fact a meeting at which matters that would ordinarily be the subject of council business were discussed and action-taking decisions were made. The court concluded that the decision to hold the meetings *in camera* was contrary to both the city's by-law and section 55 of the former *Municipal Act*.[13]

Such growing concern in the media and the public culminated with the provincial government releasing initial proposals for change in the "White Paper on Open Local Government" in the Ontario Legislature on December 19, 1991. This document, which addressed a number of related subjects such as municipal conflict of interest, staff codes of conduct, and the disposal of real property, invoked wide criticism for its crude drafting. Nevertheless, the sections dealing with open meetings, while also flawed, withstood closer scrutiny.

After considerable public debate and further revision, the new legislation was introduced as Bill 163, the *Planning and Municipal Statute Law Amendment Act, 1994*. Following prolonged debate amidst further public hearings, the Act came into force on January 1, 1995. In a significant reversal of the former law, that legislation stipulated that all meetings shall be open to the public, subject to:

- one mandatory and seven discretionary exceptions; and
- the right of the head of council or presiding officer to expel any person for improper conduct at a meeting.

In a major departure from past practice, the open or closed status of a council/committee meeting in Ontario is now determined by the subject-matter considered, not by the type of meeting being held.

The 1995 amendments to Ontario's *Municipal Act* have been carried over into the *Municipal Act, 2001* with some minor revisions.

Municipal Act, 2001

The open and closed meeting provisions found in section 239 of the *Municipal Act, 2001* are applicable to both municipal councils and local

---

13 *Southam Inc. et al. v. Ottawa (City) and the Attorney General of Ontario* (1991), 5 O.R. (3d) 726 (Div. Ct.).

boards. The word "meeting" means "any regular, special, committee or other meeting of a council or local board."[14]

With respect to the phrase "local board," the Act's general definition section provides that:

> "local board" means a municipal service board, transportation commission, public library board, board of health, police services board, planning board, or any other board, commission, committee, body or local authority established or exercising any power under any Act with respect to the affairs or purposes of one or more municipalities, excluding a school board and a conservation authority.[15]

However, subsection 238 (1) more specifically states that, for the open/closed meeting requirements in section 239, "local board" does not include police services boards or public library boards.

Furthermore, the word "committee" in sections 238 and 239 means "any advisory or other committee, subcommittee or similar entity of which at least 50 per cent of the members are also members of one or more councils or local boards." The addition of the percentage requirement in this definition is a change from the old *Municipal Act*, which defined "committee" as including "any advisory or other committee, subcommittee or similar entity composed of members of one or more councils or local boards."[16] It has been suggested that this modification has further broadened the term "committee," thereby including some entities that were not previously subject to the open/closed meeting requirements of the statute.[17] Conversely, it is arguable that this new definition may result in fewer "committees" being subject to these requirements. This would be true with respect to various municipal advisory committees that are often comprised solely of community volunteers.

Ultimately, the all-encompassing nature of these definitions seems intended to include virtually all meetings of every municipal council, local board, committee or "similar entity," excluding police services and library boards.

---

14 *Ibid.*, s. 238 (1).

15 *Ibid.*, s. 1 (1).

16 *Municipal Act*, R.S.O. 1990, c. M.45, s. 55 (1).

17 "New Ontario Municipal Act, 2001 (Bill 111)," City of Toronto Report to the Policy and Finance Committee (October 24, 2001) at p. 10.

Mandatory Closing

A meeting or part of a meeting of a municipal council or local board *must* be closed to the public "if the subject-matter relates to the consideration of a request under the *Municipal Freedom of Information and Protection of Privacy Act*." However, this only occurs "if the council, board, commission or other body is designated as head of the institution for the purposes of that Act."[18] Alternatively, where a municipal council by by-law, or local board in writing, has designated a committee to act as head of the institution, then the mandatory closure provision would similarly attach to the specific committee.[19]

Discretionary Closings

A meeting or a part of a meeting of a municipal council, a local board or a committee thereof may be closed to the public if the subject-matter being considered falls within one of the seven categories expressly set out in the *Municipal Act, 2001*.[20] For convenience, those seven exemptions are set out below, followed by examples to provide guidance as to the appropriate times to invoke the discretionary, closed meeting provision. Many of these instances were drawn from the exempt provisions in Ontario's *Municipal Freedom of Information and Protection of Privacy Act*, and amendments proposed to the *Municipal Act* in 1986, which died on the Order Paper.[21]

1. The security of the property of the municipality or local board. For example:

    - information whose disclosure could reasonably be expected to prejudice the economic interests or the competitive position of the council or local board;[22]

    - information whose disclosure could reasonably be expected to be injurious to the financial interests of the coun-

---

18 *Municipal Act, 2001*, S.O. 2001, c. 25, s. 239 (3).

19 *Municipal Freedom of Information and Protection of Privacy Act*, R.S.O. 1990, c. M.56, s. 3.

20 S.O. 2001, c. 25, s. 239 (2).

21 Bill 16, *Municipal Amendment Act, 1986*, Second Reading, October 16, 1986, 2nd Sess., 33rd Leg., Ont., 35 Eliz. II, 1986.

22 *Municipal Freedom of Information and Protection of Privacy Act*, R.S.O. 1990, c. M.56, s. 11 (c).

cil or local board;[23]

- information including the proposed plans, policies or projects of the council or local board if the disclosure could reasonably be expected to result in premature disclosure of a pending policy decision or undue financial benefit or loss to a person.[24]

2. Personal matters about an identifiable individual, including municipal or local board employees. For example:

- matters relating to an individual's race, national or ethnic origin, colour, religion, age, sex, sexual orientation, and marital or family status;
- the education, medical, criminal or employment history of an identifiable individual;
- any identifying number, symbol or other particular assigned to an individual;
- the address, telephone number, fingerprints or blood type of an individual.[25]

3. A proposed or pending acquisition or disposition of land by the municipality or local board. For example:

- negotiations surrounding the sale or purchase price.

4. Labour relations or employee negotiations. For example:

- positions, plans, procedures, criteria or instructions to be implemented during employee negotiations;[26]
- hiring, disciplinary or termination matters;
- management-union negotiations during the collective bargaining process.

5. Litigation or potential litigation, including matters before administrative tribunals, affecting the municipality or local board. For example:

---

23 *Ibid.*, s. 11 (d).

24 *Ibid.*, s. 11 (g).

25 *Ibid.*, s. 2 (1), definition of "personal information."

26 *Ibid.*, s. 11 (e).

- matters before all courts, and administrative tribunals such as the Ontario Municipal Board, the Ontario Labour Relations Board or other labour arbitrators, the Ontario Human Rights Commission, the Workplace Safety and Insurance Board and the Ontario Highway Transport Board.

6. The receiving of advice that is subject to solicitor-client privilege, including communications necessary for that purpose. For example:

    - verbal or written legal advice, whether given in contemplation of or for use in litigation or not.[27]

7. A matter in respect of which a council, board, committee or other body has authorized a meeting to be closed under another Act.

This last exemption will be discussed below in greater detail.

Not surprisingly, these seven limited exemptions attempt to balance the principle of confidentiality inherent in these matters and the requirement for municipal councils or local boards to conduct some business *in camera,* against the public's right to know how local government operates. Despite the guidance that can be derived from the above-noted comparisons, these seven discretionary exemptions in the *Municipal Act, 2001* do not correspond directly to the confidential exemptions found in the privacy legislation. This can lead to some curious situations. For example, can a municipal council meet in closed session to consider a public-private partnership proposal that includes sensitive, technical information owned by the business? It would appear that, absent an extremely broad interpretation of the "security of the property of the municipality" provision, the council could not discuss the matter *in camera.* Interestingly, the logical approach of cross-referencing closed meeting matters with the exempt provisions found in a local government's privacy legislation was recently adopted in Saskatchewan. Pursuant to subsection 94 (2) of the *Cities Act,*[28] "councils and council committees may close all or part of their meetings to the public if the matter to be discussed is within one of the exemptions in Part III of the *Local Authority Freedom of Information and Protection of Privacy Act.*" Part III of the latter statute sets out 10 exemptions for refusing a municipal

---

27 *Ibid.,* s. 12.
28 S.S. 2002, c. C-11.1, s. 94 (2).

access to information request.[29]

Procedure

Once a municipal council or local board has determined that the subject-matter of a meeting or part of a meeting either permits or requires the issue to be dealt with *in camera,* Ontario's *Municipal Act, 2001* provides a mandatory procedure that must be followed to enable the closed session to occur. Prior to holding the closed meeting, "a council or local board shall state by resolution" the following:

- the fact of the holding of the closed meeting; and
- the general nature of the matter to be considered at the closed meeting.[30]

For example, should a council or local board decide that it would be prudent to consider, in closed session, the details of a trade union's most recent offer made during the collective bargaining negotiations, the resolution may be formulated as follows:

> BE IT RESOLVED that the next portion of the meeting be closed to the public in order to consider a labour relations/employee negotiations matter pursuant to clause 239 (2) (d) of the *Municipal Act, 2001*.

Subsequent to debating and then voting on the resolution's passage in open session, the public would be asked to leave the meeting until the matter had been considered. It must be remembered that the Act prohibits any substantive vote from occurring during such a closed meeting. Therefore, only procedural votes or those related to the giving of directions or instructions to staff can take place. This issue is addressed in greater detail in Chapter 4, Statutory Procedures. Once the matter has been considered, the open meeting would resume and the public would be re-admitted to the room for the remaining agenda items.

Meeting Closed Under Another Act

The final category in the list of seven discretionary matters that may be considered at a closed meeting of council or board is enumerated in clause 239 (2) (g) of the *Municipal Act, 2001*, as follows:

---

29 *Local Authority Freedom of Information and Protection of Privacy Act*, S.S. 1990-91, c. L-27.1, ss. 13-22.

30 *Municipal Act, 2001*, S.O. 2001, c. 25, s. 239 (4).

a matter in respect of which a council, board, committee or other body has authorized a meeting to be closed under another Act.

What then constitutes "another Act" that has authorized a meeting to be closed? Upon reflection, no obvious statutes leap to mind. Although the *Municipal Freedom of Information and Protection of Privacy Act* establishes which "information" can and cannot be accessed by the public, it does not authorize a municipal council or local board to hold a closed meeting in the absence of the public. In fact, clause 6 (1) (b) of the privacy legislation appears to be the forerunner of the revised subsection 239 (2) of the *Municipal Act, 2001* in that it states that a head may refuse to disclose a record:

> ... that reveals the substance of deliberations of a meeting of a council, board, commission or other body or a committee of one of them if a statute authorizes holding that meeting in the absence of the public.[31]

A review of a wide array of legislation concerning local government in Ontario revealed only two other statutes that would specifically authorize a municipal council or local board to hold a closed meeting: the *Emergency Management Act* and the *Statutory Powers Procedure Act*.

Subsection 2.1 (1) of the *Emergency Management Act* obligates every municipality in Ontario to "develop and implement an emergency management program" and requires every council to, "by by-law, adopt the emergency management program."[32] For obvious reasons related to security, subsection 2.1 (5) of the statute also provides that the "head of an institution, as defined in the *Municipal Freedom of Information and Protection of Privacy Act*, shall not disclose a record ... if the institution is a municipality and the head of the institution is not the council ... without the prior approval of the council of the municipality." Finally, subsection 2.1 (7) of the *Emergency Management Act* requires a council to meet in closed session "if the subject-matter being considered is the council's approval for the purpose of subsection (5)."

According to section 252 of the *Municipal Act, 2001*, a municipal council may delegate its legal requirement to hear interested parties to a committee of council before taking any action. More specifically, subsec-

---

31 *Municipal Freedom of Information and Protection of Privacy Act*, R.S.O. 1990, c. M.56, s. 6 (1) (b).

32 S.O. 2002, c. 14, s. 2.1 (1).

tion 252 (4) provides that:

> If the decision to be made by council on a matter is a statutory power of decision within the meaning of the *Statutory Powers Procedure Act*, that Act, except sections 17, 17.1, 18 and 19, applies to the committee and to the hearing conducted by it.

The *Statutory Powers Procedure Act* further states that "statutory power of decision" means a power or right, conferred by or under a statute, to make a decision deciding or prescribing, the legal rights, powers, privileges, immunities, duties or liabilities of any person or party; or the eligibility of any person or party to receive, or to the continuation of, a benefit or licence, whether the person is legally entitled thereto or not.[33]

The *Statutory Powers Procedure Act* has been held to be applicable to the following:

- a board of reference convened and acting under the *Schools Administration Act*;[34]

- an arbitration board acting pursuant to the *Fire Departments Act*;[35]

- a municipal council exercising its discretionary power under the *Police Act* to pay the legal costs incurred by a police officer in defending against charges when the officer is found not to be liable;[36]

- a municipality when refusing to permit development pursuant to a by-law enacted under the *Planning Act*;[37]

- a committee of council convened to hear requests for licence renewals;[38] and

- a committee of council convened to hold a hearing to address the proposed dismissal of a senior officer of the municipality pursu-

---

[33] R.S.O. 1990, c. S.22, s. 1 (1).

[34] *Re Thompson and Lambton Board of Education*, [1972] 3 O.R. 889 (H.C.).

[35] *Re Windsor and I.A.F.F., Local 455* (1974), 5 O.R. (2d) 690 (Div. Ct.).

[36] *Re Grant and Metro Toronto* (1978), 21 O.R. (2d) 282 (Div. Ct.). Now see, however, the *Police Services Act*, R.S.O. 1990, c. P.15, s. 50 (2).

[37] *Re Olympia and York Developments Ltd. and Toronto* (1980), 29 O.R. (2d) 353 (Div. Ct.).

[38] *Re Mariano et al. and Mississauga (City)* (1992), 9 M.P.L.R. (2d) 29 (Div. Ct.).

ant to subsection 99 (2) of the former *Municipal Act*.[39]

Therefore, once a council or local board determines that its hearing is subject to the *Statutory Powers Procedure Act*, by virtue of its exercise of a statutory power of decision, reference may be had to subsection 9 (1) of the Act which provides as follows:

9 (1) An oral hearing shall be open to the public except where the tribunal is of the opinion that,

    (a)   matters involving public security may be disclosed; or

    (b)   intimate financial or personal matters or other matters may be disclosed at the hearing of such a nature, having regard to the circumstances, that the desirability of avoiding disclosure thereof in the interests of any person affected or in the public interest outweighs the desirability of adhering to the principle that hearings be open to the public,

in which case the tribunal may hold the hearing in the absence of the public.

In three decisions dealing with subsection 9 (1) of that Act, the courts have declined to order such *in camera* hearings. In the case of *Re Pilzmaker and Law Society of Upper Canada*, it was argued that a hearing before the disciplinary committee of the Law Society of Upper Canada should be held in closed session. When the committee decided the hearing would be in public, the applicant sought a court order prohibiting the discipline hearing from continuing except *in camera*. In dismissing this motion, the court ruled that there "is an important public interest in having hearings of disciplinary bodies held in public" and concluded that there was not a strong *prima facie* case that the committee's decision was wrong.[40]

In a similar case, *Re Ottawa Police Force and Lalonde*, an application was made to a District Court Judge to hold a hearing under the *Police Act* "in secret." After reviewing subsection 9 (1), Hogg D.C.J. made the following observations in dismissing the application:

---

39 *McColl v. Gravenhurst (Town)*, [1993] O.J. No. 2424.
40 *Re Pilzmaker and Law Society of Upper Canada* (1989), 70 O.R. (2d) 126 (Div. Ct.).

> Unless there are compelling reasons to the contrary, a hearing, such as this, or a trial, that affects the public must be open to all citizens.
>
> ...
>
> While there may be cases that call for a closed hearing, the circumstances must be compelling to outweigh the desirability of an open hearing. Our courts have held that openness is the rule, covertness the exception. That while evidence may be painful or humiliating, it is tolerated because an open hearing is the best security for the proper administration of justice for achieving public confidence and respect and support. Freedom of the press to report what transpires is a fundamental safeguard of our democratic society.[41]

Both of these earlier decisions were reviewed in 1999 by an arbitrator appointed under the *Police Services Act*, and therefore exercising a statutory power of decision. The arbitrator was faced with the question of whether or not a reporter for a local newspaper should be entitled to attend at a grievance hearing regarding transfer policies. Although the arbitrator conceded that he was not certain whether the *Statutory Powers Procedure Act* specifically applied to the proceeding, his ruling followed the pattern of previous judicial decisions favouring openness:

> It may be that, if a grievance involving a public institution proceeds under the provisions of the grievance procedure in a collective agreement, greater privacy rights are afforded to the parties, and it may also be, as submitted by counsel for the board, that the provisions of section 124 of the *Police Services Act* are "in addition to," and not separate and distinct from arbitration provisions in a collective agreement. Nevertheless, in circumstances such as exist in this arbitration proceeding, where my appointment was made pursuant to the *Police Services Act*, and where I am therefore exercising a statutory power of discretion; where the employer is a public institution; and where nothing on the face of the grievance or in the opening submissions of the parties indicated that there were labour relations or personal reasons for not allowing members of the public to attend the hearing, I concluded that the proper exercise of my discretion was to open the hearing to

---

41 *Re Ottawa Police Force and Lalonde* (1986), 57 O.R. (2d) 509 at 511 (Dist. Ct.).

members of the public.[42]

It would seem clear that in the absence of compelling reasons to the contrary, most hearings under the *Statutory Powers Procedure Act* should adhere to "the statutorily expressed preference for having these hearings open."[43]

MEETINGS CASE LAW

To supplement the above-noted discussion on open/closed meetings, it is useful to canvass some of the relevant case law with respect to meetings of municipal councils or local boards across Canada.

Private Briefings = Meetings

In the 1998 decision in *City of Yellowknife Property Owners Assn. v. Yellowknife (City)*,[44] the applicant association was seeking a judicial declaration that the city council had improperly held meetings in contravention of sections 21 and 22 of the *Cities, Towns and Villages Act*.[45] The legislation provided that "every council shall hold its regular, special and committee meetings in public." However, council or its committees may, by resolution, authorize its meetings to be closed to the public where:

- it is of the opinion that to do so is in the public interest; and
- the resolution is made by at least two-thirds of the council members present.

The Trial Judge posed the legal question before the court in the following terms: "Whether certain private and confidential meetings of aldermen and members of the city administration which were described as 'Aldermen's Briefings,' were council meetings which offended ss. 21 and 22 [*supra*] because they were not held in public." These private, weekly briefing sessions were structured with elected representatives being given an agenda and briefing documents in advance, as well as minutes being taken by the city clerk. In reviewing these documents, Irvin J. found that, "the minutes disclose many decisions were taken by

---

42 *Re Ottawa-Carleton Regional Police Services Board and Ottawa-Carleton Regional Police Association* (1999), 80 L.A.C. (4th) 309 at 315.
43 *Re Pilzmaker and Law Society of Upper Canada* (1989), 70 O.R. (2d) 126 at 133 (Div.Ct.).
44 (1998), 49 M.P.L.R. (2d) 65.
45 R.S.N.W.T. 1998, c. C-8, ss. 21 and 22.

council and directions given to the administration during the six-month period, and the minutes also disclose that at seven meetings during that period, confidential matters were discussed ... which, but for the convenience provided by the briefing meeting, would have required resort to s. 22 (2) [*supra*] for an *in camera* council meeting for such contentious issues."

In determining whether or not these briefing sessions were statutory meetings, the Trial Judge reviewed both the cases of the *Economic Development Committee of Hamilton-Wentworth*[46] and the *City of Ottawa*[47] before finding as follows:

> I therefore conclude that the briefing sessions here in dispute were wide-ranging and went far beyond updating aldermen about administration activities; these dealt with many matters within the jurisdiction of council where decisions were made and instructions given by the council to the administration, and where confidential issues were dealt with without the necessity of an *in camera* resolution by s. 22 (2) [*supra*]. Thus I conclude the briefing sessions were council meetings within the provisions of s. 21 [*supra*] which were required, subject to s. 22 (2) [*supra*] to be held in public.[48]

As such, the applicant association was granted a judicial declaration to that effect.

Closed Meetings = Bad Faith

In addition to receiving a judicial declaration that statutory open meeting provisions have been breached, recent cases suggest a trend whereby a council's actions may be vulnerable if its closed meetings, under certain circumstances, constitute bad faith. In municipal law, the traditional statement of bad faith was set out by Mr. Justice Middleton in *Re Howard and Toronto (City)*:

> If it is shown that the municipal councillors have abandoned all honest attempts at legislation and are corruptly seeking by the prostitution of their legislative powers to advance the ends of

---

46 (1988), 40 M.P.L.R. 1, 33 Admin. L.R. 125, 30 O.A.C. 39 (C.A.). See also "Candid in-camera: the judicial retreat from Vanderkloet," by M. Rick O'Connor, *Municipal World*, December 1989, p. 330 at 332.

47 (1991), 5 O.R. (3d) 726 (Div.Ct.).

48 *City of Yellowknife Property Owners Assn. v. Yellowknife (City)* (1998), 49 M.P.L.R. (2d) 65 at 72.

some member of the council or some favourite individual, the courts may ... interfere.[49]

More recently, the Ontario Court of Appeal engaged in a useful discussion of bad faith in the case of *Re Equity Waste Management of Canada et al. v. Halton Hills (Town)*:

> Bad faith by a municipality connotes a lack of candour, frankness and impartiality. It includes an arbitrary or unfair conduct and the exercise of power to serve private interests at the expense of the public interest ... [50]

After reviewing the *Howard* case once again, the Court of Appeal made the following comments:

> The more recent judgment of Robins J. in *H.G. Winton Ltd. v. North York (Borough)* ... contains a similar but perhaps even broader definition of bad faith:
>
>> To say that council acted in what is characterized in law as "bad faith" is not to imply or suggest any wrongdoing or personal advantage on the part of any of its members ... But it is to say, in the factual situation of this case, that council acted unreasonably and arbitrarily and without the degree of fairness, openness and impartiality required of a municipal government ...[51]

In the 1999 decision of *Marion Community Homes Corp. v. Kingston*, the plaintiff/non-profit corporation operated a residential care facility for the elderly. It brought an action seeking damages, as well as a judicial declaration exempting it from the garbage tax rate imposed by the Ontario municipality's two by-laws. Although the plaintiff failed in its claim for declaratory relief, it was successful in obtaining modest damages arising out of the way in which the defendant municipality dealt with its exemption request. The Trial Judge ruled that, by its conduct, the township had failed in the duty it owed to the plaintiff to act in accordance with the rules of natural justice and procedural fairness. In effect, the court found that the various procedural omissions regarding meetings were evidence of the municipality's bad faith:

---

49 *Re Howard and Toronto (City)*, [1928] 1 D.L.R. 952 at 956 (Ont. C.A.).
50 (1997), 35 O.R. (3d) 321 at 340 (Ont. C.A.).
51 *Ibid.*

While some opportunity was provided to Marion Homes to address the township on these issues, both orally and in writing, at the time when the critical decision was being made, the township did not conduct itself, I find, in a responsible manner and breached its duty of procedural fairness to Marion Homes. The township failed to ensure public access to its meetings and processes on April 15, 1997 and it failed to notify Marion Homes of the April 29, 1997 date for continuation of the debate of the tax exemption or rebate issue. The township failed to provide minutes for the meetings of April 8, 15 and 29, 1997 and was derelict in its duty in this regard. The township must provide a forum in which those whose private interests are adversely affected may assert their objections. I find the township did, therefore, breach the rules of natural justice and breach its duty of procedural fairness to Marion Homes in this regard in relation to the events transpiring on April 15, 1997 and April 29, 1997 and its failure to keep the minutes of the critical meetings of April 8, 15 and 29, 1997. All of these events, I find, are badges of bad faith which I find existed on the part of the township in this regard.[52]

Closed Meetings = Cost$

In addition to the possibility that there will be some negative press arising from an *in camera* meeting of council, a more remote, albeit realistic, possibility is the fact that any action taken during a closed meeting could be subject to a challenge in a court of law. It is worth noting that, even if victorious, a municipality or local board could be subject to legal costs. Two judicial rulings in the case of *Niagara-on-the-Lake Conservancy Society v. Niagara-on-the-Lake (Town)* serve as an example of this possibility. In the first decision, the society brought a statutory application seeking a court ruling to invalidate a town resolution to relocate the library from the town hall to a building erected on a highway.[53]

The legal process was fuelled by the applicant society's allegation that the respondent town's resolution was illegal because it was conceived "in secret meetings" and was "passed in bad faith." In denying the applicant's submissions, Mr. Justice Taliano did not consider whether any of the *in camera* meetings occurred in accordance with Ontario's former

---

52 [1999] O.J. No. 5028 at paras. 25, 26 and 27; for a contrary ruling, see the decision in *Kingfisher Inns Ltd. v. Nipawin (Town)*, [1999] S.J. No. 5858, (Sask. Q.B.).

53 *Niagara-on-the-Lake Conservancy Society v. Niagara-on-the-Lake (Town)* (2000), 14 M.P.L.R. (3d) 94.

Municipal Act. Ironically, Taliano J. seems to have made his order based primarily on the fact that the "actual" decision to move the library in question had been made at one or more open meetings.

However, in a subsequent ruling on costs, Mr. Justice Taliano returned to the statutory prohibition contained in the *Municipal Act* against closed meetings and conceded that, "although the decision to move the library was not made at these two [*in camera*] meetings, nonetheless the topic was discussed ..." He went on to observe, "this is a highly dangerous practice and in this case has rightly aroused suspicion that the town was conducting business behind closed doors, in contravention of the *Municipal Act*."[54]

Although the court found that the applicant had not made out its case, Mr. Justice Taliano stated, "nevertheless, this court had and continues to have, serious misgivings about the propriety of the town's practice of meeting behind closed doors to discuss issues of importance to the citizens of the community. To reward the town by ordering the applicant [society] to pay costs of the proceeding is neither fair nor equitable under the circumstances." Ultimately, the court awarded the town only a small portion of its costs in this application, which it fixed at $1,200 all inclusive and issued the following warning to other local government bodies intent on regularly meeting in closed session:

> It therefore seems to me that the town has, by its penchant for closed-door meetings, aroused the suspicions of a distrustful community concerned with legitimate issues concerning preservation of the town's uniqueness. As long as the town continues to meet behind closed doors, it will inevitably invite the scrutiny, expense and inconvenience of court challenges to certain of its decisions. When such circumstances arise, the town should not be able to point to the trophy case and boast that cost sanctions will necessarily attach to those who seek to challenge the town's authority. The town had a victory in this case, but in my opinion, it is a hollow one.[55]

The Future

Clearly, municipalities should be wary of the various judicial penalties for non-compliance with the statutory requirements regarding

---

54 (2001), 20 M.P.L.R. (3d) 84 at 86.

55 *Ibid.*, at p. 88. See also *Niagara-on-the-Lake Association of Ratepayers v. Niagara-on-the-Lake (Town)*, [2003] O.J. No.1925.

open/closed meetings, as well as the cost consequences and negative media exposure of holding numerous, albeit legally closed meetings in general. In addition to these concerns, a new variation on this old theme arose when a local newspaper launched a formal complaint with the Ontario Press Council against a council for meeting in secret. In September 2001, *The Hamilton Spectator* filed a complaint with the Ontario Press Council against the City of Hamilton as a result of an alleged closed meeting between the mayor and members of council. Opting for this administrative challenge instead of a court battle "so taxpayers wouldn't be faced with a huge legal bill," the newspaper's editor-in-chief set out the reasons for the complaint:

> As a newspaper, we feel very strongly about public transparency in government. The lack of transparency at city hall, and the reputation this city has for wheeling and dealing behind closed doors, has hurt the city ... We felt it was absolutely crucial we send a clear and unequivocal message that, as far as the Spectator's concerned, this was an inappropriate action and we will seek recourse to prevent it from happening again.[56]

On March 20, 2002, the Ontario Press Council upheld the complaint in the following ruling:

> *The Hamilton Spectator* complained that Hamilton city council flouted its own procedural by-law and the Ontario *Municipal Act* by failing to give formal notice of an August 27, 2001 meeting called by Mayor Robert E. Wade to consider concerns about council's working relationship with senior management.
>
> The mayor maintained that, with the lack of an agenda, the absence of staff members and the fact no specific decisions were reached, councillors had not contravened the city's by-law or the *Municipal Act*.
>
> Noting that municipal councils are required to declare by resolution that they are holding a closed meeting and to identify the general nature of the matter to be considered, the Ontario Press Council says it believes the city council acted improperly.
>
> While the newspaper happened to learn of the meeting and the subject of discussion, the Press Council is concerned that, unless councils follow due process or there happens to be a leak, *in cam-*

---

56 *The Hamilton Spectator*, September 8, 2001, p. A-8.

era meetings might never come to public attention.

On a more general plane, the Press Council sees open meetings as an issue of freedom of press and the right of the public to information about the activities of their elected representatives. It accepts that legislative rules by which meetings may be closed are reasonable. But it is strongly critical of attempts to circumvent the rules by declaring that a meeting is an informal get-together.[57]

As we look to the future, it is appropriate to also make a brief observation on the scant legislative references concerning the ability of local government bodies to hold electronic meetings. Although the past decade has borne witness to significant technological advances, few statutes in Canada address the issue of "e-meetings" in any meaningful way. To being with, Ontario's *Municipal Act, 2001* omits any reference to councils having electronic meetings. A brief survey of the enabling legislation in other provinces found only Alberta's *Municipal Government Act*, British Columbia's *Local Government Act*, Manitoba's *City of Winnipeg Charter* and Saskatchewan's *Cities Act* had succinct, permissive provisions to allow e-meetings.[58]

However, these clauses focused largely on the technical ability of participants to see, hear and speak to each other, and for the public to watch and/or listen to the debate. Ironically, the most detailed, legislative examination of e-meetings arises from a regulation enacted pursuant to Ontario's *Education Act*.[59] Simply entitled "Electronic Meetings," Ontario Regulation 463/97 identifies a variety of issues arising from e-meetings including conflict of interest concerns and matters surrounding closed meetings.

It is anticipated that in a country as vast as Canada, the ability of local government bodies to hold e-meetings will become an increasingly routine affair in the future.

---

57 This ruling can be found on the Ontario Press Council's website at: www.ontpress.com.

58 *Municipal Government Act*, R.S.A. 2000, c. M-26, s. 199; *Local Government Act*, R.S.B.C., c. 323, s. 222.1; *Cities Act*, S.S. 2002, c. C-11.1, s. 99; *City of Winnipeg Charter*, S.M. 2002, c. 39, ss. 74 and 81; and see British Columbia's *Community Charter* (Bill 14), s. 128, which will provide municipalities with the opportunity to conduct council meetings using electronic devices, as well as the detailed summary of this provision online: www.mcaws.gov.bc.ca/charter/opportunity/electronic_meetings.htm

59 R.S.O. 1990, c. E.2, ss. 8 (1) and 208.

Chapter 3
LOCAL BOARD MEETINGS

> *This morning I threw up at a board meeting. I was sure the cat was out of the bag, but no one seemed to think anything about it; apparently it's quite common for people to throw up at board meetings.*
>
> Playwright Jane Wagner (1986)

Regrettably, the 1995 amendments to Ontario's *Municipal Act* did not have universal application with respect to all local boards. A number of other statutes – including the *Education Act*, the *Public Libraries Act* and the *Police Services Act* – were revised prior to the amendments made to the *Municipal Act* to specify closure requirements based on subject-matter. Those statutes, however, were drafted in a manner, each different from the other. They also differed from the 1995 revisions to the *Municipal Act* and some continue to be different from those in the *Municipal Act, 2001*. Finally, a number of other provincial statutes also contemplate councils holding "public meetings" that are open to the public with rules that may vary from those set out in the *Municipal Act, 2001*.[1]

In the open and closed meeting provisions set out in sections 238 and 239 of Ontario's *Municipal Act, 2001*, the following definitions are provided for guidance with respect to "local boards:"

> "committee" means any advisory or other committee, subcommittee or similar entity of which at least 50 per cent of the members are also members of one or more councils or local boards;

> "local board" does not include police services boards or public library boards.

---

[1] For example, see the *Development Charges Act*, S.O. 1997, c. 27, s. 12.

Furthermore, subsection 1 (1) of the Act provides the following broad definition:

> "local board" means a municipal service board, transportation commission, public library board, board of health, police services board, planning board, or any other board, commission, committee, body or local authority established or exercising any power under any Act with respect to the affairs or purposes of one or more municipalities, excluding a school board and a conservation authority.

Therefore, the open and closed meeting sections in the *Municipal Act, 2001* have wide application and include any committee and local board as defined, subject to the four specific exemptions:

- police services boards;
- library boards;
- school boards; and
- conservation authorities.

Why were such bodies singled out for exemption? While, logically, such open local government legislation should be all-encompassing, it nevertheless acknowledges that the statutes applicable to meetings of the exempted bodies had already been reformed to recognize variations on the open meeting concept.

This chapter will concentrate on the specific requirements of the various Acts applicable to these four exempted bodies and the limitations and variances with the general legislation applicable to all municipal councils and most other local boards.[2]

Police Services Board

The *Police Services Act* includes within its principles:[3]

---

[2] For a thorough discussion of local boards subject to the *Municipal Act, 2001*, see Joanna Kouris, "Local Boards: How to Identify Them under Ontario's new Municipal Act," *Municipal World*, October 2003, at p. 31.

[3] *Police Services Act*, R.S.O. 1990, c. P.15, s. 1, par. 2.

Chapter 3
LOCAL BOARD MEETINGS

The importance of safeguarding the fundamental rights guaranteed by the *Canadian Charter of Rights and Freedoms*[4] and the *Human Rights Code*.[5]

It is suggested that the recognition of such rights is reflected in the specific provisions governing the conduct of board meetings. In this regard, the *Police Services Act* provides as follows:

35 (1) The board shall hold at least four meetings each year.

35 (2) A majority of the members of the board constitutes a quorum.

35 (3) Meetings and hearings conducted by the board shall be open to the public, subject to subsection (4), and notice of them shall be published in the manner that the board determines.

35 (4) The board may exclude the public from all or part of a meeting or hearing if it is of the opinion that,

(a) matters involving public security may be disclosed and, having regard to the circumstances, the desirability of avoiding their disclosure in the public interest outweighs the desirability of adhering to the principle that proceedings be open to the public; or

(b) intimate financial or personal matters or other matters may be disclosed of such a nature, having regard to the circumstances, that the desirability of avoiding their disclosure in the interest of any person affected or in the public interest outweighs the desirability of adhering to the principle that proceedings be open to the public.

An analysis of the foregoing provisions reveals that the meetings of a police services board are open to the public, subject to specific exceptions that permit the board to exclude the public from all or part of a meeting or hearing if the board is of the opinion that:

- matters involving public security may be disclosed; or

---

[4] *Canadian Charter of Rights and Freedoms, Constitution Act, 1982*, c. 11 (U.K.), Schedule B, Part I.

[5] *Human Rights Code*, R.S.O. 1990, c. H.19.

- intimate financial or personal matters or other matters may be disclosed.

These two exceptions will apply where "the desirability of avoiding their disclosure in the public interest outweighs the desirability of adhering to the principle that proceedings be open to the public." In the second instance, set out in clause 35 (4) (b), the interest of any person affected is also recognized.

Furthermore, section 37 mandates that each police services board "shall establish its own rules and procedures in performing its duties under this Act and, except when conducting a hearing under subsection 65 (9), the *Statutory Powers Procedure Act* does not apply to a board."

The express exclusion of police services boards in Ontario from the open meeting provisions in the *Municipal Act, 2001* may be less clear in some other jurisdictions. For example, a recent court challenge in Alberta was brought against the Edmonton Police Commission for holding *in camera* meetings allegedly in contravention of the *Municipal Government Act*.[6] In the case of *Kirchmeir v. Edmonton (City)*, the court ruled that, as the commission had been established under the *Police Act*,[7] "the provisions of the *Municipal Government Act* do not apply to the conduct of police commission meetings as the commission is not a council committee created under that Act."[8]

Public Library Board

The *Public Libraries Act*[9] states that:

> "board" in Part I means a public library board, a union board, a county library board or a county library co-operative board and in Part II means an Ontario library service board;

Prior to 2002, the Act set out the following criteria for the holding of regular and special meetings of a library board:[10]

---

6   S.A. 1994, c. M-26.1, s. 1 (1) (f).
7   R.S.A. 1980, c. P-12.01, s. 28 (1).
8   *Kirchmeir v. Edmonton (City)*, [2001] A.J. No. 161, at par. 16.
9   R.S.O. 1990, c. P.44, s. 1.
10 *Ibid.*, s. 16.

16 (1) A board shall hold regular meetings at least once monthly from January to June and from September to December, both inclusive, and at such other times as it considers necessary.

(2) The chair or any two members of a board may summon a special meeting of the board by giving each member reasonable notice in writing, specifying the purpose for which the meeting is called.

(3) Despite any other Act, board meetings shall be open to the public, except that where the board is of the opinion that intimate financial or personal matters may be disclosed at a meeting and that the desirability of protecting against the consequences of their public disclosure outweighs the desirability of holding the meeting in public, the board may hold that meeting in the absence of the public.

(4) Despite subsection (3), the chair may exclude any person from a meeting for improper conduct.

(5) The presence of a majority of the board is necessary for the transaction of business at a meeting.

(6) The chair or acting chair of a board may vote with the other members of the board upon all questions, and any question on which there is an equality of votes shall be deemed to be negative.

An analysis of the former legislation revealed that meetings of a library board "shall" be open to the public, subject to an exception where the board is of the opinion that intimate financial or personal matters may be disclosed. As with the police services board legislation (although the exact language differs), this exception would only apply where "the desirability of protecting against the consequences of the public disclosure outweighs the desirability of holding the meeting in public."

However, with the passage of the omnibus *Municipal Statute Law Amendment Act, 2002*,[11] subsections 16 (3) and (4) have been repealed and a new section 16.1 has been added to the *Public Libraries Act*. This latter provision largely adopted the open/closed meeting requirements found in sections 238 and 239 of the *Municipal Act, 2001*, with some minor amendments.

---

11 S.O. 2002, c. 17.

School Board

The *Education Act*[12] contains the following relevant definitions:

"board" means a district school board or a school authority;

"district school board" means,

    (a)   an English-language public district school board;

    (b)   an English-language separate district school board;

    (c)   a French-language public district school board; or

    (d)   a French-language separate district school board.

"school authority" means,

    (a)   a board of a district school area;

    (b)   a board of a rural separate school;

    (c)   a board of a combined separate school zone;

    (d)   a board of a secondary school district established under section 67;

    (e)   a board established under section 68; or

    (f)   a board of a Protestant separate school.

The Act further stipulates the following criteria for access to meetings and records:[13]

207 (1) The meetings of a board and, subject to subsection (2), meetings of a committee of the board, including a committee of the whole board, shall be open to the public, and no person shall be excluded from a meeting that is open to the public except for improper conduct.

207 (2) A meeting of a committee of a board, including a committee of the whole board, may be closed to the public when the subject-matter under consideration involves:

    (a)   the security of the property of the board;

---

12 R.S.O. 1990, c. E.2, s. 1.

13 *Ibid.*, s. 207.

(b) the disclosure of intimate, personal or financial information in respect of a member of the board or committee, an employee or prospective employee of the board or a pupil or his or her parent or guardian;

(c) the acquisition or disposal of a school site;

(d) decisions in respect of negotiations with employees of the board; or

(e) litigation affecting the board.

(3) The presiding officer may expel or exclude from any meeting any person who has been guilty of improper conduct at the meeting.

An analysis of the foregoing legislation reveals that, subject to five specific exceptions for closed committee meetings:

- meetings of a board; and
- meetings of a committee of the board, including a committee of the whole board;

shall be open to the public and no person shall be excluded except for improper conduct.

In the 1985 case of *Vanderkloet et al. v. Leeds and Grenville County Board of Education*,[14] the Ontario Court of Appeal was asked to determine whether or not a resolution of the board concerning the re-organization of three schools within its jurisdiction were valid. At issue was the fact that Mr. Justice Holland of the Ontario High Court of Justice had held that the resolutions enacted by the board constituted a "closing" of one of the schools and were passed contrary to the statutory guidelines requisite upon the closing of a school. His Honour found that the resolutions were invalid by reason of procedural unfairness because the board reached a decision:

> ... without any notice to the public or public participation, and it seems clear that it did so *in camera,* going into public session only to formally pass the resolution.

---

14 (1985), 51 O.R. (2d) 577, 21 Admin. L.R. 36, 30 M.P.L.R. 230, 20 D.L.R. (4th) 738, 11 O.A.C. 145 (Ont. C.A.). Leave to appeal to the Supreme Court of Canada refused (1986), 54 O.R. (2d) 352n, 65 N.R. 159n, 15 O.A.C. 238n (S.C.C.).

In its controversial decision, the Court of Appeal overturned the decision of the Motions Court Judge, stating in part:

> ... I do not think that the requirement that the meeting of the board should be open to the public precludes informal discussions among board members, either alone or with the assistance of their staff. Nor does the statute require that the board prepare an agenda to be distributed to the public in advance of a board meeting. In acting as they did, I do not think that the board violated any of the statutory provisions governing their conduct, and were not required to make public any staff reports prepared for their assistance and guidance.

Although this passage is cited by those defending public authorities in subsequent "closed meetings" cases, it has been suggested that the Ontario Court of Appeal's later ruling in the *Hamilton-Wentworth* [15] case and the Divisional Court decision in the *Ottawa* [16] case constitute a judicial withdrawal from the position set out in the *Vanderkloet* decision.[17]

Conservation Authorities

Unlike the other three exempt bodies discussed above, the *Conservation Authorities Act*[18] does not establish precise procedures regarding the open or closed meetings of such authorities. However, two provisions are of significance. Subsection 15 (1) of the Act provides:

> The first meeting of an authority shall be held at such time and place as may be determined by the minister and, in each year thereafter, the authority shall hold at least one meeting before the 1st day of March and at least one meeting after the 1st day of July and such other meetings as it considers necessary to effectively conduct the affairs of the authority.

---

15 *Southam Inc. v. Economic Development Committee of the Regional Municipality of Hamilton-Wentworth* (1988), 40 M.P.L.R. 1, 33 Admin. L.R. 125, 30 O.A.C. 39 (C.A.). See also "Candid in-camera: the judicial retreat from Vanderkloet," by M. Rick O'Connor, *Municipal World*, December 1989, p. 330 at 332.

16 *Southam Inc. et al. v. Ottawa (City) and the Attorney General of Ontario* (1991), 5 O.R. (3d) 726 (Div. Ct.).

17 See M. Rick O'Connor, "Candid In Camera: Judicial Retreat from Vanderkloet," *Municipal World*, December 1989, p. 330; and *Humber Heights of Etobicoke Ratepayers Inc. v. Toronto District School Board*, [2003] O.J. No. 1381.

18 R.S.O. 1990, c. C.27.

Although the Act does not expressly mandate that the authorities' meetings be open or closed to the public, section 30 provides that, "subject to the approval of the Minister [of Natural Resources], an authority shall make regulations providing for the calling of meetings of the authority and prescribing the procedure at those meetings," within one year after its establishment. Presumably, the public's right to attend the meetings of conservation authorities would be set out in their respective procedure by-law or regulation.

Comparison of Statutes

The foregoing review of the statutes applicable to the four exempted boards again raises the concern that open local government legislation in Ontario should have been harmonized with the enactment of the Municipal Act, 2001. Clearly, while there are distinctions to be made between the affected bodies, serious omissions remain evident. For example, the statute applicable to police services boards fails to mention meetings of a committee of those boards. Nor does such legislation specifically address the issue of security of the board's property, acquisition or disposition of land, labour relations or employee negotiations, litigation or solicitor/client privilege – all being standard in camera provisions applicable to many other local boards subject to the Municipal Act, 2001.

While the legislation applicable to a school board is broader than some of the other exceptions, and more closely parallels the meetings provisions in the Municipal Act, 2001, the language used is different and such matters as "advice that is subject to solicitor/client privilege" are not even mentioned. Such variations will likely lead to court decisions specific to the enabling statute of each body and cause further public and media confusion surrounding access to their meetings.

Conclusions

As with most municipal councils across Canada, the closed meetings of local boards may be subject to the same judicial scrutiny if challenged in court. The May 2003 judgment of the British Columbia Supreme Court in the case of *Hospital Employees Union v. Northern Health Authorities (British Columbia)*[19] is instructive – even though it involved provincial, and not local, boards.

---

19 [2003] B.C.J. No. 1173.

In December 2001, the British Columbia government made various changes to the manner in which it operated health care services, including the creation of five regional health boards. Under pressure to produce budgets and redesign plans that were consistent with the province's health care goals, the chair of each regional health board determined that the board's initial meeting (to discuss the budget and redesign plans) would be closed to the public. This decision was subsequently the central focus of a judicial review by the Health Employees Union (HEU), which argued that the *in camera* meetings were contrary to subsection 8 (3) of the *Health Authorities Act*:[20]

> Meetings of a board are open to the public, but the board may exclude the public from a meeting if the board considers that, in order to protect the interests of a person or the public the desirability of avoiding disclosure of information to be presented outweighs the desirability of public disclosure of the information.

In examining the issue "of whether the regional health boards improperly exercised their statutory power of decision in deciding to hold their first board meeting *in camera*," Mr. Justice Macaulay found that "the content of the minutes strongly supports the suggestion by counsel for the HEU that the decision to exclude the public was made by the chair before the meeting in order to accommodate the government timetable for public disclosure and not for any reason connected to the balancing test mandated by subsection 8 (3)" of the statute. In fact, at least one regional director deposed that a reason for not conducting board affairs in public was because:

> The premature public disclosure of prospective plans and strategy, particularly on controversial issues, has the potential to discourage or stifle these processes. The presence of the public can inhibit free and open discussion and debate, and can discourage innovative planning, which, in my opinion, negatively impacts on the public interest in efficient and effective health care administration.[21]

Mr. Justice Macaulay found that statement to be "a cynical favouring of the interests of the bureaucracy over that of the public, as well as a stun-

---

20 R.S.B.C. 1996, c. 180, s. 8 (3).
21 *Hospital Employees Union v. Northern Health Authorities (British Columbia)*, [2003] B.C.J. No. 1173, at para. 85.

ning disregard for the legislative intent behind section 8." Ultimately, the judge agreed with the HEU's interpretation of section 8:

> On balance, the evidence indicates that the boards viewed public meetings as an opportunity for public submissions and consultation. Section 8, however, is directed only towards public presence, something very different from public consultation. I am satisfied that, even if the boards tacitly approved the decision to hold the first meeting *in camera*, they failed completely to address the statutory requirement that the public be present except in the limited circumstances set out in section 8. In my view, any presumption of regularity was successfully rebutted.[22]

The decision in this case not only guides British Columbia's regional health boards on how to meet in closed session, but also reminds all local boards to follow their respective statutory procedures in order to properly hold an *in camera* meeting.

---

22 *Ibid.*, at para. 90.

Chapter 4
STATUTORY PROCEDURES

> *Municipalities are entirely the creatures of provincial statutes. Accordingly, they can only exercise those powers which are explicitly conferred upon them by a provincial statute.*
>
> Honourable Mr. Justice F. Iacobucci (1993)

In most jurisdictions, the relevant provincial legislation establishes a number of statutory procedures related to the holding of meetings, to which municipal councils and local boards are required to adhere.[1] The purpose of this chapter is to summarize some of these specific legislative requirements with reference to Ontario's *Municipal Act, 2001*. Chapter 5, Procedure By-law, will discuss the procedure by-laws that municipal councils and local boards are obligated to enact pursuant to the Act, in order to govern the calling, place and proceedings of meetings. The provisions in those by-laws will likely supplement the statutory procedures set out in this chapter.

Inaugural Meeting of Council

Following a regular municipal election in Ontario, the *Municipal Act, 2001* prescribes that the first meeting of a new council shall be held "at the time set out in the municipality's procedure by-law but in any case not later than 31 days after its term commences."[2] The council is deemed to be organized after a regular election or a by-election when the "declarations of office" have been made by a sufficient number of councillors to form a quorum. Furthermore, the council is required to "hold its meetings and keep its public offices within the municipality or an adjacent municipality" at a place identified in its procedure by-law.[3]

---

1 For example, see Chapter 2, footnote 6.
2 *Municipal Act, 2001*, S.O. 2001, c. 25, s. 230.
3 *Ibid.*, c. 25, s. 236.

Special Meetings of Council

Under section 240 of the *Municipal Act, 2001*, the traditional statutory procedure for calling a special meeting of council is subject to any provisions set out in the municipality's procedure by-law. This condition reverses the previous statutory procedure in this instance, apparently granting to each council or local board ample parameters to establish its own rules regarding the calling of such special meetings.

In the event that the procedure by-law does not address special meetings, the Act provides for the following:

- the head of council may, at any time, call a special meeting; or
- the clerk shall call a special meeting upon receiving a petition of the majority of the members of council, to be held for the purpose and at the time specified in the petition.

Head of Council

As in some other provinces, the head of council in Ontario acts as the chief executive officer of the municipal corporation and possesses unique powers not shared by the other members of council. Formerly variously described as a warden, mayor, or reeve, the head of council is endowed with the following statutory duties and responsibilities:

225. It is the role of the head of council,

    (a)   to act as chief executive officer of the municipality;

    (b)   to preside over council meetings;

    (c)   to provide leadership to the council;

    (d)   to represent the municipality at official functions; and

    (e)   to carry out the duties of the head of council under this or any other Act.[4]

---

4   *Ibid.*, s. 225; for example, see also British Columbia's *Local Government Act*, R.S.B.C. 1996, c. 323, s. 218; Newfoundland's *Municipalities Act*, S.N. 1999, c. M-24, s. 21; and Nova Scotia's *Municipal Government Act*, S.N.S. 1998, c. 18, s. 15.

In addition, the head of council is charged with the legislated duty of presiding at all council meetings[5] and is also responsible for signing all by- laws passed at the meetings over which he or she presided.[6]

Where the head of council is absent, refuses to act, or the office is vacant, council may, by by-law or resolution, appoint a member of council to act in the place of the head of council.[7] Furthermore, the council may, with the consent of the head of council, appoint a member of council to act in the place of the head of council "on any body, other than the council of another municipality, of which the head is a member by virtue of being head of council."[8]

Explusion for Improper Conduct

In addition to the statutory duties described above, the head of council, or other presiding officer, has the legislative authority to "expel any person for improper conduct at a meeting."[9] As the phrase "improper conduct" is not defined, there remains a great degree of flexibility when being interpreted by a presiding officer. Balanced against the severity of the penalty in this provision (expulsion from the meeting), it is likely that the "improper conduct" contemplated would have to be equally severe, possibly to the point of completely disrupting the meeting.

It is also important to note that this expulsion power is not limited to municipal councillors, but includes "any person" who is behaving improperly in the opinion of the head of council or presiding officer. This broad authority, usually applied in only the most extreme circumstances, may be used in conjunction with a municipality's ability to restrict or bar a person's access to future meetings in accordance with the provisions of the relevant trespass legislation.[10]

In one rare instance, this type of approach resulted in a city obtaining an injunction against a citizen who had, on numerous occasions, disrupted both council and committee meetings. In that 1993 case, *Port Coquitlam (City) v. Osberg*, the municipality sought a court order bar-

---

5   *Municipal Act, 2001*, S.O. 2001, c. 25, s. 241 (1).
6   *Ibid.*, s. 249.
7   *Ibid.*, s. 242.
8   *Ibid.*, s. 226.
9   *Ibid.*, s. 241 (2).
10 In Ontario, this would be the *Trespass to Property Act*, R.S.O. 1990, c. T.21.

ring the individual from attending further council meetings and restrained her from entering any part of city hall, save and except for the public reception desk.[11] In granting the order, Chief Justice Esson stated that the "court will not lightly interfere in that way with a citizen's right to express herself, to be present at meetings and to have access to the offices of the municipality." He went on to confirm that "neither the defendant nor anyone else has the right to deliberately obstruct the workings of our institutions"and that "the plaintiffs, not only for the benefit of the mayor and the other officers of the city, but of the general body of ratepayers to whom they are responsible, have a right to protect civic government from conduct such as that in which the defendant has indulged herself since 1987."[12]

In contrast to the *Osberg* ruling is the 2001 judgment in the Ontario case of *R. v. Behrens*.[13] In that instance, five members of Toronto Action for Social Change, an organization involved in non-violent political protests and peaceful protests, were charged under the *Trespass to Property Act*. The charges arose after the defendants had entered upon the adjoining grounds of the Legislative Building at Queen's Park, despite being prohibited from doing so by the Speaker of Ontario's Legislative Assembly. Although the Crown suggested that this was "strictly a simple trespass matter and nothing more," the defendants argued that their Charter rights to assemble and express themselves had been violated. After a thorough review of the relevant law, Quon J.P. dismissed the trespass charges as follows:

> In accordance with the [case law], it would be untenable for the government to use the law of trespass to quell the voices of dissent and the freedom of expression on state-owned property. The government should not wantonly use the law of trespass to evict legitimate peaceful protesters or stop their voices. This form of expression, expressing dissatisfaction with a government policy and publicizing a particular political view while on state-owned prop-

---

11 *Port Coquitlam (City) v. Osberg*, [1993] B.C.J. No. 1005, cited in 2 D.M.P.L. Vol. 2, issue 8, at p. 139.

12 *Ibid.*, at para. 12.

13 [2001] O.J. No. 245.

erty, is a value cherished and is protected by section 2 (b) [of the Charter].[14]

Therefore, despite the ruling in the *Osberg* case, it is suggested that the courts will be loathe to support any trespass bans that appear to infringe a person's Charter rights.

In another rather unusual case, *R. v. Ellis*,[15] a charge had been laid against the defendant under the *Criminal Code*[16] for causing a disturbance in a council chamber. The Honourable Justice K. Johnston found in part that:

> ... the defendant said things in an elevated voice that some people call shouting and some people do not call shouting.
>
> I am not satisfied that the decision of council to go into a committee of the whole was in fact a legitimate decision and I find as a fact the reason they chose to go into a committee of the whole at that point was because they wanted to get rid of Mr. Ellis because they did not like to hear what he had to say.
>
> ... the issue is clearly ... whether or not a disturbance sufficient to warrant criminal sanction was caused on this evening.

The court concluded that the accused had not caused a disturbance worthy of attracting criminal sanctions and that the decision to go into committee of the whole was in fact wrongly motivated by virtue of the fact that it was a convenient method of silencing Mr. Ellis, or so they thought.[17]

A similar ruling occurred in a 1992 Quebec decision. However, it concerned the interpretation of a municipal by-law and not the *Criminal Code*. In *Ste-Catherine (Ville) v. Fyfe*,[18] the respondent asked the mayor a number of questions regarding the forced retirement of her husband, a municipal firefighter, during a council meeting. The mayor had the po-

---

14 *Ibid.*, par. 103.

15 (Ont. Ct. Prov. Div.), Peterborough, July 6, 1992, Johnston, Ont. C.J., *Municipal World*, August 1992, p. 3.

16 R.S.C. 1985, c. C-46, s. 174 (1) (a) (i).

17 For a discussion of this case, see the editorial "Eviction for improper conduct in a council chamber," *Municipal World*, August 1992, at pp. 3, 21. *R. v. Ellis*, (Ont. Ct. Prov. Div.), Peterborough, July 6, 1992, Johnston, Ont. C.J.

18 (1992), 14 M.P.L.R. (2d) 304.

lice remove the respondent from the room and charge her with breaching a by-law that prohibited the disruption of a "public performance, show, lecture or similar gathering." Although an appeal court subsequently ruled that a session of a municipal council was "a similar gathering" as set out in the by-law, it also found that:

> ... a violation of the by-law as it related to the question period did not necessarily constitute a disruption of public order or disorderly conduct likely to generate trouble. Contradicting the mayor did not *per se* constitute disruption and it was the municipal court's duty to re-assess the evidence and rule on the issue.

Members of Council

During the 1996 consultation phase that precipitated the release of Ontario's *Municipal Act, 2001,* a reporting letter, simply called "Stage 2 of the Municipal Reform Initiative," emphasized the need to statutorily delineate the responsibilities of elected representatives from those of municipal staff:

> The sub-panel would like to underscore that there should be a sharp line drawn between the governing powers exercised by a council and the administrative responsibilities of municipal staff. Council is responsible for setting out municipal policy. The staff are charged with researching, providing advice and implementing council's policy direction. This type of clear statement in legislation will prevent ambiguity.[19]

In response to these concerns, the *Municipal Act, 2001* clarified the role of the municipal councillor in the following areas:

224. It is the role of council,

    (a)   to represent the public and to consider the well-being and interests of the municipality;

    (b)   to develop and evaluate the policies and programs of the municipality;

    (c)   to determine which services the municipality provides;

---

19 "Stage 2 of the Municipal Reform Initiative," correspondence from Dr. Peter Meyboom to the Honourable Al Leach, Minister of Municipal Affairs and Housing (December 6, 1996).

(d) to ensure that administrative practices and procedures are in place to implement the decisions of council;

(e) to maintain the financial integrity of the municipality; and

(f) to carry out the duties of council under this or any other Act.

Similar statutory duties have been established in other provinces for members of council.[20]

Quorum

A "quorum" is the minimum number of members of a council or local board required to be present at a meeting in order to legally transact business. In Ontario, the legislation applicable to a council meeting provides that, in most cases, a quorum is a "majority of the members of a municipal council."[21] The practical effect of this requirement is to relax the majority voting requirements for smaller councils. For instance, on a council of five members, a quorum would be three; however, a simple majority of the quorum (being two members) is all that is now required for a council to pass any measure.

Similar "majority" provisions apply to certain local boards.[22] Members, however, must check the enabling legislation specifically applicable to the local board and/or committee, as in certain instances this simple majority principle for a quorum is not observed. For example, with respect to the quorum for conservation authorities, the statute provides that "a quorum consists of one-third of the members appointed by the participating municipalities, except where there are fewer than six such members, in which case two such members constitute a quorum."[23]

In addition, when determining a quorum, all municipal councils and local boards must have regard to the provisions of other relevant provincial statutes. For example, section 7 of Ontario's *Municipal Conflict of Interest Act* states that when the number of councillors who cannot par-

---

20 For example, see Alberta's *Municipal Government Act*, S.A. 1994, c. M-26, s. 153.

21 *Municipal Act, 2001*, S.O. 2001, c. 25, s. 237 (1); note that it also sets out various exceptions for certain upper-tier municipalities.

22 For example, see the *Education Act*, R.S.O. 1990, c. E.2, s. 208 (11); and *Police Services Act*, R.S.O. 1990, c. P.15, s. 35 (2).

23 *Conservation Authorities Act*, R.S.O. 1990, c. C.27, s. 16 (2).

ticipate in a matter "is such that the remaining members are not of sufficient number to constitute a quorum, then despite any other general or special Act, the remaining number of members shall be deemed to constitute a quorum, provided such number is not less than two."[24]

Public Notice and Consultation

Related to the open and closed meeting provisions discussed earlier are the notice and consultation requirements under the *Municipal Act, 2001*. The former legislation contained a vast number of different notice requirements. In 1996, the consultation process emphasized that municipalities should develop and implement their own notice requirements, since they are "in the best position to determine the most appropriate means for giving notice in a particular situation." In light of this sentiment, it was recommended that "municipalities have the authority to determine whether and how to give notice in the case of both their proposed and past by-law."[25]

Not surprisingly, the notice requirements in section 251 of the *Municipal Act, 2001* succinctly delegate this matter to each municipality:

> Where a municipality is required to give notice under a provision of this Act, the municipality shall, except as otherwise provided, give the notice in a form and in the manner and at the times that the council considers adequate to give reasonable notice under the provision.

The first observation to be made with regard to this provision is that there is no statutory requirement to have a separate consultation by-law. Secondly, most municipalities will likely enact a notice by-law as early as possible in order to avoid any procedural difficulties or delays that may arise in the absence of one. It is recommended that municipal staff should review and harmonize all of the relevant notice provisions that their municipality previously adhered to and consolidate them in a single notice by-law. In doing so, reference should be had to section 2 of the Act, whereby "each municipality is given powers and duties under this Act and many other Acts." Therefore, in seeking to develop a harmonized notice by-law, municipalities cannot override the relevant notice

---

24 *Municipal Conflict of Interest Act*, R.S.O. 1990, c. M.50, s. 7.
25 "Stage 2 of the Municipal Reform Initiatives," correspondence from Dr. Peter Meyboom to the Honourable Al Leach, Minister of Municipal Affairs and Housing (December 6, 1996), at p. 13.

provisions set out in the *Municipal Act, 2001* or other provincial statutes.

For example, there are numerous provisions in the *Municipal Act, 2001* that require a municipality to give notice (to the public or other specified persons) with regard to its intent to pass a specific type of by-law, including:

- give notice to the public of its intention to pass a by-law for permanently closing/altering a highway (subsections 34 (1) and (2)); and

- given notice to a local board before passing a by-law either dissolving or making prescribed changes to the board (subsection 216 (4)).

In reviewing this matter, staff should also reference the statutory definition of the word "newspaper," as set out in the *Interpretation Act*.[26] Finally, it is important to recall that such notice provisions may be challenged in the courts on a variety of grounds, including whether or not they are "reasonable." Having said that, it is worth observing that the *Municipal Act, 2001* also contains special "public notice" requirements, including a rather vague provision related to adopting or amending a budget.[27] Whether there is any substantive difference between the statutory requirement to give "reasonable notice" versus "public notice" remains to be seen.

Open Voting

The *Municipal Act, 2001* also prescribes a number of matters with regard to the voting process to be followed by councils and local boards. To begin with, the statute expressly states that, "except as otherwise provided, every member of council shall have one vote."[28] In addition, the legislation also provides that "a tie vote shall be deemed to be lost, except as otherwise provided by any Act."[29]

On the issue of "recorded votes," any member of council may request that a particular vote be recorded and each member present, and not dis-

---

26 R.S.O. 1990, c. I.11, s. 29 (1).
27 *Municipal Act, 2001*, S.O. 2001, c. 25, s. 291.
28 *Ibid.*, s. 243.
29 *Ibid.*, s. 245.

OPEN LOCAL GOVERNMENT

qualified from voting by virtue of any legislation, must then openly announce his or her vote. In such circumstances, a failure to vote by a member who is present is deemed to be a negative vote.[30] In Ontario, the *Municipal Act, 2001* does not expressly address the issue of a member abstaining from a vote. By comparison, Alberta's *Municipal Government Act* requires a council member to abstain from voting on a by-law or resolution if he or she "was absent from all of the public hearings" where the matter was discussed.[31] The practical effect of this issue not being in the *Municipal Act, 2001* means that members seeking to truly abstain and not be counted may do so by leaving the council chamber before the vote is called. What is clear from all of these variations is that a member of council must be present in order to have his or her vote recorded. This clarity should end those few situations where assumptions are made with respect to how certain absentee or "phantom" councillors may have voted.[32]

Furthermore, it is important to note that when a question is put by the presiding officer and "carried" without a dissent or a call for a recorded vote, then the matter will be deemed to be carried unanimously by those present.[33]

The *Municipal Act, 2001* also contains a prohibition against all methods of "secret voting" and further provides that if such a secret vote is taken, it "is of no effect."[34] This prohibition against secret voting is best described as a ban on "anonymous voting." As such, the restriction has never been seen to be a ban against voting while participating in an *in camera* meeting, provided that such voting was not done by secret ballot. An exception to the prohibition against any "method of secret voting" is with respect to the election of a head of council, since the Act ex-

---

30 *Ibid.*, s. 246; see also *Thunder Bay Seaway Non-Profit Apartments v. Thunder Bay (City)* (1991), 5 O.R. (3d) 667 at 674 (Ont. Div. Ct.) under *Municipal Act*, R.S.O. 1990, c. M.45, s. 61 (1).

31 S.A. 1994, c. M-26.1, s. 184.

32 See "Phantom Councillors: Absent Brant County Councillors Should Not Be Permitted to Vote," *Brantford Expositer*, p. A12, January 25, 2002.

33 See for example the comments of Greene J. in *R. v. Jaimet*, [1940] 4 D.L.R. 264 at 267, (Ont. S.C.) who said that under such circumstances, "it seems to me that ... it should be held that the vote was unanimous."

34 *Municipal Act, 2001*, S.O. 2001, c. 25, s. 244.

pressly states that the "head of council may be appointed by secret ballot."[35]

Closed Voting

Reference should also be had to the statutory provisions that address votes during a closed meeting. Briefly, the Act provides that "a meeting shall not be closed to the public during the taking of a vote." At first glance, the introduction of such a mandatory requirement may appear both reasonable and consistent with the intentions of most local governments to function as open and accountable public bodies. However, subsection 239 (6) provides that "a meeting may be closed to the public during a vote" if:

(a) subsection 239 (2) or (3) permits or requires the meeting to be closed to the public; and

(b) the vote is for a procedural matter or for giving directions or instructions to officers, employees or agents of the municipality, local board or committee of either of them or persons retained by or under a contract with the municipality or local board.

Prior to 1995, it was apparent that, at previous lawfully closed committee meetings in Ontario, any number of votes could be taken upon motions prior to a final vote on the matter. The *Municipal Act, 2001* further clarifies that the only votes permitted during such *in camera* council or committee deliberations must fall within one of two exceptions: procedural matters, or giving instructions or direction to staff. All other votes, including those infamous "straw" votes, as well as the so-called definitive or final ones, must be made in open session. A practical example may be useful in illustrating how these statutory requirements may be implemented.

---

[35] *Ibid.*, s. 233 (5): for a history of the circumstances relative to this unusual provision, see the editorial "Secret ballots - are they ultra vires of the Legislature and municipalities?" *Municipal World*, May 1977, p. 114.

Case Study

In order to discuss a pending acquisition of land, a committee of a council or local board in Ontario has resolved to hold a portion of its meeting in closed session, pursuant to clause 239 (2) (c) of the *Municipal Act, 2001*.[36] The staff report being considered by the committee contains a recommendation on the maximum purchase price to be offered to the vendor. Should the committee agree with the staff recommendation, then a vote could be taken during the course of the closed meeting in order to direct staff to proceed with the negotiations to acquire the land pursuant to the price specified in the staff report. This approach would enable the committee members both to direct their staff as necessary and to maintain the confidentiality of their bargaining position in order to obtain the best price available on behalf of their constituents. Similarly, should the committee members feel that the staff offer to purchase is too generous, then this *in camera* voting mechanism would also permit sufficient opportunity to instruct staff on how much they are to offer the vendor on the proposed land acquisition.

Alternatively, a vote of a procedural nature may occur during the course of a closed meeting. To continue from the previous scenario, the situation may arise when the committee would like additional financial or factual information from staff that is not on hand at the meeting. As such, the committee could then vote *in camera* to "defer" the matter until a later date when the requested information could be made available. In a similar fashion, should a committee seek to maintain the item's confidentiality until approved by the full council, the matter could be the subject of an *in camera* vote to "refer" it to council without any substantive recommendation.

It is important to remember that these are specific exceptions to the general rule that "a meeting shall not be closed to the public during the taking of a vote." Therefore, once the negotiated price for the land purchase discussed above is agreed to, then the issue would be brought back before the entire municipal council or local board to be the subject of a substantive vote at an open meeting. Following such public consideration of the issue, the council or board must be aware, however, of the

---

36 Local boards should review their own statutory requirements with regards to this case study. For example, if the local board in question was subject to the *Education Act*, R.S.O. 1990, c. E. 2, the *in camera* committee meeting may be pursuant to clause 207 (2) (c) while the disposal of surplus real property would be in compliance with section 194 and O.Reg. 444/98 as amended.

fact that all of its previous deliberations of the subject-matter, even though dealt with *in camera,* may be open to public scrutiny.[37]

Clearly stated, the two exceptions to the rule are intended to facilitate the decision-making process for local government only to the extent necessary. Premised upon the public's right to know, such exceptions are not to be employed as procedural mechanisms to enhance *in camera* actions.

Appeal of a Vote – Abuse of Process

Should a member wish to "appeal" a vote that has apparently been carried by a council or local board, he or she may first request that a recorded vote be taken in order to clarify the final result. In most cases, barring reconsideration of the matter pursuant to the procedure by-law, there would not appear to be any other appeal mechanism with respect to the matter before the council or local board. What about an appeal to a third party, such as an administrative tribunal or the courts? Two cases shed some light on this unusual approach, which may be viewed as an abuse of process.

In a 1987 case before the Ontario Municipal Board (OMB) known as *Copthorne*, an alderman from the City of Toronto was personally made a party to an appeal before the board pursuant to the *Planning Act*. Although the appeal was allowed in part, the OMB ordered costs against the alderman involved, and made the following comments with regard to his actions in the case:

> The board would also be remiss if it did not say that although there is nothing in law to forbid an alderman from appealing his council's decision, the board believes it is an abuse of process, unless clearly related to an adverse impact occurring against a clearly private interest of the alderman's, i.e. zoning for a wrecking yard next door to his home. The *Municipal Act*, R.S.O. 1980, c. 302, established that councils operate by majority vote when it comes to decision-making. It does not contemplate any appeal by the minority. Thus, to take an appeal to this board as any other ratepayer can, is in those circumstances an "abuse." The sanction, though, is to stop the proceedings, not necessarily to allow costs. There is an old saying, "you win some and you lose some," and that is in the

---

37 For example, see subsection 6 (2) of the *Municipal Freedom of Information and Protection of Privacy Act*, R.S.O. 1990, c. M.56.

board's opinion how aldermen should operate within council. Surely, if an alderman can appeal either to the board, the courts or to Cabinet every time he/she loses a vote at council, municipal activities would come to a halt.[38]

Leave to appeal this order to the Divisional Court was subsequently denied. The court rejected the applicant's argument that the board had taken the position that a member of council did not have status before it. Associate Chief Justice Callaghan was keen to observe that although the board may not like the fact that an alderman who had voted on the matter in council launched the application before it, it did not deprive him of his right to be heard.[39]

More recently, the OMB had another opportunity to revisit the same issue of a councillor's actions in an appeal of a council decision before the board. In this case, a planning issue had been formally resolved by the city council's adoption of Minutes of Settlement, which the member both moved and voted for. At the subsequent OMB hearing, that same councillor took on various roles including: "community leader, spear-heading the opposition by obtaining the assistance of staff and [the municipal] council;" "agent for ratepayers;" a "pay master;" and "acted as the community's lawyer, without finding out the proper responsibilities that a lawyer has before [the] board." The OMB characterized the councillor's actions as having "overstepped the boundaries of appropriate political activism by actively quarterbacking this case to ensure that the hearing would go on despite the Minutes of Settlement." The board concluded by observing, "if he wished to help [his community], he ought not to have voted in favour of the Minutes of Settlement and should have respected the standard for municipal councillors in *Copthorne*."[40]

Therefore, while it may remain an option for members of municipal councils or local boards to appeal the decisions of these bodies, in accordance with a statute granting such a right of appeal to the general public, to either the courts or relevant administrative tribunals, it is

---

38 *Re Copthorne Holdings Ltd.* (1987), 36 M.P.L.R. 122 at 139 (OMB).

39 *Martin v. Toronto (City)* (1987), 36 M.P.L.R. 141 at 143 (Ont. Div. Ct.).

40 *Toronto (City) v. Vaughan (City)* (April 3, 1998), an unreported decision of Member Ted Yao, OMB. File Nos. 0970126, R970140, M970047 and M970075: See M. Rick O'Connor, Councillor Misconduct at the Ontario Municipal Board (1998), 4 D.M.P.L. 247.

worth remembering that such a route of appeal may be found to be an abuse of process and have costs or related consequences attached to it.

Ultra Vires

Municipalities and local boards are often called "creatures of statute," that are bound by the legislative constraints of their respective enabling charters or statutes. As such, they are established to exercise only those powers that have been expressly delegated to them by the provincial legislatures. Consequently, any action deemed to be outside the powers of a municipal council can be nullified by the courts. The ability of the courts to review the actions of such government bodies, with a view to determining whether their acts are within the scope of their delegated powers, has resulted in the development of the common law doctrine of *ultra vires*. Ian MacF. Rogers defines the doctrine as follows:

> If there is no legislative authority, express or implied, vested in the corporation to deal with the subject-matter, then the by-law, resolution or other act is beyond its power and is a nullity.[41]

Despite this restriction, municipal councils and local boards will, from time to time, undertake actions in areas outside of the generally accepted mandate for local government. It is perhaps not surprising that the use of a municipal referendum, in various jurisdictions across Canada, has contributed significantly to the case law with respect to *ultra vires*. For example, in the case of *Baird v. Oak Bay (District)*, the British Columbia Supreme Court dismissed an application to set aside a municipal by-law to hold a local referendum on whether electors supported the goal of the general nuclear disarmament, and whether or not they wanted to encourage the federal government to continue its efforts to negotiate and implement a balanced reduction in nuclear weapons and other weapons of mass destruction.[42]

In another British Columbia case, *Shell Canada Products v. Vancouver (City)*, the confusion that can arise when interpreting the doctrine of *ultra vires* was demonstrated by the conflicting decisions of all levels of court in that instance. The facts of the case were relatively straightforward. The City of Vancouver sought to make a symbolic gesture against international companies with business links to South Africa. Therefore,

---

41 Ian MacF. Rogers, *The Law of Canadian Municipal Corporations*, 2nd ed. (Toronto: Carswell, 2002), p. 362.
42 (1982), 21 M.P.L.R. 278.

it passed two resolutions proclaiming that the city would not do business with Shell Canada Products Limited until the parent company divested itself of its South African holdings. At trial, the British Columbia Supreme Court allowed Shell Canada's challenge and ruled that the city had to act within its legislated jurisdiction and could not pursue a philosophical or political interest not set out in that legislation.[43] The decision at trial was subsequently reversed by the British Columbia Court of Appeal, which found that, as there was no express limitation on the city's commercial power in the statute, it should not be inferred by a court.[44] However, the Court of Appeal's decision was ultimately overturned by the Supreme Court of Canada on a slim majority. In holding that the resolutions of the city were *ultra vires*, Mr. Justice Sopinka found that their purpose was to "affect matters beyond the boundaries of the city without any identifiable benefit to its inhabitants," a breach of the territorial limit placed on the council's jurisdiction.[45]

One of the most recent decisions dealing with the *ultra vires* doctrine was an application to quash two by-laws of the City of Toronto that changed the term of office for council members of the Toronto Transit Commission from three years to 18 months, and provided for appointments to be made by a simple majority vote of council. It was argued that this simple majority requirement was in conflict with subsection 26 (1) of the *City of Toronto Act, 1997 (No. 2)*, which statutorily required that "the appointment of a member requires the affirmative vote of at least two-thirds of the members of council present and voting." In quashing both of the by-laws in question, the court summarized the law as follows:

> As creatures of statute, municipalities have only those powers which are expressly conferred upon them by statute or which are fairly implied therefrom. Where subordinate legislation, such as a municipal by-law, effectively adds or alters substantive requirements specifically set out in governing legislation, it is *ultra vires* to the extent of the inconsistency.

---

43 (1990), 49 M.P.L.R. 185.
44 (1991), 6 M.P.L.R. (2d) 116.
45 [1994] 1 S.C.R. 231.

In my opinion, city council had no authority under its governing legislation, namely the *City of Toronto Act, 1997 (No. 2)* to change the specifically mandated majority to a simple majority.[46]

Other Relevant Statutes

In addition to adhering to all of the provisions in the enabling legislation for a municipality or local board, reference must also be had to other relevant statutes. These will include, as previously noted, such statutes as the *Interpretation Act* or the *Statutory Powers Procedure Act*. As well, local government staff must remain vigilant for any new statutes affecting municipalities and local boards. Such legislation seems to be on the rise in Ontario, perhaps a side-effect of years of provincial downloading. Two brief examples will suffice.

The *Ontarians with Disabilities Act, 2001*, for instance, requires certain municipalities to develop accessibility plans and to establish accessibility advisory committees to advise council on the implementation effectiveness of said plans.[47] Similarly, the *Emergency Management Act* obligates every municipality to develop and implement an emergency management program that must be adopted by by-law.[48] The failure of a local government to be cognizant of and respond to any statutory duties arising from these other Acts could result in an allegation of non-compliance.

---

46 *Moscoe v. Toronto (City) et al.*, [1999] O.J. No. 3012, at p. 4.

47 S.O. 2001, c. 32.

48 S.O. 2002, c. 14.

Chapter 5
PROCEDURE BY-LAW

There is no general rule without some exception.

17th Century Proverb

The municipal legislative process is dominated by the enactment of by-laws by the council, often in a manner reminiscent of either the federal or provincial legislature when passing a Bill into law. It is important, however, not to overstate the obvious parallels between these two processes. The latter levels of government generally adhere to the parliamentary system of democratic law-making, replete with its centuries of colourful history and legal precedents. Municipal governments, on the other hand, have few, if any, contemporary reference materials in either statute or jurisprudence form to provide guidance in the way they govern themselves.[1]

True, the *Municipal Act, 2001* in Ontario, and similar statutes in other provincial jurisdictions, provide some statutory directions regarding the first meeting of a newly-elected council, the place, time and nature of council meetings, the quorum requirements and the rules for voting.[2] Unfortunately, there is little else to assist councillors in addressing such issues as the proper rules of debate, or how to properly reconsider an item previously rejected by their council, or even how to adopt a valid and legally binding by-law or resolution.

The overall purpose of a procedure by-law is to assist in the effective decision making of a municipal council or local board. In the absence of

---

1 For example, see the suggested code of rules in Sir John George Bourinot's 1894 essay, "A Canadian Manual on the Procedure at Meetings of Municipal Councils and Other Public Bodies," as well as Chapter XX, being a draft Procedure By-law for Municipal Council, in Arthur Beauchesne's *Procedure at Meetings in Canada* (Toronto: Canada Law Book, 1954).

2 For details of these issues, see Chapter 4, Statutory Procedures.

the more restrictive confines of partisan, party politics, the legislative process for councils and local boards is often forged in the heat and light of persuasive debate, and ultimately enacted by consensus. It is in this atmosphere that an effective procedure by-law will operate to keep the business at hand running reasonably smooth.

Parliamentary Procedure

When faced with procedural problems, some municipal councils and local boards have looked to either parliament or their respective provincial legislature to see how they resolved these issues. In this respect, careful reference may be made to the classic procedural treatises by Bourinot, Beauchesne, May or Robert.[3] Despite these traditional resource aids, and contrary to popular misconception, there has never been any specific set of rules or procedures – parliamentary or otherwise – that would legally bind municipal councils or local boards in their decision-making process. In fact, in the absence of a procedure by-law specifically incorporating such parliamentary rules, they would have no inherent application to how Canadian local governments operate.

For example, in Ontario, there is no general legislative requirement that municipal by-laws must, like statutes, receive three readings prior to enactment.[4] Unfortunately, certain by-laws passed under other legislation, such as the *Drainage Act*, do require three readings. It has been observed that this inconsistent approach may give rise to confusion, and demonstrates "the need for clear municipal practice rules" on such matters.[5] Similarly, there is no general, statutory requirement for a House of Commons-style question period when a municipal council or local board is considering a particular course of action. To the contrary, a Quebec municipality's by-law, which limited the number of questions

---

[3] Sir John George Bourinot, *Bourinot's Rules of Order*, 3rd ed. revised by G.H. Stanford (Toronto: McClelland and Stewart, 1977); Arthur Beauchesne, *Beauchesne's Rules & Forms of the House of Commons of Canada*, 6th ed. by A. Fraser, W.F. Dawson and J.A. Holthy (Toronto: Carswell, 1989); Erskine May, *Treatise on the Law, Privileges, Proceedings and Usage of Parliament*, 19th ed. by D. Lidderdale (London: Butterworths, 1976); and General Henry M. Robert, *Robert's Rules of Order*, 9th ed. by S.C. Robert (U.S.A.: Scott Foresmen, 1990).

[4] Conversely, section 187 of Alberta's *Municipal Government Act*, R.S.A. 2000, c. M-26, provides that, "every proposed by-law must have 3 distinct and separate readings."

[5] *Drainage Act*, R.S.O. 1990, c. D.17, s. 75 (1) (a); see also "Three Readings of By-laws" by M.J. Smither and C.P. Stobo, *Municipal World*, May 1992, p. 12 at 13.

that could be asked at council meetings by the public and established an overall time limit on such "question periods," was upheld in court.[6]

A procedure by-law expressly incorporating some version of parliamentary procedure, such as *Bourinot's Rules of Order,* may create other problems, both real and perceived. Typically, procedure by-laws that adopt parliamentary procedures do so in the following manner:

> The proceedings of the council/board shall be governed by the provisions of this by-law and, except as provided herein, the rules of parliamentary procedure as contained in *Bourinot's Rules of Order* shall be followed.

The immediate perception one may have from reading this clause is that the procedure by-law is so defective or incomplete that constant reference to the parliamentary rules of procedure cited is likely required. Alternatively, where a procedure by-law contains a sufficiently detailed code of conduct to effectively govern proceedings, a reference incorporating parliamentary procedure may be redundant.

Therefore, it is recommended that municipal councils and local boards should not automatically adopt, in their entirety, such publications on parliamentary rules in their procedure by-laws. In the alternative, it is suggested that a glossary of parliamentary procedures and terms could be appended to the by-law as a separate and distinct schedule, to be used solely as a reference for the assistance and guidance of the council or board. Similarly, a procedure by-law need not "adopt" *Bourinot's Rules of Order,* but could merely provide that, in the case of a conflict with or omission of the rules of procedures, *Bourinot's Rules of Order* may be consulted as an interpretive aid in resolving the problem.

Mandatory Procedure By-laws

For more than a century, municipal councils and local boards in Ontario were not even obligated by statute to enact by-laws governing their proceedings.[7] In the provincial "White Paper on Open Local Government" the requirement to enact a procedure by-law was to remain optional. This draft legislation, however, reserved to the minister the right to prescribe by regulation "standards for the calling, place and proceedings of

---

6   *Laplante v. Sainte-Liboire (Municipalité)* (1990), 4 M.P.L.R. (2d) 220.
7   For example, the *Municipal Act,* R.S.O. 1990, c. M.45, s. 102, merely provided an option for councils to enact procedure by-laws.

meetings of councils and local boards."[8] This proposal was criticized by such organizations as the Association of Municipalities of Ontario (AMO) for being "largely intrusive in the every day conduct of municipalities." According to AMO, the preferable alternative was to make the passage of a procedure by-law mandatory for every municipal council and local board in Ontario.[9] Such procedure by-laws are now mandatory in Ontario was subsection 238 (2) of the *Municipal Act, 2001*:

> Every municipality and local board shall pass a procedure by-law for governing the calling, place and proceedings of meetings.

The *Municipal Act, 2001* further provides for the following with respect to procedure by-laws:

- the first meeting of a new council shall be held at the time set out in the municipality's procedure by-law (s. 230);

- council shall hold its meetings and keep its public offices within the municipality or an adjacent municipality at a place set out in the municipality's procedure by-law (s. 236); and

- a municipality and local board shall give notice of an intention to pass a procedure by-law (s. 238 (4)).

Inclusion of Statutory Procedures

Chapter 4, Statutory Procedures, reviewed a host of statutory procedures found in the *Municipal Act, 2001* that municipal councils must adhere to when calling and holding meetings. In this respect, it is important to remember that such local by-laws governing procedure are subject to legislative provisions in the *Municipal Act, 2001* that already address the same issues. In effect, a procedure by-law enacted by a municipal council could not derogate from the statutory requirements set out in the enabling legislation. To do so would imperil any action taken by the council that was in breach of the legislation.

---

8   White Paper on Open Local Government (1992), p. 33 at s. 55.1 (2).
9   Association of Municipalities of Ontario Response to Open Local Government (March 1992), p. 39.

For example, in the case of *Southam Inc. et al. v. Ottawa (City)*,[10] the city council's decision to hold an *in camera* "retreat" at the Calabogie Resort was challenged on the basis that the gathering was really a council meeting that pursuant to both the *Municipal Act* and the city's procedure by-law, should have been open to the public. The Divisional Court subsequently agreed that the retreat was, in fact, an *in camera* meeting held contrary to both the Act and the by-law. Ultimately, the court determined that the council decision to hold such an *in camera* meeting exceeded its jurisdiction and issued an order quashing and setting aside that decision.

Therefore, a procedure by-law must adhere to the provisions governing meetings contained in the relevant enabling legislation, and any other provincial statutes that establish such legislative standards. Alternatively, a procedure by-law may only regulate those aspects of meetings upon which provincial legislation is either permissive or altogether silent.

Despite these requirements, a procedure by-law should not merely reiterate all the meeting and procedural provisions set out in the *Municipal Act, 2001*. The reasons for this recommendation are varied. To begin with, there is always the possibility that the by-law's drafters could inadvertently alter the wording of the statutory provision and thus modify its effect, leaving the council or local board in breach of the Act, albeit unintentionally.

Alternatively, even if the provisions are copied verbatim from the statute, the legislation may subsequently be amended or a regulation enacted, and those revisions may not always be carried forward into the by-law in a timely fashion. In such a case, the council or board may purportedly be adhering to a statutory requirement that was, in fact, repealed or revised long ago.

Finally, if a procedure by-law incorporates a number of statutory provisions, there exists the potential of apparently overriding these legislative requirements when a municipal council or local board votes to suspend or waive its own procedure by-law.

The challenge is to develop a procedure by-law that clearly identifies and refers to all procedures to be observed by councils and local boards,

---

10 *Southam Inc. et al. v. Ottawa (City)* (1991), 5 O.R. (3d) 726.

but which does not incur any of the foregoing concerns. The problem may be overcome by including a schedule to the procedure by-law identifying all of the mandatory provisions from the *Municipal Act, 2001* and other statutes, once again, for reference only. Many problematic issues can be resolved simply by treating references to parliamentary procedures and statutory provisions as separate schedules that do not form part of the procedure by-law.

Procedure By-law Structure

Keeping in mind the foregoing concerns, municipal councils and local boards are, nevertheless, free to borrow from either the parliamentary precedents currently in existence or those procedure by-laws previously enacted by other local government bodies. Extreme caution is urged, however, in reproducing unabridged such procedure by-laws from other organizations blindly, albeit in good faith. Detailed council procedures appropriated from a major metropolitan area may be practically worthless to a small council or local board of five members that already operates reasonably well.[11] To that end, it is suggested that each municipal council and local board develop its own, home-grown procedure by-law.

While such rules will, no doubt, take various forms, it is suggested that the most effective procedure by-laws should be based upon the following general framework,[12] which also identifies the relevant *Municipal Act, 2001* provisions for convenience:

- title;
- recitals;
- definitions;
- duties of the head of council and/or members of council (ss. 224 and 225);
- time and place of first/regular meetings (ss. 230 and 238(2));
- special meetings (s. 240);

---

11 For example, the City of Ottawa's by-law governing council and committee procedures, being By-law No. 2002-247, is 44 pages in length.

12 See the former Regional Municipality of Ottawa-Carleton By-law No. 238 of 1991; see also W. Knott, *Developing a Municipal Procedural By-law*, AMCTO How-to Series, Manual #36 (June 1992).

- where head of council absent (s. 242);
- open and closed meetings (s. 239);
- quorum requirements (s. 237);
- voting in council (s. 243)
    - recorded vote (s. 246)
    - secret ballot prohibited (ss. 233 and 244)
    - tie vote (s. 245)
    - the putting of questions;
- rules of conduct and debate (s. 241);
- resolutions and motions;
- by-laws (s. 5 (3));
- committee proceedings and reporting;
- adjournments;
- suspension of rules;
- Schedule "A" – extracts from the *Municipal Act, 2001* and other legislation for reference only;
- Schedule "B" – glossary of terms and parliamentary procedures for the guidance of the council/local board.

Routine interpretation and enforcement of the procedure by-law will primarily be carried out by the meeting's presiding officer and subject only to appeal to the municipal council or local board itself, as the case may be.

Conduct of Members

One observation may be made with regard to the ability of a council to regulate "the conduct of members" within the confines of a procedure by-law. Section 102 of the former *Municipal Act* in Ontario established the general regulatory power to enact by-laws "for the health, safety, morality and welfare of the inhabitants of the municipality ... and for governing the conduct of its members as may be deemed expedient and are not contrary to law."[13]

It was argued that the effect of this clause was significant, as it no longer restricted a council's authority to regulate "the conduct of its members" strictly within the narrow confines of a meeting as set down in a procedure by-law. In effect, the power of a council to govern by by-law "the conduct of its members" could have been broadened to include any circumstance within the context of the affairs of the municipality. For example, such a by-law could attempt to regulate such matters as the conduct of councillors before and after a council meeting, the relationship between councillors and staff and other sensitive issues such as lobbying. Without clear limitations being set down in the former Act, there was a concern that a council could impose a regime to regulate the conduct of its members, which could have the effect of infringing on a member's fundamental rights or freedoms as guaranteed by the *Canadian Charter of Rights and Freedoms*.

In light of these concerns, it is perhaps not surprising that the *Municipal Act, 2001* only mandates the passage of a procedure by-law that governs "the calling, place and proceedings of meetings," thus reverting to the pre-1995 provision regulating members' conduct solely within the confines of meetings. Nevertheless, the existence of the natural person powers in section 8 of the *Municipal Act, 2001* may provide a municipal council with the ability to enact rules regulating the conduct of their members. This particular issue will be examined in greater detail in Chapter 10, Members' Code of Conduct.

Waiver Clause

Even if all municipal councils and local boards adopt comprehensive procedure by-laws, it is inevitable that, in some unique emergency situ-

---

13 This was a change from the pre-1995 *Municipal Act*, R.S.O. 1990, c. M.45, in which s. 102 provided as follows: "Every council may pass such by-laws and make such regulations ... for governing the proceedings of the council, the conduct of its members and the calling of meetings."

ations, the decision-makers will be inclined not to follow their own rules. Therefore, most procedure by-laws include a clause that will enable the council or local board to suspend or waive any of its internal rules.

In some instances, it may be desirable to establish a special two-thirds or three-quarters vote of the whole council to suspend the rules, in order to preserve the integrity of the procedure by-law. Such a weighted vote could ensure that the circumstances when the rules are waived are truly rare. Requiring endorsement by more than a simple majority of members present may act as a barrier to those members merely seeking to evade the rules of procedure for their own purposes.

Special Meetings

As noted in Chapter 4, section 240 of the *Municipal Act, 2001* provides councils and local boards with the authority to establish their own local requirements to hold a special meeting. Traditionally, it had been held that a special meeting was only to be called for the purpose stated in the notice, and that the only business to be transacted must relate to the matter set out in the notice. Council decisions on matters not specified in the notice were thus subject to judicial challenge.

However, the new Act clearly provides that it is up to council, via its procedure by-law, to determine what can be considered at a special meeting. Therefore, some thought should be given to a provision specifically addressing the consideration of a matter not set out in the notice to the special meeting. Based on the waiver clause discussed above, a weighted vote of two-thirds of the whole council may be appropriate for council to consider a matter of which notice had not been given.

Violations

Although not expressly set out in the *Municipal Act, 2001*, the head of council is usually the sole arbiter on all points of procedure, subject to an appeal to the complete council.[14] Most procedure by-laws contain a specific section that identifies sanctions to be invoked against those who persist in breaching the rules. These penalties may range from asking a member to merely apologize for his or her inappropriate behaviour to directing their removal from a meeting. One of the most common

---

14 Note that the *Municipal Act, 2001*, S.O. 2001, c. 25, s. 225 (b) requires the head of council to "preside over council meetings" while s. 225 (c) provides that he or she is "to provide leadership to the council."

sanctions is to formally reprimand a member by a vote of censure. One Ontario newspaper reported a council's censure of its own mayor in the following fashion:

> Following a strained discussion, council voted 5-4 to censure the mayor over comments he made to a local columnist about an *in camera* meeting. Censuring a member of council has never occurred before and some politicians said there is no such thing. But several councillors said it is an official reprimand that speaks for itself and requires no further action.[15]

What, then, is the legal effect of a municipal council's failure to properly interpret or adhere to its own procedure by-law? The answer is somewhat complex, dependent upon whether the breach relates directly to a number of different factors.

On the one hand, Canadian courts have been reasonably consistent in holding that a municipal council's non-compliance with its own procedure by-law is merely an irregularity that does not automatically nullify the council's actions.[16] The classic ruling in support of this proposition was rendered by Chief Justice Meredith in the 1917 decision in *Merritton (Village) v. Lincoln (County)*, in which he stated that it is "well settled that failure to conform with the rules of procedure of a municipal council does not invalidate a by-law passed by it."[17] In 1928, in the case of *Re Howard and Toronto (City)*, the Ontario Court of Appeal cited with approval the earlier comments of Meredith C.J.O., but added the following caveat:

> The court cannot prescribe the procedure to be adopted by the council, and cannot quash a by-law for error in procedure, except in cases where there has been a failure to observe the formalities (by way of notice or otherwise) prescribed by the statute as a condition precedent to the exercise of its powers or unless the proceedings are so inequitable and unfair as to evidence a fraudulent misuse by the council of its powers.[18]

---

15 "Council Censures Mayor," *Sarnia Observer*, October 8, 2000, p. A1.
16 Ian MacF. Rogers, *The Law of Canadian Municipal Corporations*, 2nd ed, (Toronto: Carswell, 1994), at pp. 259-261, par. 48.22.
17 *Merritton (Village) v. Lincoln (County)*, 41 O.L.R. 6 at 14.
18 *Re Howard and Toronto (City)*, 61 O.L.R. 563 at 575-576.

This general proposition was subsequently endorsed by Mr. Justice Crossland in the 1990 Ontario case of *Blyth v. Northumberland (County)*, in which he stated, "a court will not quash a by-law for the reason that in passing it the council failed to observe its own procedure unless such procedure is statutory and obligatory."[19]

Thus, where a council's departure from its procedure by-law would constitute a breach of either a mandatory statutory requirement or natural justice, then any action taken by the council in such circumstances may be quashed by the courts.

Despite these generalizations, the Ontario Court of Appeal in the case of *Southam Inc. v. Economic Development Committee of the Regional Municipality of Hamilton-Wentworth* dealt with a situation where the committee held an *"in camera* workshop," whereas the region's procedure by-law required all committee meetings to be held in public.[20] Although the "informal gathering" took place without an agenda; and no reports, recommendations or resolutions were made; nor were any minutes kept; the Court of Appeal held that a "meeting" had occurred in contravention of the procedure by-law. The court then made a declaration that the committee had exceeded its jurisdiction contrary to the procedure by-law.

Prayer

No review of procedure by-laws governing local government meetings in the new millennium would be complete without a reference to the traditional prayer said before many councils and local boards get down to business. The seminal case in this area is the Ontario Court of Appeal's 1999 ruling in *Freitag v. Penetanguishene (Town)*.[21] At the beginning of the town council meetings, the mayor would invite all councillors to rise with him to recite the Lord's Prayer. The applicant, who regularly attended these meetings, applied for a judicial declaration that the mayor's practice of reciting the Lord's Prayer violated his right to freedom of religion guaranteed by clause 2 (a) of the *Canadian Charter of Rights and Freedoms*. Although the application was dismissed at trial, the Ontario Court of Appeal allowed his appeal. The court ruled that the

---

19 *Blyth v. Northumberland (County)* (1990), 75 O.R. (2d) 576 at 582-583.
20 *Southam Inc. v. Economic Development Committee of the Regional Municipality of Hamilton-Wentworth* (1988), 40 M.P.L.R. 1, 33 Admin. L.R. 125, 30 O.A.C. 39 (C.A.). See also the discussion in Chapter 2.
21 (1999), 4 M.P.L.R. (3d) 1.

mayor's authority to preside over a council meeting emanated from the *Municipal Act,* while his ability to open the meeting derived from the town's procedure by-law. Therefore, the mayor's action in standing and reciting the Lord's Prayer was governmental conduct subject to the *Charter.* Furthermore, the purpose of the recitation was to impose a Christian moral tone on the deliberations of the council, in breach of clause 2 (a).

While it is arguable that the use of a non-denominational "prayer," like that used to begin parliament, may have produced a different result, some municipal councils have ceased this practice altogether.[22]

Ironically, two years later, the Ontario Court of Appeal dismissed a very similar challenge aimed at Ontario's Legislative Assembly on the basis that parliamentary privilege protected its internal procedures from such applications. In its unanimous decision, the court was clear to distinguish its earlier ruling in the *Penetanguishene* decision as being "of little guidance to the issues in the case at bar" for the following reasons:

> In terms of comparing the case decided by Feldman J.A. to the case at bar, it must first be noted that in *Freitag v. Penetanguishene, supra,* the offending body was a municipal council, not a provincial legislative assembly. This is an extremely significant difference. A municipal council is a creation of the legislature and only has those powers granted and delegated to it by the province. In the case at bar, the court is being asked to scrutinize the actions of a provincial legislative body that enjoys constitutional status. It is the direct successor to the "mother of all parliaments" in the United Kingdom. The Assembly elected the Speaker from within its membership and clothed the Speaker with far-reaching powers to oversee all of the business of the House. With or without the Standing Orders, the Speaker's activities as they relate to the internal procedures of the legislature are protected by the same constitutionally-entrenched privileges that protect the independence of the legislature itself.[23]

---

22 See for example, "Religion removed from council ceremony," *The Kingston Whig-Standard,* November 18, 2003.

23 *Ontario (Speaker of the Legislative Assembly) v. Ontario Human Rights Commission et al.* (2001), 54 O.R. (3d) 595 at 610.

Revisions

Although most municipal councils and local boards are statutorily obligated to adopt procedure by-laws, those that have already done so should not sit idly by. Procedural changes can be initiated by either the provincial legislature or the courts.

Therefore, it is recommended that the procedure by-law be reviewed once during each municipal term of office. This review would establish a regular opportunity to determine if any amendments are required to address procedural queries or difficulties that repeatedly arose during the last term of council.

Conclusions

Despite the stated intention of procedure by-laws to promote more effective and democratic decision making, occasions will undoubtedly arise whereby these same procedural rules may be used and even abused in order to meet the machinations of a particular member of council or local board. These regrettable instances may be mitigated where all councillors or board members have a thorough understanding of the rules governing their meetings. Alternatively, it is anticipated that the positive effect of enacting such a procedure by-law will be to require public notice and access to such meetings, thereby increasing public participation in the municipal legislative process in due course.

Chapter 6
SALE OF SURPLUS LAND

> *We agree with the Trial Judge that, in the circumstances of this case, the order in which the procedures [were] required by the by-law did not matter. All required procedures did take place and the sale must be upheld.*
>
> Ontario Court of Appeal (2001)

During the past two decades, the political debate in Ontario concerning the methods to achieve more open and accountable decision making for local government bodies generally focused on an oft-cited, three-part platform.[1]

The leading plank was that municipal councils and local boards had to become more open and accessible to the general public, with fewer substantive decisions being made *in camera*. The second initiative proposed was an overhaul of the province's existing municipal conflict of interest legislation. The third and final component of the campaign was to establish minimum standards for the sale of surplus municipal land.

This chapter will discuss the statutory duties imposed by this latter reform strategy in Ontario, and provide some insight on how to achieve compliance with these responsibilities.

Background

In the past, municipal councils and local boards in Ontario were largely free to sell their surplus land in whatever fashion they deemed appropriate. Indeed, the pre-1995 version of section 193 of the *Municipal Act*

---

[1] See for example the following comments of the province's three previous Ministers of Municipal Affairs: the Honourable John Sweeney on April 19, 1990, Legislature of Ontario Debates, 2nd Sess., 34th Parl., p. 654; the Honourable Dave Cooke, December 19, 1991, Legislature of Ontario Debates, 1st Sess., 35th Parl., pp. 4455-4456; and the Honourable Ed Philip, June 16, 1994, Legislature of Ontario Debates, 3rd Sess., 35 Parl., p. 7108.

was more or less a clause designed to restrict judicial review of such sales:

193. Sale of land by council – when not to be open to question
The determination of a council as to the time when, the manner in which, the price for which or the person to whom any property of the corporation that the council may lawfully sell, shall be sold, is not open to question, review, or control by any court, if the purchaser is a person who may lawfully buy and the council acted in good faith.[2]

However, the provincial government introduced Bill 152, being *An Act to Amend the Municipal Act and certain other Acts related to Municipalities* with First Reading on April 19, 1990.[3] Among other things, Bill 152 proposed to amend the *Municipal Act* to statutorily require every council and local board to establish, by by-law, a number of procedures governing the sale of surplus property. Although this Bill subsequently died on the Order Paper, it was likely the origin of those revisions made to the *Municipal Act* some four years later in the *Planning and Municipal Statute Law Amendment Act, 1994*. In fact, the underlying rationale for such revisions seemed to lay in the correlation between the elements in the three-pronged approach to reforming local government. This interrelationship was identified by Bob Rae on the day that Bill 152 was first introduced into the legislature:

> I think the government has to understand the questions we have raised in this House over the last number of years on this very critical question of conflict of interest. The major issues that have been raised by the way in which decisions have been taken in certain municipalities and the extraordinary pressure that is brought to bear on municipalities by the development process itself and by the development industry have got to be understood. We have to have laws to provide that protection and to build that protection into our decision-making process.

> You do not have to be a genius to understand that in southern Ontario in the last decade we have seen one of the greatest building and expansion booms in our history. I would say there has never been a time in Canadian history when a boom of this kind has not

---

2 *Municipal Act*, R.S.O. 1990, c. M.45, s. 193.
3 Bill 152, *An Act to Amend the Municipal Act and certain other Acts related to municipalities*. First Reading, April 19, 1990, 2nd Sess., 34th Parl.

been accompanied by potential and real conflicts of interest. Anybody who reads Canadian history would understand that is the temptation that is there, that is the process that is there. We are dealing with human beings, and that is the problem we face.[4]

A similar sentiment was expressed in the "Report of the Municipal Conflict of Interest Consultation Committee" when it commented on the proposal that a member disclose certain financial interests:

> Included in the range of suggestions was a limited disclosure of real property assets only. This proposal is based on the fact that the overwhelming majority of conflict of interest complaints relate to real property matters. It was proposed, therefore, that as a minimum, disclosure should focus on the member's real property interests. In general, people do not object to this principle because information of this kind is available to the public through the local registry office.[5]

Application of the Municipal Act, 2001

Section 268 of the *Municipal Act, 2001* concerns the sale of surplus land. Subsection 268 (1) states, "Every municipality and local board with authority to sell land shall pass a by-law establishing procedures, including the giving of notice to the public, governing the sale of land."[6] The next provision clarifies that the term "sale" includes a lease of 21 years or longer.

While this provision may be appropriate where a council or board is leasing a building or land in excess of 21 years, it is suggested that this definition may also, rather unintentionally, include easements that have been granted for similar periods of time. In plain terms, an easement is a legal right to utilize another person's land for a particular use, such as running utility lines over or under it. Therefore, it would appear that where a municipal council or local board seeks to grant such an easement to a utility commission, it would be subject to the procedural requirements set out in this provision. Since the granting of such an easement could be a rare occurrence for many councils and local boards, following these requirements would not appear to pose a significant

---

4 Legislature of Ontario Debates, 2nd Sess., 34th Parl., p. 655.
5 "Report of the Municipal Conflict of Interest Consultation Committee," (July 1991), pp. 46-47.
6 S.O. 2001, c. 25, s. 268 (1).

problem. Although it may be somewhat awkward to pass a resolution declaring the easement "to be surplus" in accordance with clause 268 (3) (a), and similarly to give public notice of this matter, the infrequency of such an occurrence militates against undue anxiety.

Subsection 1 (1) of the Act defines "local board" to mean:

> ... a municipal service board, transportation commission, public library board, board of health, police services board, planning board, or any other board, commission, committee, body or local authority established or exercising any power under any Act with respect to the affairs or purposes of one or more municipalities, excluding a school board and a conservation authority.

The statutory requirements described above do not apply to school boards, since they already have specific guidelines that address how they may sell or dispose of real property.[7]

Property Disposal By-law

The Act requires that every municipality and local board with the authority to sell land "shall pass a by law establishing procedures, including the giving of notice to the public, governing the sale of land." Unlike its predecessor legislation, this section does not specifically note anything that may be in such a property disposal by-law.[8]

Subsection 268 (3) of the Act also establishes the following mandatory conditions that must be met prior to the sale of land by either a municipality or local board:

- the property in question must be declared to be surplus, by by-law or resolution;

- at least one appraisal of the fair market value of the land must be obtained; and

---

[7] *Education Act*, R.S.O. 1990, c. E.2, s. 194 and see O.Reg. 444/98, Disposition of Surplus Real Property, amended to O.Reg. 303/03.

[8] See *Municipal Act*, R.S.O. 1990, c. M.45, s. 193 (3), which expressly stated that such by-laws could establish different procedures for different classes of real property and incorporate a procedure for the sale of real property of a council or local board required by this or any other Act; note that section 10 of the *Municipal Act, 2001* appears to provide a general authority to differentiate in such matters.

- notice must be given to the public of the proposed sale.[9]

It is assumed that most municipal councils and local boards will establish their own specific procedures to meet these three pre-conditions and incorporate them within the confines of a distinct property disposal by-law. However, reference should be had to the other relevant provisions of the Act and section 268. For example, clause 239 (2) (c) of the *Municipal Act, 2001* permits a meeting of a municipal council or local board to be closed if the subject-matter being considered is " a proposed or pending acquisition or disposition of land." Although this provision provides sufficient discretion to discuss the pending sale of surplus land *in camera,* the voting restrictions set out in subsection 239 (6) still require that the resolution or by-law declaring the land to be surplus must be passed during the open session of a meeting. Even greater latitude is available with regard to providing notice to the public of the proposed sale of land. Remember, section 251 of the Act provides a council or board with sufficient leeway to determine the degree of public notice necessary to satisfy the Act. These types of decisions will likely depend upon the class of land being sold or disposed of.

Finally, subsection 268 (10) expressly exempts the following classes of land from the three requirements set out in subsection 268 (3):

- land sold under section 110 (agreements for the provision of capital facilities); and
- land to be used for the establishment and carrying on of industries and industrial operations and incidental uses.

Appraisals

Some additional comments may be constructive in assisting councils and boards to meet the statutory requirement to "obtain at least one appraisal of the fair market value of the land" prior to its sale. First of all, the term "fair market value" is not defined in the *Municipal Act, 2001*. However, Ontario's *Expropriations Act* does define the "market value of land expropriated" as "the amount that the land might be expected to realize if sold in the open market by a willing seller to a willing buyer."[10]

---

9 *Municipal Act, 2001*, S.O. 2001, c. 25, s. 268 (3).
10 *Expropriations Act*, R.S.O. 1990, c. E.26, s. 14 (1).

This definition may provide some guidance as to the intent of the phrase "fair market value."

Secondly, the term "appraisal" does not seem to require the services of an accredited appraiser, as did the earlier draft provision in Bill 152.[11] Therefore, many councils and local boards should be able to have their own staff provide such an evaluation.

In addition, there may exist any number of factors that make it difficult to determine the fair market value of a particular piece of land, not the least of which may be the uniqueness of the property itself. Therefore, in the absence of either legislation or regulatory guidelines and formulas to determine "market value," Canadian courts have approved a variety of assessment methods.

In the classic decision in *Sun Life Assurance Co. of Canada v. Montreal (City)*, the Supreme Court of Canada concluded that any one of the following five methods could be employed in order to determine a property's market value:

- recent free sale of the property itself;
- recent free sales of identical properties;
- recent free sales of comparable properties;
- depreciated replacement cost;
- economic or revenue-producing capacity of the property.[12]

It is reasonable to assume that in each of the assessment methods cited above, there is an inherent sense of contemporariness. For example, the *Assessment Act* not only provides that any land assessed "shall be based on its current value or average current value," but further defines the phrase "current value" to mean "the amount of money the fee simple, if unencumbered, would realize if sold at arm's length by a willing seller to a willing buyer."[13] Therefore, although the *Municipal Act, 2001* does not expressly state that the appraisal of the fair market value must be, for

---

11 Bill 152, s. 195 (7) (b) stated, "obtain at least one appraisal of the fair market value of the property from an accredited appraiser."

12 *Sun Life Assurance Co. of Canada v. Montreal (City)*, [1950] 2 D.L.R. 785 (S.C.C.); affirmed [1952] 2 D.L.R. 81 (P.C.).

13 *Assessment Act,* R.S.O. 1990, c. A.31, ss. 19 and 1.

example, no more than one year old, implicit in such terminology is the intent that the appraisal reflect the fair market value of the real property at the time the council or board declares it to be surplus. Failure to use a current appraisal would not necessarily constitute a breach of the Act. It may, however, lead to a host of undesirable and potentially embarrassing inquiries from the media, other interested parties and the general public about the sale and the reason why such a stale, out-of-date appraisal was used.

It is perhaps worth noting that even the statutory requirement to obtain an appraisal of the property's fair market value will not resolve conclusively all disputes regarding the proper price for a parcel of land. Take, for example, the response by the Honourable Gilles Pouliot, Minister of Transportation, to a 1994 inquiry concerning a substantial discrepancy arising from two opposing appraisals:

> I thank the member for sharing in the concern of the Township of Howard in his constituency. We have a mandate at Transportation to dispose of surplus land at market value. Simply put, the Township of Howard hires an appraiser who says that this specific parcel of land is worth $2,500.00. The Ministry of Transportation also has appraisers. Our appraiser says it's worth $11,000. There is a discrepancy between $11,000 and $2,500.
>
> What we factor in is the possibility of housing on the specific piece of land. That's why there is the discrepancy. We would be only willing and happy to avail ourselves of the opportunity to explain our practices to the Township of Howard.[14]

Exemptions from Appraisals

Subsection 268 (8) exempts the following classes of land from the statutory requirement to obtain an appraisal of the fair market value of the land prior to its sale:

1. Land 0.3 metres or less in width acquired in connection with an approval or decision under the *Planning Act*.

2. Closed highways if sold to an owner of land abutting the closed highways.

---

14 This was a response to a question from Pat Hayes (Essex-Kent) on May 30, 1994. See Legislature of Ontario Debates, 3rd Sess., 35th Parl., p. 6487.

3. Land formerly used for railway lines if sold to an owner of land abutting the former railway land.

4. Land that does not have direct access to a highway if sold to the owner of land abutting that land.

5. Land repurchased by an owner in accordance with section 42 of the *Expropriations Act*.

6. Land sold under section 107 (power to make grants or loans), section 108 (power to establish a counselling service to small businesses) and section 109 (power to establish a community development corporation).

7. Easements granted to public utilities or telephone companies.

In addition, the legislated prerequisite to obtain a fair market value of the surplus land to be sold does not apply to certain "public bodies." Therefore, subsection 268 (9) exempts the following public bodies from this statutory requirement:

(a) a municipality;

(b) a local board (including a school board or conservation authority); and/or

(c) the federal or provincial Crown and their agencies.

Public Register

Similar to a number of other aspects of this legislation that favour increased public access, subsection 268 (5) of the *Municipal Act, 2001* requires that every municipality and local board "shall establish and maintain a public register *listing* and *describing* the land owned or leased by the municipality or local board." In order to comply with this statutory requirement, the information to be included in this public register could be organized in the following manner:

- divide the register to distinguish between leased versus owned properties;

- subdivide these properties further in a geographic manner (eg. an upper-tier municipality may divide the real property it owns or leases in each lower-tier municipality, or simply by north/south/east/west);

- list the properties according to the assessment roll number for more convenient retrieval;
- provide the legal description of the land;
- provide the municipal description of the property if available; and
- provide an adequate description of what is on the land itself, including whether it is a barren agricultural lot or has a five-storey office complex on it, and the land's general uses.

Finally, it is recommended that once a particular lot of land is no longer owned or leased by the council or local board, the reference to it in the public register should be deleted promptly.

Despite the requirement to establish a public register describing lands owned or leased by a municipality or local board, subsection 268 (11) excludes the following classes of land from such a register:

1. Land 0.3 metres or less in width acquired in connection with an approval or decision under the *Planning Act*.
2. Highways.
3. Land formerly used for railway lines.

In spite of the express exclusion of "highways" from the public register for land required by subsection 268 (5), there will, in all likelihood, be a similar register listing most "municipal highways." This probability arises because of the regulation issued under the *Municipal Act, 2001* to establish minimum standards of repair for highways and bridges or *any class of them*."[15] Briefly, the regulation creates six classes of highways (based on the applicable speed limit and average daily traffic) and each municipality must determine into which category each highway under its jurisdiction falls.

Compliance Certificates

In an effort to assure purchasers that the sale of the surplus land will not subsequently be challenged in court, the *Municipal Act, 2001* provides that the clerk of a municipality or the secretary of a local board may issue a certificate of compliance verifying that the municipality or board

---

15 S.O. 2001, c. 25, s. 44 (4), emphasis added; and see Minimum Maintenance Standards for Municipal Highways, O.Reg. 239/02, as amended.

has complied with both the statutory provisions and those contained in the property disposal by-law.[16] The Act also mandates that any compliance certificate so issued "shall be included in a deed or transfer of land and, unless a person to whom the land is sold has notice to the contrary, shall be deemed to be sufficient proof that [section 268] has been complied with."[17]

Obviously, most prudent purchasers will require such a compliance certificate as part of the transaction. Although the form and content of such certificates will not be prescribed by the regulations, the Open Local Government Working Group on Forms and Regulations did recommend to the minister that the following matters be included in a compliance certificate:

- a statement that the land was declared surplus by by-law or resolution, and the date;
- a property description sufficient to identify the property, as recommended for the notice of intent to dispose;
- a statement that an appraisal was obtained, and the date, in appropriate cases;
- the approved sale price/consideration;
- a statement of any exemption from the declaration, notice and appraisal requirements relied on by the council/board where applicable;
- a statement that public notice of intent to dispose was given, the method of giving notice and the date of the public meeting; and
- a statutory declaration by the municipal clerk/secretary of the local board attesting to all of the above.[18]

In addition, the clerk or secretary would also be required to attest that the provisions of this section and the procedure by-law were adhered to. A draft certificate of compliance is set out in Appendix A to this chapter.

---

16 *Municipal Act, 2001*, S.O. 2001, c. 25, s. 268 (6).

17 *Ibid.*, s. 268 (7).

18 "Report of the Open Local Government Working Group on Forms and Regulations" (August 1994), p. 19.

Judicial Review

In light of the legislated requirement that most municipalities and local boards enact a property disposal by-law, it is not surprising then that the previous statutory restriction on courts reviewing such sales of real property has been made subject to a council or board adhering to such a procedural by-law, as well as the other statutory requirements found in subsection 268 (4):

> The manner in which the municipality or local board carries out the sale of its land, if consistent with this section and with the by-law under subsection (1), is not open to review by any court if the municipality or local board may lawfully sell the property, the purchaser may lawfully buy it and the municipality or local board acted in good faith.

Recently, the Ontario courts had an opportunity to address both the statutory requirements of this provision in the former *Municipal Act*, as well as allegations with regard to a procedural error in relation to a property disposal by-law. In the case of *Wight Milling Ltd. v. Bloomfield (Village)*,[19] the village had called for tenders with respect to the purchase of surplus property. Tenders were received from two adjacent property owners. Notice of the proposed sale, which was published prior to the municipality receiving the market value appraisal, did not state the date for the close of tenders, but did indicate the date that council intended to enact a by-law authorizing the sale. The plaintiffs put in a bid of $132,010 for the property in question, while the other bidder submitted a bid approximately $20,000 higher. After the village rejected the plaintiff's attempt to submit a new bid in a sealed envelope, the plaintiff brought an action to quash the by-law authorizing the sale to the higher bidder.

At trial, Mr. Justice O'Flynn found that "before the court can review the sale of the property and the reasonableness of [the village's] decision to accept Mr. Nyman's tender for $152,000," the plaintiff must prove that:

(a) council failed to act in a manner that was consistent with section 193 [now section 268] of the *Municipal Act*;

(b) council failed to act in a manner that was consistent with Procedural By-law 781; and

---

19 (2000), 12 M.P.L.R. (3d) 268.

(c) council failed to act in good faith.

Although the plaintiff admitted that the council had acted in good faith throughout the process, it alleged that the municipality had breached subsection 193 (4) [now subsection 268 (3)] of the Act with respect to the statutory conditions precedent to the sale of the property by the municipality. O'Flynn J. found that the statutory conditions precedent set out in that provision "do not require the council to obtain an appraisal before notice to the public is given." Therefore, the court found that the Village of Bloomfield had, in fact, complied with the mandatory provisions of the legislation.

In a related allegation, the plaintiff argued that a procedural error had occurred in relation to the village's by-law, governing the sale of real property. In addressing this matter, Mr. Justice O'Flynn found that "the procedure in issue is not statutory and obligatory" and that "the error is of a purely technical nature and is not fatal to the process." As such, the court dismissed the plaintiff's claim.

On appeal, the Ontario Court of Appeal unanimously upheld the Trial Judge's ruling. In reviewing the decision of Mr. Justice O'Flynn, the Court of Appeal found as follows:

> O'Flynn J. held that the error in procedure was of a purely technical nature and not fatal to the process respecting the sale of the land. He held that the sequence of the procedures did not matter so long as all procedures took place. In effect, O'Flynn J. held that the actions of council were consistent with the by-law. Alternatively, he exercised his discretion on review and, since the error was procedural in the circumstances of this case, decided not to set aside the sale of the land.
>
> We agree with the Trial Judge that, in the circumstances of this case, the order in which the procedures [were] required by the by-law did not matter. All required procedures did take place and the sale must be upheld.[20]

Recently, a similar case occurred involving the sale of a landlocked parcel of surplus property in the City of Windsor. The two corporate applicants sought to judicially review the relevant council resolution by al-

---

20 (2001), 21 M.P.L.R. (3d) 181 at 182.

leging bad faith and discrimination on the part of the municipality. On February 13, 2003, the Divisional Court of Ontario unanimously dismissed the application. Although the endorsement did not directly address the provisions in the former *Municipal Act* with respect to the disposal of surplus property, the court did make the following instructive comments concerning bad faith:

> The applicants have failed to show on the evidence any improper motive of the council to favour or to hurt any of the interested parties. Finally, it cannot be said that the resolution was passed without regard to the public interest. The resolution requires that the subject land be offered for sale to [the purchaser] at the independently appraised market value. In our view, that requirement protects the public interest.[21]

Conclusions

In addition to all of the above, it is important to note that section 268 does not apply to the sale of land for tax arrears as set out under Part XI of the *Municipal Act, 2001*.

Furthermore, subsection 268 (13) provides that the Minister of Municipal Affairs and Housing may make the following regulations with regard to this particular section:

(a) exempting the sale of prescribed classes of land from all or any of the provisions of this section;

(b) removing the requirement to obtain an appraisal of land that is being sold to a prescribed public body; and

(c) prescribing classes of land that are not required to be contained in the public register of land under this section.

---

21 *General Motors Products of Windsor Ltd. et al. v. Windsor (City) et al.*, Superior Court of Justice (Ont. Div. Ct.), Court File No. 1291, an unreported decision dated February 13, 2003, at par. 17.

APPENDIX "A"

CERTIFICATE OF COMPLIANCE
[MUNICIPALITY'S NAME]
Municipal Act, 2001, S.O. 2001, c. 25, s. 268

IN THE MATTER OF the sale of the land described as:

[MUNICIPALITY'S NAME]

I, the undersigned, pursuant to the *Municipal Act, 2001*, S.O. 2001, c. 25, subsection 268 (6), hereby certify that to the best of my knowledge and belief:

1. A procedural by-law required by the *Municipal Act, 2001*, subsection 268 (1) was in force at the time the resolution declaring the above-described surplus land was passed.

2. The measures necessary for giving notice to the public required by the procedural by-law have been carried out.

3. The appraisal required by the *Municipal Act, 2001*, subsection 268 (3) was obtained.

_____   _____
Date   Clerk/Deputy Clerk

Chapter 7
BIAS: OPEN VS. CLOSED MINDS

> *Unless it can be shown that an elected councillor has prejudged an issue to the extent that he or she is no longer capable of persuasion, bias is not proved.*
>
> Madam Justice B.M. Helper (1996)

While the rules and procedures for members of municipal councils or local boards who have a traditional "conflict of interest" in a matter about to be considered are enunciated in various pieces of legislation, a similar statutory mechanism does not exist for applying the "rule against bias" in the municipal realm. Arising from one of the primary principles of natural justice, the definition of bias has traditionally been ascribed to the Latin phrase *nemo judex in sua causa*, meaning "no one shall be a judge in their own cause." Much of the case law related to the alleged bias of a decision-maker appears to fall within one of the following three categories:

- an association between one of the parties and a decision-maker;
- involvement by a decision-maker in a preliminary stage of the decision; and/or
- attitude of a decision-maker toward the outcome.[1]

Legal scholars agree that a finding of bias against a decision-maker "will generally cause a statutory delegate to lose his jurisdiction, and will render any administrative action void and thereby subject to successful judicial review."[2]

---

1 Jones, J.M. Evans, H.N. Janisch, D.J. Mullan and R.C.B. Risk, *Administrative Law*, 2nd ed. (Toronto: Emond Montgomery, 1984), p. 220.

2 D.P. Jones and A.S. de Villaro, *Principles of Administrative Law* (Toronto: Carswell, 1985), p. 244.

In 1990, the Supreme Court of Canada issued two concurrent judgments that established the test necessary to meet the rule against bias as it applied to councillors endeavouring to participate in the municipal decision-making process. A brief summary of the law as it existed prior to these seminal decisions will be helpful to understand the judicial evolution of the rule against bias in the rough and tumble world of municipal politics.

Pre-1990: Reasonable Apprehension of Bias Test

In the field of administrative law, one of the rationale underlying the concept of natural justice is that "justice should not only be done, but should manifestly and undoubtedly be seen to be done."[3] Thus, the courts have long since "established that it is not necessary to demonstrate that a decision-maker is actually biased."[4] The traditional test to determine bias before most administrative tribunals and the courts has been whether or not the actions of the judge or adjudicator raise a "reasonable apprehension" or suspicion of bias in all of the circumstances. An excellent explanation of this test was set out by England's Lord Denning in the following fashion:

> There must be circumstances from which a reasonable man would think it likely or probable that the justice or chairman, as the case may be, would, or did, favour one side unfairly at the expense of the other. The court will not inquire whether he did, in fact, favour one side unfairly. Suffice it that reasonable people might think he did. The reason is plain enough. Justice must be rooted in confidence: and confidence is destroyed when right-minded people go away thinking: "The judge was biased."[5]

In Canada, the test of reasonable apprehension of bias was first made applicable to the decision-makers in the exercise of their municipal functions in the 1904 case of *Re L'Abbé and Blind River*.[6] In that early case, the applicant sought to quash a by-law limiting the number of liquor licences in the municipality on the basis that the reeve was a mort-

---

[3] *R. v. Sussex Justices: Ex parte McCarthy*, [1924] I K.B. 256, Lord Chief Justice Hewart, at p. 259.
[4] Jones, J.M. Evans, H.N. Janisch, D.J. Mullan and R.C.B. Risk, *Administrative Law*, 2nd ed. (Toronto: Emond Montgomery, 1984), p. 267.
[5] *Metropolitan Properties v. Lannon*, [1969] 1 Q.B. 577 at 599, (Eng. C.A.).
[6] *Re L'Abbé and Blind River* (1904), 7 O.L.R. 230.

gagee of one of the two existing taverns. After setting out the law with regard to a municipal councillor's pecuniary interests in such matters, Boyd C. observed that:

> There may be also substantial interest other than pecuniary, and then the question arises, on all the circumstances, as to whether there is a real likelihood of bias – a reasonable probability that the interested person is likely to be biased with regard to the matter in hand.[7]

Almost 75 years later, the Ontario Divisional Court once again explored the concept of disqualifying bias in a case that can now be seen as a harbinger to the Supreme Court of Canada's decisions a decade later. At issue in the case of *Re McGill and Brantford (City)* was whether the local council had, prior to a public hearing, conclusively prejudged an issue and committed the municipality to the closure of various city streets as part of a major revision of the highway scheme.[8]

Speaking on behalf of the unanimous court, Mr. Justice Henry stated:

> [t]here is no need to restate the principle *nemo judex in sua causa*, but in the case at bar there are special elements to be considered, particularly the impact of that principle on a body whose role it is to legislate for the community it governs.

Henry J. explained further that of "fundamental importance is the proper recognition of the function of a municipal council in the body politic."[9] In addressing the rule against bias, Mr. Justice Henry emphasized the true legislative nature of municipal councils and concluded that bias was, to some degree, an inherent feature in their decision-making process:

> The fact is that the legislature has required the hearing to be conducted by the very persons who are expected to have formed at least a tentative view, and to have made decisions to carry forward the plan at least to the stage where the formal closing of the roads is to take place. It must be assumed that the legislature knew the functions and the mode of developing such a project from its in-

---

7   *Ibid.*, at 234.
8   *Re McGill and Brantford (City)* (1980), 28 O.R. (2d) 721.
9   *Ibid.*, at 726.

ception to the advanced stages, and nonetheless designated the council as the body to hold the hearing. In these circumstances, all that can be required of the council is to put aside their tentative views individually and collectively, hear the objections, consider them honestly and fairly, see if they can be accommodated and then make the final decision. No more and no less can be expected of them.[10]

Ultimately, the Divisional Court determined that the applicants had not shown disqualifying bias since the city council had not made an "irrevocable" decision to pass the roads closure by-law before the public hearing had occurred. The irrevocable decision test set out in the *McGill* case was subsequently approved by the Supreme Court of Canada in its companion decisions on bias and municipal councils.

The recognition by the Ontario Divisional Court in *McGill* that "the ultimate decision of the council to close the roads by by-law is a legislative, not a judicial problem," produced an interesting result. Briefly, a quasi-judicial power is one that is primarily judicial in its focus, but is undertaken by officials rather than full-fledged judges. Nevertheless, as the exercise of a quasi-judicial power will often result in a decision affecting the legal rights of individuals, there exists a common law duty for such decision-makers to adhere to the more formal rules of natural justice and to act in a fair and impartial manner. Alternatively, since the enactment of a municipal by-law in *McGill* was found to be a legislative matter, then the so-called rules of natural justice were not applicable. This judicial conclusion was subsequently altered by the Ontario government during its 1983 revisions to the *Planning Act* at section 60:

> Where, in passing a by-law under this Act, a council is required by this Act, by the provisions of an official plan or otherwise by law, to afford any person an opportunity to make representation in respect of the subject-matter of the by-law, the council shall afford such person a fair opportunity to make representation but throughout the course of passing the by-law the council shall be deemed to be performing a legislative and not judicial function.[11]

---

10   *Ibid.*, at 730.
11   *Planning Act, 1983*, S.O. 1983, c. 1, s. 60 [Now R.S.O. 1990, c. P.13, s. 61].

By approving this amendment, the provincial government codified its response to the sometimes conflicting common law.[12] Therefore, the general conclusion that the power to pass municipal by-laws constitutes the exercise of a legislative power that would not usually require adherence to the rules of natural justice is subject to statutory requirements such as those set out in the *Planning Act*. The provision, in effect, obligates a municipal council in Ontario to hold a fair hearing when enacting such planning by-laws.[13]

Post-1990: Amenable-to-Persuasion Test

In the appeals in *Old St. Boniface Residents Assn. Inc. v. Winnipeg (City)* and *Save Richmond Farmland Society v. Richmond (Township)*,[14] the Supreme Court of Canada rendered, in its judgments, a new threshold test applicable to biased councillors in the municipal decision-making process. In *Old St. Boniface*, a city councillor had been personally involved in the planning of a proposed condominium development on municipal property and had supported the project at *in camera* hearings of the city's finance committee. Before a rezoning by-law could be passed, the appellants sought a declaratory judgment from the courts quashing the committee's recommendation on the ground that the councillor was biased.

Save Richmond Farmland also concerned a rezoning application. In that case, an alderman campaigned for municipal office on a platform that favoured a rezoning of the lands in question. Prior to a public hearing on the rezoning issue, the alderman was interviewed by the media. It was alleged that he said he would listen to the public, but would not change his mind about the by-law. Appellants petitioned for judicial review of the matter, and sought an order preventing the alderman from participating further based on the concept of disabling bias.

Speaking on behalf of the majority in the *Old St. Boniface* case, Mr. Justice Sopinka clearly refuted the contention that the traditional test of reasonable apprehension of bias was the proper one to apply to municipal councillors. In doing so, Sopinka J. reviewed in detail all the factors

---

12 See *Wiswell v. Metro Corp. Greater Winnipeg* (1965), 51 D.L.R. (2d) 754 (S.C.C.); *Re Angil Const. Ltd. and West Gwillimbury (Township)*, [1971] 2 O.R. 713 (H.C.J.).

13 *Re Spence and York (City)* (1985), 17 O.M.B.R. 53 (H.C.J.).

14 *Old St. Boniface Residents Assn. Inc. v. Winnipeg (City)* (1990), 2 M.P.L.R. (2d) 217; and *Save Richmond Farmland Society v. Richmond (Township)* (1990), 2 M.P.L.R. (2d) 288, 46 Admin. L.R. 264.

and practical circumstances that could affect the decisions of a municipal council before focusing his comments on the zoning by-law question before him:

> Furthermore, with respect to the enactment of zoning by-laws and amendments to zoning by-laws, it is well known that numerous committees are involved at which members of council are expected to vote before being called upon to hear representations and decide the question. Moreover, in the preparation and processing of a development, a municipal councillor is often involved in assisting parties supporting and opposing the development with respect to their presentations. In the course of this process, a councillor can and often does take a stand either for or against the development. *This degree of prejudgment would run afoul of the ordinary rule which disqualifies a decision-maker on the basis of a reasonable apprehension of bias. Accordingly, it could not have been intended by the legislature that this rule apply to members of council with the same force as in the case of other tribunals whose character and functions more closely resemble those of a court.*[15]

Having rejected the more traditional approach to the rule against bias, Mr. Justice Sopinka then pronounced a new threshold requirement, clearly derived from the irrevocable decision test in the earlier *McGill* case. The evidentiary burden to be met, in what has subsequently been called the "amenable-to-persuasion" test, was described by Sopinka J. in the following terms:

> In my opinion, the test that is consistent with the functions of a municipal councillor and enables him or her to carry out the political and legislative duties entrusted to the councillor is one which requires that the objectors or supporters be heard by the members of council who are capable of being persuaded. The legislature could not have intended to have a hearing before a body who has already made a decision which is irreversible. The party alleging disqualifying bias must establish that there is a prejudgment of the matter, in fact, to the extent that any representations at variance with the view which has been adopted would be futile. Statements

---

15 *Old St. Boniface Residents Assn. Inc. v. Winnipeg (City)* (1990), 2 M.P.L.R. (2d) 217 at 237 (emphasis added).

by individual members of council while they may very well give rise to an appearance of bias will not satisfy the test unless the court concludes that they are the expression of a final opinion on the matter, which cannot be dislodged. In this regard, it is important to keep in mind that support in favour of a measure before a committee and a vote in favour will not constitute disqualifying bias in the absence of some indication that the position taken is incapable of change. The contrary conclusion would result in the disqualification of a majority of council in respect of all matters that are decided at public meetings at which objectors are entitled to be heard.[16]

Thus, the Supreme Court of Canada dismissed the appeal in *Old St. Boniface*. Similarly, the court rejected the appellant's arguments in the *Save Richmond Farmland* case on the basis that they had not met the threshold standard of the amenable-to-persuasion test.

Interestingly enough, it is in the concurring decision of Mr. Justice La Forest in the *Save Richmond Farmland* case that the first serious concerns are alluded to with respect to the viability of the newly-proclaimed amenable-to-persuasion test. In examining the legal arguments that comprised the concurring judgments in the British Columbia Court of Appeal, La Forest J. stated his preference for the "closed mind" test of Madam Justice Southin over that of Lambert J.A. who had espoused the amenable-to-persuasion standard. In the former instance, Southin J.A. had reasoned that "it would be unjust to find fault with municipal councillors who maintained a closed mind on the development issue."[17] La Forest concurred, stating, "I think that Southin J.A. is correct when she holds that a 'closed mind' (provided it is not a corrupt mind) should not disentitle an alderman from participating in the electoral process."[18] In support of this logic, La Forest J. drew the following critical conclusions with respect to the amenable-to-persuasion test:

> This [amenable-to-persuasion test] sounds good in theory, but breaks down in practice. Southin J.A.'s approach might seem drastic, but is the more realistic of the two. There is no way of

---

16 *Ibid.*, at 241.

17 *Save Richmond Farmland Society v. Richmond (Township)* (1990), 2 M.P.L.R. (2d) 288 at 301.

18 *Ibid.*, at 303.

gauging the "openness" of a person's mind, and indeed it would be pointless to attempt to do so. In the result, it seems to me that if this court is to adopt the "amenable-to-persuasion" test, this is bound to lead to a lot of posturing. Politicians who have campaigned on a given issue, and owe their election to it, can be expected to make solemn pronouncements to the effect that they remain "amenable-to-persuasion" if a truly convincing argument is presented to them.[19]

Recent Case Law

This judicial prediction concerning political "posturing" could make it virtually impossible to meet the high burden of proof necessary to establish bias at the level of municipal decision making. A brief review of some of the cases decided subsequent to the enunciation of the amenable-to-persuasion test by the Supreme Court of Canada will suffice to show that the concerns first espoused by Mr. Justice La Forest have been realized.[20]

Save St. Ann's Coalition v. Victoria (City) – The first case to apply the amenable-to-persuasion test was determined by the British Columbia Court of Appeal and concerned another rezoning issue. In *Save St. Ann's Coalition v. Victoria (City)*, two councillors who had been appointed members of the Provincial Capital Commission by the city council voted in favour of a commission-approved proposal to rezone certain historic property owned by the commission.[21] The by-law passed council by a narrow 5 to 4 margin and opponents sought to have it struck down by the courts on the grounds of bias. In dismissing the appeal, Mr. Justice Lambert found it "significant" that the two councillors in question filed affidavits in which each stated:

> I consider myself to be free to vote either for or against the passage of the by-laws and had a completely open mind when listening to the presentations, both verbal and written, which were made at the public hearing preceding the adoption of the by-laws.[22]

---

19 *Ibid.*, at 301.

20 See John Mascarin, "Tolerance for the Biased Municipal Councillor: The amenable to Persuasion Test," 2 M.P.L.R. (2d) 322; and M. Rick O'Connor, "Bias and the Open-Minded Councillor," 11 M.P.L.R. (2d) 250.

21 *Save St. Ann's Coalition v. Victoria (City)* (1991), 5 M.P.L.R. (2d) 331.

22 *Ibid.*, at 336

As neither of the councillors were cross-examined on their affidavits, Lambert J.A. could only conclude that "we are left with those statements of their state of mind, unchallenged."[23] In the absence of such a direct challenge, the appellants instead argued that a number of newspaper articles left the inference that the councillors were incapable of changing their minds. This type of inferential evidence was given short shrift by the court, who determined it fell far short of the heavy onus established in the *Old St. Boniface* case.

Brentwood Golf Course v. Central Sannich (District) – A second British Columbia decision, released shortly after the *Save St. Ann's* case, went one step further in attempting to meet the evidentiary onus in the amenable-to-persuasion test. In the case of *Brentwood Golf Course v. Central Sannich (District)*, the issue focused on the repeal of a zoning by-law by a newly-elected municipal council.[24] The golf course petitioned for judicial review of this reversal on a variety of grounds, including an allegation of bias.

To meet the high onus established in the amenable-to-persuasion test, the petition included an affidavit from a reporter for a local newspaper who deposed that the mayor had stated "he intended to use his mayoralty powers to rescind the rezoning of the Brentwood Lakes Golf Course."[25] The court observed that other affidavits had attributed similar statements to two other members of the council. Although the mayor and one alderman had been cross-examined on their affidavits, neither could recall making such statements. The mayor did depose, however, that "if the statement had been made, it followed on the heels of a political debate between himself and former Mayor Cullis regarding the final approval of the golf course proposal."[26]

Despite the additional evidence in this case, the court held that the petitioners had not met the evidentiary burden for the amenable-to-persuasion test. Associate Chief Justice Campbell summarized his findings as follows:

---

23 *Ibid.*
24 *Brentwood Golf Course v. Central Sannich (District)* (1991), 6 M.P.L.R. (2d) 1.
25 *Ibid.*, at 22.
26 *Ibid.*

It is significant that Mayor Jones, Alderman Tobin and Alderman Mar, in their respective affidavits, each affirmed his obligation as an elected official to keep an open mind. Each deposed that he read the guidelines and agenda for the conduct of the public hearing, and that his decisions had not been reached until he considered these submissions and the facts as a whole during council deliberations. This evidence remained uncontroverted by the cross-examination of Mayor Jones and Alderman Tobin.[27]

Marianno et al. v. Mississauga (City) – In 1992, the Ontario Divisional Court received its first opportunity to apply the amenable-to-persuasion test in the case of *Mariano et al. v. Mississauga (City)*.[28] The applicants in this case sought judicial review of a city council resolution that refused to renew their amusement arcade, billiard tables, lunch counter and tobacco licences. The matter of the licence renewals was determined by the council upon receipt of a 17-page report from a committee comprised of three councillors who heard testimony from numerous witnesses, including the ward councillor, who had received a number of complaints about the applicants' establishment.

In the application for judicial review, the applicants argued that, as the ward councillor was of such firmly held views, he was incapable of persuasion. Mr. Justice Craig reviewed the evidence of the ward councillor as follows:

His affidavit indicates that he did not consider himself to have closed his mind nor to have come to any irreversible conclusions concerning the licence renewal. He was prepared to consider, and did consider with an open mind, the submissions to council on various occasions in the past. However, on the basis of submissions [from the counsel for the applicants] and on the committee report before council, Councillor McKechnie determined that he could not support the renewal of the licences.[29]

Craig J. subsequently concluded that there was no evidence to show that the councillor was incapable of persuasion.

---

27 *Ibid.*, at 22-23.
28 *Mariano et al. v. Mississauga (City)* (1992), 9 M.P.L.R. (2d) 29.
29 *Ibid.*, at 37.

Atkins v. Calgary (City) – In this 1994 decision of the Alberta Court of Appeal, the applicants appealed an unsuccessful application to quash an amendment to a land use by-law on a variety of grounds, including bias. In rejecting the appeal, Kerans J.A. provided the following summary of the law on bias:

> This issue is almost the other face of the hearing issue. The idea of a reasonable apprehension of bias, seen as a predisposition toward one conclusion over another, makes little sense except in the context of a trial, or 'pure' judicial hearing. The decision-maker in such a case must arrive with an open mind. On the other hand, in the case of a public policy fight, the councillor may arrive at the hearing with a publicly stated position. Indeed, she may have been elected precisely because she took that position. To the extent, then, that the process under review moves down the spectrum from a purely judicial mode to something more political, one cannot equate fairness with the *tabula rasa* mentality expected of a juror.
>
> This was the precise issue in *Old St. Boniface Residents Association Inc. v. Winnipeg (City) et al.*, [1990] 3 S.C.R. 1170. Rejecting the approach earlier taken by it in *Wiswell v. Metropolitan Winnipeg (Municipality)*, [1965] S.C.R. 512, the Supreme Court held that, where political and legislative duties are engaged, fairness requires only that the predisposition of the legislators not be so firm that submissions are futile because minds are utterly closed. That is quite different from a claim that fairness commands that minds must be utterly open.
>
> I note that this rule imposes a tough burden upon those who complain they did not receive a fair hearing. Critics say that it is very difficult to show that minds are closed. See John Mascarin, "Tolerance for the Biased Municipal Councillor: The Amenable to Persuasion Test" (1991), 2 M.P.L.R. (2d) 322; and an article by M. Rick O'Connor, "Bias and the Open-Minded Councillor" (1993), 11 M.P.L.R. (2d) 250. And, to be sure, few have succeeded in the complaint. See *Save St. Ann's Coalition v. Victoria (City)* (1991), 2 B.C.A.C. 296; 5 W.A.C. 296; 5 M.P.L.R. (2d) 331 (C.A.); *Brentwood Lakes Golf Course v. Central Saanich (District)* (1991), 6 M.P.L.R. (2d) 1 (B.C.S.C.); *Mariano v. Mississauga (City)* (1992), 55 O.A.C. 68; 90 D.L.R. (4th) 104 (Div. Ct.). I do not find this toughness troubling. The point, I think, of the *Old St.*

Boniface rule is that courts should respect the political process. The rule catches only the rare (I hope) case where the political process has descended to farce.[30]

Save the Eaton's Building Coalition v. Winnipeg (City) – This 2002 case represents one of the recent judicial reviews of the law with respect to allegations of bias against a municipal council. The facts of this case revolve around the coalition's efforts to prevent the demolition of the Eaton's building in downtown Winnipeg. In unanimously dismissing the coalition's appeal, the Manitoba Court of Appeal emphasized the appellant's failure to overcome the test's high standard:

> I agree with the conclusions reached by the learned motions judge on the subject of bias relative to both the decision of the property committee concerning the conditional use order and the decision of city council itself to amend the zoning by-law. The city council, and its property committee, are unlike the usual administrative tribunals. While they do have an adjudicative function, it is secondary to a responsibility to initiate – in this case, to initiate a development which most members of city council hope and believe will aid in the revitalization of the city centre. It is not surprising that members of city council, including the mayor, should become advocates of the project. But councillors remain charged with a responsibility to consider the merits of each step with a mind that is not firmly closed. There is no evidence that the members of the property committee and, save for one outspoken councillor, the members of city council itself viewed the conditional use order or the zoning amendment with closed minds. The threshold for establishing bias as set forth by the Supreme Court in *Old St. Boniface Residents Assn. Inc. v. Winnipeg (City)*, [1990] 3 S.C.R. 1170, has not been overcome.[31]

Of significance is the fact that, on March 27, 2003, the Supreme Court of Canada dismissed the coalition's appeal, thereby refusing an opportunity to review the amenable-to-persuasion test.

Mushka v. Candle Lake (Resort Village) – A March 31, 2003 decision of the Saskatchewan Court of Queen's Bench appears to raise the bar a

---

30 *Atkins v. Calgary (City)*, (1994), 24 M.P.L.R. (2d) 141 at 149.
31 *Save the Eaton's Building Coalition v. Winnipeg (City)* (2002), 218 D.L.R. 694, at p. 699.

little higher for applicants seeking to overturn a council decision on the basis of bias. In *Mushka et al. v. Candle Lake (Resort Village)*, the plaintiffs had purchased a residentially-zoned lot in the hopes of locating and renovating a mobile home on it – a plan that was prohibited without council approval.[32] After a stop work order was issued, the plaintiffs' brought an action seeking judicial review of three related council resolutions. At trial, all three resolutions were quashed on the basis that the resort village had not complied with the principles of procedural fairness.

However, in her comments on the allegation that the mayor was biased, Madam Justice Ryan-Froslie found that the closed mind of a single member of council was insufficient to taint the whole council:

> The evidence in this case discloses the mayor, Dale McLeod, was biased in making the decisions in issue. It is clear from his testimony that he did not approach the Mushkas' situation with an open mind. He made it quite clear that his mind was closed and that nothing the Mushkas could have said or done would have changed his mind. Such bias should have disqualified Mr. McLeod from participating in the decision. He was, however, only one member of the council for the resort village. He could not pass the resolutions in issue except as part of a quorum of that council. There was no evidence that any other member of the council was biased. Mr. McLeod's bias is insufficient to taint the whole council.[33]

If this judicial interpretation is upheld and/or adopted in future cases, it will become even more difficult to bring a successful application in bias, especially on large councils with many members. This is due to the fact that the ruling by Madam Justice Ryan-Froslie would appear to require a plaintiff to prove a level of bias that was sufficient to taint the whole municipal council.

In more than a decade since the Supreme Court's two decisions on bias, it is possible to draw some useful observations from the subsequent jurisprudence on the amenable-to-persuasion standard. First, most municipal councillors have been able to meet the amenable-to-persuasion

---

32 *Mushka v. Candle Lake (Resort Village)*, [2003] S.J. No. 242.

33 *Ibid.*, at par. 59.

test by submitting affidavits or testifying that they are of an open mind and, therefore, free to vote either for or against the passage of a particular by-law.[34] As Mr. Justice Lambert expressed in the *Save St. Ann's* case, a "mind open to that extent is more than is required to meet the test in the *Old St. Boniface* case."[35] Second, it is clear that inferential evidence from newspaper articles will not be sufficient for those alleging bias to meet the high onus established in the amenable-to-persuasion test.

Other Administrative Boards

It is important to recognize that, although the amenable-to-persuasion test applies to allegedly biased councillors addressing a variety of legislative and policy issues before a municipal council, these same individuals may face the stricter, more traditional reasonable apprehension of bias test when sitting as members of other boards or tribunals. In 1992, the Supreme Court of Canada revisited its earlier rulings in *Old St. Boniface* and *Save Richmond Farmland* in an effort to address this distinction.

The case of *Newfoundland Telephone Co. Ltd. v. Board of Commissioners of Public Utilities* dealt with an allegation of bias against the member of an administrative board responsible for regulating the telephone company.[36] While the public utilities board was investigating telephone rates, an appointee to the board commented to the media that he would not let "them fat cats" in the telephone company get to keep their salary increases. During the subsequent hearing on those rates, the appointee made similar remarks to the press. In his analysis of which test for bias was applicable, Mr. Justice Cory made the following general statements in which he outlined the broad scope of administrative boards in Canada and identified varying standards of natural justice dependent upon the nature and functions of the board in question:

> It can be seen that there is a great diversity of administrative boards. Those that are primarily adjudicative in their functions will be expected to comply with the standard applicable to courts.

---

34 For example, see the two decisions of the British Columbia Supreme Court in *Striegel v. Tofino (District)* (1994), 20 M.P.L.R. (2d) 218; and *Watson v. Burnaby (City)* (1994), 22 M.P.L.R. (2d) 136.

35 *Save St. Ann's Coalition v. Victoria (City)* (1991), 5 M.P.L.R. (2d) 336.

36 *Newfoundland Telephone Co. Ltd. v. Board of Commissioners of Public Utilities* (1992), 89 D.L.R. (4th) 289.

That is to say that the conduct of the members of the board should be such that there could be no reasonable apprehension of bias with regard to their decision. At the other end of the scale are boards with popularly elected members such as those dealing with planning and development whose members are municipal councillors. With those boards, the standard will be much more lenient. In order to disqualify the members a challenging party must establish that there has been a prejudgment of the matter to such an extent that any representations to the contrary would be futile. Administrative boards that deal with matters of policy will be closely comparable to the boards composed of municipal councillors. For those boards, a strict application of a reasonable apprehension of bias as a test might undermine the very role which has been entrusted to them by the legislature.[37]

In 1993, the Alberta Court of Appeal considered this same rationale in the case of *Hutterian Brethren Church of Starland v. Starland No. 47 (Municipal District).*[38] This case concerned two appeals before the Development Appeal Board (DAB), whose composition included several municipal councillors. In determining the appropriate test for bias, Mr. Justice Côté reviewed both the *Old St. Boniface* ruling and the decision in the *Newfoundland Telephone* case, and then rejected the amenable-to-persuasion test in favour of the reasonable apprehension of bias. Among his reasons, Côté J.A. stated that "the committee in *Old St. Boniface* was legislative, which is not true of this DAB. That its members happen to be councillors does not make it a legislative body."[39]

Conclusions

In summation, the following guidelines are suggested in determining the test of bias to be applied to a municipal councillor in specific circumstances.

---

37 *Ibid.*, at 299.
38 *Hutterian Brethren Church of Starland v. Starland No. 47 (Municipal District)* (1993), 9 Alta. L.R. (3d) 1; see also *Anderson v. Twin Rivers School Division No. 65*, an unreported decision of the Alberta Court of Queen's Bench, June 2, 1994 (Murray J.); by contrast, see the remarks of the Alberta Court of Appeal in *Crown Parking Co. v. Calgary (City)*, 22 M.P.L.R. (2d) 1 at 5, wherein the Court of Appeal observed that while "the municipal councillors sitting on a development appeal board may offer an appearance of bias, that is the framework contemplated by the *Planning Act*."
39 *Ibid.*, at 11.

Amenable-to-persuasion test – This test may be reasonably assumed where legislative functions are being performed, which the member must then approach with an open mind. This is true even though the council may be mandated by the statute to provide a certain amount of procedural fairness, which may give the proceedings the air of a quasi-judicial hearing.[40]

Reasonable apprehension of bias – While it would appear that this stricter test is no longer applicable to most decision-makers sitting as members of council, the same may not always be true in circumstances where such persons sit as members of other administrative boards or tribunals. Indeed, if the function and character of the board or tribunal is primarily adjudicative or quasi-judicial in nature, then it will likely be subject to the stricter standard applicable to a court, being the reasonable apprehension of bias.

---

40 *Planning Act*, R.S.O. 1990, c. P.13, s. 61.

Chapter 8
LIBEL, SLANDER & DEFAMATION

> *The jury found that I defamed the officers and the first thing I did was go over and apologize sincerely for having caused hurt in the job and their personal lives. I've learned from this and I think members of council will learn from this. There are limits to what we can say.*[1]
>
> Toronto Councillor Kyle Rae (June 18, 2001)

As local governments across Canada achieve increasing levels of "openness," the law as it relates to libel, slander and defamation becomes an issue of greater consequence to both elected and appointed officials. The traditional advice, "If you are not sure it is true – do not say it," may appear to offer a total solution to the problem. In a political environment, however, that contention is:

- simplistic;
- in most instances, unworkable; and
- in some circumstances, plain bad advice.

Elected representatives and municipal staff often have a responsibility to convey information to a council, committee or local board that has been impossible to conclusively verify. Members or employees may also hold strong professional and personal opinions on an issue, based on the available facts. In such circumstances, silence – predicated on the fear of a defamation lawsuit – may be both impossible and inappropriate if the individual is to fully discharge the duties of his or her public office. All elected and appointed officials should therefore be familiar with both the scope of benefits and the profound limitations imposed by

---

[1] "Rae defamed police over raids – councillor must pay officers $170,000, jurors decide," *Toronto Star* (June 19, 2001): in criticizing police regarding a liquor inspection at a lesbian party, Councillor Rae defamed seven officers by calling them "rogue cops," "goons," "renegades" and "cowboys" in media interviews.

the general legal principles of libel and slander and, in particular, the concept of qualified privilege.

Double-edged Sword

For local government elected members and staff, "defamation" (a lay term meant to encompass both libel and slander) may prove to be a double-edged sword. Ultimately, a person involved in a defamation action may be either:

- a defendant, as a result of an imprudent or malicious remark, or of words published, which adversely affect the reputation of another person; or

- a plaintiff, responding to words published by a ratepayer, the media or another person.

This chapter will examine the multi-faceted nature of defamation, explore the availability of various legal defences, and cite case examples to show the response of the courts to particular circumstances involving local government representatives.

Categories of Defamation

The law of defamation is "essentially aimed at the prohibition of the publication of injurious false statements" by either spoken or written words.[2] In 1995, the Supreme Court of Canada set out the following rationale regarding the importance of protecting one's "good reputation" in the case of *Hill v. Church of Scientology of Toronto*:

> The other value to be balanced in a defamation action is the protection of the reputation of the individual. Although much has very properly been said and written about the importance of freedom of expression, little has been written of the importance of reputation. Yet, to most people, their good reputation is to be cherished, above all. A good reputation is closely related to the innate worthiness and dignity of the individual. It is an attribute that must, just as much as freedom of expression, be protected by society's laws ... False allegations can so very quickly and completely destroy a good reputation. A reputation tarnished by libel can seldom regain its former luster. A democratic society, therefore, has

---

[2] *Hill v. Church of Scientology of Toronto* (1995), 126 D.L.R. (4th) 129 at 169 (S.C.C.).

an interest in ensuring that its members can enjoy and protect their good reputation so long as it is merited.[3]

Generally, defamation falls into two distinct categories:

- criminal law, as set out in the *Criminal Code of Canada*; and
- civil law, codified in various provincial statutes and illustrated by case law.

Criminal law – In relative terms, libel and slander under the *Criminal Code* is seldom resorted to, being confined to circumstances of blasphemous libel;[4] defamatory libel;[5] and hate propaganda.[6] As these charges are unlikely to be the basis for local government violations, this chapter will focus on the civil law aspects of this subject.

Civil law – In civil law, both libel and slander are said to have their roots in a class society, where the protection of reputation was paramount. The distinctions between libel and slander as separate torts occurred in the division made between the ecclesiastical courts and common law courts. It is not clear that this distinction has any relevance today.[7]

Slander is spoken defamation. In contrast, libel, in its original context and in most current circumstances, concerns the written or printed word. It may now extend, however, to other circumstances such as a radio or television broadcast, although difficulty in obtaining evidence in the form of tapes or other recordings may complicate an action. At last count, nine provincial and territorial agents had eliminated the distinction between libel and slander, seeking to address such matters in the same manner.[8]

---

3   *Ibid.*, at 160.
4   *Criminal Code*, R.S.C. 1985, c. C-46, s. 296.
5   *Ibid.*, ss. 297-317.
6   *Ibid.*, ss. 318-320.
7   "The Law of Defamation, An Issues Paper," March 1989, Publications Ontario, 103233, at p. 2.
8   For example, see: Alberta's *Defamation Act*, R.S.A. 1980, c. D-7; Manitoba's *Defamation Act,* C.C.S.M., c. D20; New Brunswick's *Defamation Act*, R.S.N.B. 1973, c. D-5; Newfoundland's *Defamation Act*, R.S.N. 1990, c. D-3; Prince Edward Island's *Defamation Act*, R.S.P.E.I. 1988, c. D-5; Nunavut and the Northwest Territories' *Defamation Act*, R.S.N.W.T. 1988, c. D-1; Yukon Territory's *Defamation Act*, R.S.Y.T. 1986, c. 41; and Nova Scotia's *Defamation Act,* R.S.N.S. 1989, c. 122.

Injurious falsehoods – words that cause damage but do not injure a person's reputation – are not considered libelous. If such words are maliciously published, however, it may be possible to bring an action for defamation.[9]

Elements of Proof

The threshold of what may constitute defamatory matter is very low, and may range from trivial insults, to the most calculated divestiture of the important aspects of the plaintiff's reputation.[10] Although there is no definitive formulation of "defamation," it generally occurs when a published statement tends to lower the reputation or discredit a person in the minds of right-thinking members of society generally.

There is no need to prove damages and the statement need not be false. Further, the feelings of the plaintiff are not relevant. It is what the community thinks of the statement that matters. The court must be satisfied that the following three key elements have been established:

- publication occurred;
- the plaintiff was identifiable; and
- the words were defamatory.

Where this test is met, there is a presumption that the words are false and the plaintiff has been damaged. Having said that, extreme caution is urged to any councillor or member of a local board contemplating a defamation lawsuit. This complex area of the law is fraught with strict procedural requirements contained in most libel and slander statutes. Therefore, independent legal advice is strongly recommended prior to commencing any such action. Two recent libel decisions will suffice to demonstrate the serious nature of this concern, not only as it relates to the statutory timelines and limitation periods in Ontario's legislation, but also with respect to the latest advances in technology.

In the case of *Bahlieda v. Santa*, the plaintiff, the city clerk for Thunder Bay, initiated a lawsuit against a councillor over alleged defamatory

---

9 *The Dictionary of Canadian Law,* Deluxe Edition, p. 516.
10 "The Law of Defamation, An Issues Paper," March 1989, Publications Ontario, 103233, at p. 19.

material placed on his website in May 2001.[11] The plaintiff stated that she did not discover the alleged libel until mid-July 2001. As such, she only served a notice of intention to file a libel action on November 14, 2001 and the statement of claim on January 8, 2002. The defendant/councillor subsequently brought a motion for partial summary judgment, wherein he maintained that placing material on the Internet constituted a "broadcast" within the definition of that word as set out in the *Libel and Slander Act*.[12] In essence, the legal foundation for this motion was that a "broadcast" within the meaning of the legislation triggered both the notice provisions found in subsection 5 (1), as well as the limitation period in section 6. Therefore, the defendant argued that the plaintiff's failure to deliver a notice of claim within six weeks of discovering the impugned material (pursuant to s. 5 (1)) and her failure to issue a statement of claim within three months (pursuant to s. 6) meant that part of the claim was statute-barred. After reviewing the provisions in the Act, the relevant case law, and the various expert reports, Madame Justice Helen Pierce agreed with the defendant councillor's legal argument and granted the motion for partial summary judgment. However, on October 22, 2003, the Ontario Court of Appeal unanimously overturned the ruling of the motions court judge. In allowing the plaintiff's appeal, Chief Justice McMurtry concluded that "summary judgment applications are not a substitute for trial and thus will seldom prove suitable for resolving conflicts in expert testimony particularly those involving difficult, complex policy issues with broad social ramifications.[13]

Exceptions - Exclusions

Certain circumstances are excluded – for example, they include defamation of:

- the dead; or
- a group.

---

11 *Bahlieda v. Santa*, [2003] O.J. No. 1159.
12 R.S.O. 1990, c. L.12.
13 [2003] O.J. No. 4091, at para. 6.

In the case of *McCann v. The Ottawa Sun*,[14] the plaintiff, a resident and the mayor of the City of Pembroke, Ontario, unsuccessfully sought damages for libel against a sports columnist. An article about the conduct of some fans at a hockey game included the following, unflattering sentence: "These people are from places like Embrun, Arnprior, Renfrew and Pembroke where inbreeding, wood-burning stoves, moonshine stills, outhouses, human manure on the boots and baying hounds in the night reign supreme."[15]

The claim was made both on the plaintiff's own behalf and as a representative of a class of citizens known as the residents of the City of Pembroke. In rejecting the claim, the court agreed with the defendant newspaper's argument that group defamation only lies where "a group is so small and limited in scope that the words complained of must be taken to refer to each and every person in that group."

The "group" exception will not apply if a defamatory statement "points to a particular member or particular members of the group."[16] Whether a five-member council or a three-member committee would constitute such a group remains to be judicially determined. Furthermore, limitations affecting the publication of racist propaganda and sexist and ethnic jokes generally make such offensive matters not actionable, no matter "how false, malicious or damaging."[17] Such anti-social behaviour may, however, be punishable as a crime under the *Criminal Code* anti-hate legislation,[18] or as an offence under human rights legislation.[19]

---

14 (1993), 16 O.R. (3d) 672.

15 *Ibid.*, at 674.

16 *Bai et al. v. Sing Tao Daily Ltd. et al.* (2003), 226 D.L.R. (4th) 477 at 482 (Ont. C.A.); but see also *Malhab v. Métromédia CMR Montréal Inc. et al.* (2003), 226 D.L.R. (4th) 722 (Que. C.A.) where allegations of a general group prejudice were sufficient to found a class action suit.

17 "The Law of Defamation, An Issues Paper," March 1989, Publications Ontario, 103233, at p. 51; however, see Manitoba's *Defamation Act*, which states in s. 19 (1): The publication of a libel against a race, religious creed or sexual orientation likely to expose persons belonging to the race, professing the religious creed, or having the sexual orientation to hatred, contempt or ridicule, and tending to raise unrest or disorder among the people, entitles a person belonging to the race, professing the religious creed, or having the sexual orientation to sue for an injunction to prevent the continuation and circulation of the libel; and the Court of Queen's Bench may entertain the action.

18 *Criminal Code*, R.S.C. 1985, c. C-46, ss. 318-320.

19 *Canadian Human Rights Act, 1976-77*, c. 33; *Human Rights Code*, R.S.O. 1990, c. H.19.

Historically, when an action has been commenced, the court has presumed that the statement made was false. The defendant has been required to prove either the accuracy of the statement, or rely on the applicability of a common law or statutory defence.

Defences

As a result of the low threshold as to what constitutes defamation, most court cases deal with whether the defendant has made out one of the available defences. There are various defences that may be invoked, including:

- justification (i.e. truth);
- fair comment;
- consent;
- absolute or qualified privilege; and
- in the case of a "newspaper" (as defined), an appropriate retraction has been made.[20]

Justification

In most Canadian jurisdictions, proof of the accuracy of the statement, or truth, is a complete defence to the defamation action. The danger inherent in this approach, however, is that if the defence of justification is advanced and rejected by the court, aggravated damages will usually be sought by the plaintiff on the grounds that the defence itself "reiterated the libel."

In 1912, the Ontario Court of Appeal accepted the defence of justification in the case of *Holland v. Hall*.[21] In that instance, the defendant accused the plaintiff of seeking to return to municipal council as mayor in order to sell the town more dry goods, as he had in his previous electoral term. The truth won out when the evidence established that the plaintiff had, indeed, sold goods to the town while sitting as mayor during the previous term, a clear breach of the *Municipal Act* in those days.

---

20 *Libel and Slander Act*, R.S.O. 1990, c. L.12, s. 9 (1); "Newspaper" is defined in part as "... being published ... at least 12 times a year."

21 22 O.W.R. 209 (C.A.).

More recently, the defence of justification was accepted by the Supreme Court of British Columbia in a rather unique defamation case. In 2000, the plaintiff, a city councillor, sought the Liberal Party nomination in his provincial riding. While completing a detailed party questionnaire, the plaintiff disclosed that, 15 years earlier, he had been convicted of a breach of undertaking and given a conditional discharge for an assault charge. At the request of the Liberal Party, the plaintiff withdrew his candidacy. However, newspapers subsequently published stories alleging that the Liberal Party rejected the plaintiff after learning that he had pleaded guilty to assaulting a resident "with a noxious substance" and that he also defied a court order to "stay away from the assault victim before she could testify." During a lengthy trial, the defendants pleaded justification, although they acknowledged that they were incorrect in stating that the assault was "with a noxious substance." The plaintiff countered by arguing that the plea of justification could not succeed because the defendants could not prove the truth of the allegation in its entirety.

Mr. Justice McEwan accepted the defence of justification and dismissed the defamation claim in the following fashion:

> Here, the plaintiff's past activity resulting in criminal charges was misdescribed by the phrase "with a noxious substance" when in fact the unobjectionable description could have included two incidents: an assault "with his hand in which he held a pen like wrench"; and an assault wherein the victim was "pinned on the bed" and "... struck on the head, face and back." I simply do not think there is a credible case that the published description inflated or exaggerated the actual occurrence. This is an "error in detail" of no practical consequence in the circumstances.[22]

In Quebec,[23] in the case of a newspaper or other publication, it is not a sufficient defence to merely prove the accuracy of the statement. In that province, it is necessary to show that the statement was both true and published without malice in the public interest according to the terms of Quebec's Civil Code. It is also important to note that a resident of Que-

---

22 *Jay v. Hollinger Canadian Newspapers, Limited Partnership*, [2002] B.C.J. No. 2679 at par. 89.

23 Quebec Civil Code as quoted by the Canadian Business Press in "Seven key things you should know about publishing libel."

bec may take action under Quebec law, regardless of where the publication is located.[24]

Fair Comment

To invoke the defence of fair comment, the statements must reiterate facts that are true and related to a matter of legitimate public interest, and must contain "fair comment" thereon.[25] In Ontario, the *Libel and Slander Act* states in part that where an action arises from words consisting:

- partly of allegations of fact; and
- partly of expressions of opinion;
- a defence of fair comment shall not fail by reason only that the truth of every allegation of fact is not proved;
- if the expression of opinion is fair comment having regard to such of the facts alleged or referred to in the words complained of as are proved.[26]

Despite this elasticity, it therefore follows that if all of the purported "facts" are wrong, there is no basis for "fair comment." For example, in the 1976 British Columbia case of *Thompson v. N.L. Broadcasting*, a radio broadcaster aired editorials that alleged wrongdoing by the mayor. At trial, the defendant broadcaster pleaded the defences of justification and fair comment.[27] Ruling the allegations to be false, the court rejected the defence of justification. With respect to the defendant's reliance on fair comment, the court found that "if the facts are false, the defence of fair comment, based thereon, fails."

Conversely, the defence of fair comment was successful in the 1995 case of *Carey v. Phillips (c.o.b. The Boissevain Recorder)*.[28] The plaintiff reeve of the Rural Municipality of Winchester, Manitoba had sought

---

24 For a recent review of the law of defamation as it relates to a municipal councillor in Quebec, see the Supreme Court of Canada's decision in *Prud'homme v. Prud'homme*, [2002] S.C.C. 85, File No. 28117.

25 The comment must be the honest opinion of the person publishing it: *Chernesky v. Armadale Publishers Ltd.*, [1979] 1 S.C.R. 1067. See also "The Law of Defamation, An Issues Paper," March 1989, Publications Ontario, 103233, at p. 63.

26 R.S.O. 1990, c. L.12, s. 23.

27 1 C.C.C.I. 278 (B.C.S.C.).

28 [1995] M.J. No. 169.

the resignation of a member of council following an investigation of allegedly false expense claims. When the councillor refused, the plaintiff met with the local RCMP and indicated that a criminal conviction would force the councillor to resign. At the criminal trial, the councillor was acquitted of fraud, leading the defendant newspaper to publish an "open letter" by the councillor's lawyer, which concluded with the following colourful words:

> The 18 month unsuccessful investigation, prosecution, and persecution of [councillor] Gordon Holden can only be described as a fiasco. Such an ignominious failure even at the municipal level but under a system of "responsible government" should cause Reeve Ivan Carey to consider his involvement and resign his office.[29]

The plaintiff reeve claimed that the publication of the open letter defamed him and therefore brought an action against the newspaper which relied on the defence of fair comment.

Ultimately, the court found that, as the underlying factual basis of the publication was true and the comments were made on a matter of public interest, the defence of fair comment succeeded.

Consent

For the defence of consent to succeed, the court must be satisfied that the prior consent of the plaintiff was obtained permitting the use of the information. In addition, the consent may be either express or implied and the defendant must remain within the limits of the consent granted. For example, in the case of *Syms v. Warren*, the plaintiff chair of the Manitoba Liquor Control Commission and Liquor Licensing Board was rumoured to have arranged the quashing of impaired driving charges against him.[30] Subsequently, the plaintiff agreed to a radio interview, hosted by the defendant, for the purpose of denying the rumours. When the interview had ended, the defendant aired a telephone call from a female caller who alleged the rumours were true. At trial, the defendant raised the defence of the plaintiff's consent to the publication of the defamatory comments. In rejecting the defence, the court found that the defendant had exceeded the parameters of the plaintiff's consent:

---

29 *Ibid.*, at par. 16.
30 *Syms v. Warren* (1976), 71 D.L.R. (3d) 558.

I am ... satisfied that the plaintiff did not consent to a continuation of the discussion of the rumour. The consent of the plaintiff extended only to such publication as was necessary to fulfill the purpose indicated by Warren, that is, to participate in the program to deny the rumour and the comments of Warren that would be made in regard thereto. Even if the plaintiff was aware that the topics discussed on the program were often subsequently discussed with listeners telephoning the program, I can find nothing in the consent of the plaintiff or in any of the evidence to indicate the plaintiff agreed to Warren opening the topic for public discussion.[31]

Privilege

A defamatory statement may not be actionable if the occasion on which it is made is "privileged." This is true even if the defamatory statement is false.

There are two types of privilege: absolute privilege and qualified privilege. On December 20, 2002, the Supreme Court of Canada, in a defamation case involving a city councillor from Repentigny, Quebec, confirmed that "[e]lected municipal officials do not enjoy the parliamentary privilege enjoyed by members of the National Assembly of Quebec or the federal Parliament." The court went on to observe that the "English and Canadian courts, however, have held that words spoken at a meeting of a municipal council are protected by qualified privilege."[32]

Absolute Privilege

The defence of absolute privilege had its historical origins in the English Civil War and was confirmed in the English Bill of Rights of 1668. Article 9 of the Bill states, "the freedom of speech and debates on proceedings in parliament ought not to be impeached or questioned in any court or place outside the parliament."[33]

Over the centuries, absolute privilege has protected federal members of parliament, as well as the members of provincial legislatures at both

---

31 *Ibid.*, at 562.

32 *Prud'homme v. Prud'homme*, [2002] S.C.C. 85, File No. 28117 at par. 49.

33 David A. Potts, "Qualified Privilege for Municipal Councillors" *Municipal World*, December 1997, p. 10.

common law and after being codified in legislation.[34] There is, however, no absolute privilege for the comments made by municipal councillors during the course of a debate in council chambers, despite calls for such legislative protection.[35]

Despite this drawback, the defence of absolute privilege may still be available to municipal councillors on two other, albeit rarer occasions: when they are involved in litigation; or when they act as a statutory tribunal. In the former case, litigants are generally protected by absolute privilege during the course of judicial proceedings. In the seminal 19th century English decision on this matter, the court enunciated the principle as follows:

> The authorities are clear, uniform and conclusive, that no action of libel or slander lies whether against judges, counsel, witnesses or parties, for words written or spoken in the ordinary course of any proceeding before any court or tribunal recognized by law.[36]

Therefore, as a party to a lawsuit, an elected representative may be protected by absolute privilege for his or her actions during the judicial proceedings, including testimony given under oath or sworn in an affidavit.

In a manner related to such legal proceedings, it is possible that a municipal council may avail itself of the defence of absolute privilege in the rare instance when it is acting as a statutory tribunal. In the 1971 case of *Perry v. Heatherington*, Justice Munroe likened such a tribunal to a court of justice:

> The law is clear that the privilege applies wherever there is an authorized inquiry, which, though not before a court of justice, is be-

---

34 See, for example, *Legislative Assembly Act*, R.S.O. 1990, c. L.10, s. 37, which states: "A member of the Assembly is not liable to any civil action or prosecution, arrest, imprisonment or damages, by reason of any matter or thing the member brought by petition, bill, resolution, motion or otherwise, or said before the Assembly or a committee thereof."

35 For example, see the following comments on absolute privilege by AMO to the Province of Ontario's Standing Committee on Administration of Justice (September 1994): "The association urges the province to extend to municipal councillors and members of local boards the same privileges granted to them. The inclusion of section 37 in the *Legislative Assembly Act* provides safeguards for provincial members against potential libel suits. As part of their duties and responsibilities, municipal councillors are also faced with these potential liabilities and thus should be provided with the same measures of protection."

36 *Dawkins v. Lord Rokeby* (1873), L.R. 8 Q.B. 255 at 263; aff'd (1875), L.R. 7 H.L. 744.

fore a tribunal which has similar attributes, which acts in a manner similar to that in which courts of justice act.[37]

In a 1926 decision of the Ontario Court of Appeal, the defence of absolute privilege was afforded to a county auditor appointed by the municipality under the *Municipal Act* to investigate and undertake an accounting of road expenditures. The court's rationale was based on the quasi-judicial nature of the auditor's position:

> The matter was being investigated by a quasi-judicial officer who had power in his inquiry to administer an oath. He required these men to make a statement under oath, and it was their duty to make full disclosure of the facts within their knowledge.[38]

In the absence of these two, rather unique, occasions, municipal councillors must rely on the lesser defence of "qualified privilege."

Qualified Privilege

When qualified privilege is established, protection is generally afforded to a councillor's defamatory comments. The facts do not need to be true and the opinions expressed do not need to be based on the facts stated or alluded to. In 1911, the Ontario Court of Appeal issued the following eloquent ruling with respect to the successful application of the defence of qualified privilege as it related to the statement by an alderman, who had suggested that the plaintiff had "robbed the city:"

> Aldermen are legislators in as true and in as many instances as important a sense as members of parliament or of the legislature – it is their right and their duty to speak their mind fully and clearly without evasion or equivocation – they should show no fear, favour, or affection; and it is their duty, as well as their right, to use all legitimate means, rhetorical or otherwise to impress their fellow legislators with the righteousness of their views – they have no need to be mealy-mouthed, and should call a spade a spade.[39]

It is crucial to appreciate that it is the occasion that is the basis of qualified privilege, not the particular words used. In the 1917 House of

---

37 *Perry v. Heatherington*, [1971] 5 W.R. 670 (B.C.S.C.).
38 *Nixon v. O'Callaghan* (1926), 60 O.R. 76 (C.A.).
39 *Ward v. McBride* (1911), 24 O.L.R. 555 at 568 (C.A.).

Lords' case of *Adam v. Ward*,[40] it was held that a qualified privilege occasion arises when the person who makes the communication has:

- an interest; or
- a duty – legal, social or moral,

to make the communication to the person to whom it is made, and such person has a corresponding interest or duty to receive it.

This reciprocity between the interested parties is essential. Lord Diplock, in the slander case of *Horrocks v. Lowe*, confirmed that:

> What is said by members of a local council at meetings of the council or of any of its committees is spoken on a privileged occasion. The reason for the privilege is that those who represent the local government electors should be able to speak freely and frankly, boldly and bluntly, on any matter which they believe affects the interest or welfare of the inhabitants. They may be swayed by strong political prejudice, they may be obstinate and pig-headed, stupid and obtuse; but they were chosen by the electors to speak their minds on matters of local concern and so long as they do so honestly they run no risk of liability for defamation of those who are the subjects of their criticism.[41]

In *Bay-Tower Homes Limited et al. v. Illingworth*,[42] an Ontario Court determined that, despite the fact that the defendant mayor made his comments to the council at a council meeting with the knowledge that the press was present, the defence of qualified privilege still applied.

This "occasion" for which the defence of qualified privilege may arise in the municipal realm need not be limited to debates on the council chamber floor. In the 1993 case of *Bauman v. Turner*,[43] the British Columbia Court of Appeal found that a letter by the mayor of the District of Squamish had been written on the occasion of qualified privilege. Briefly, the case concerned a dispute over a proposed water source between the mayor and the plaintiff, a resident who was a geological engi-

---

40 [1917] A.C. 309 at 334 (H.L.).
41 *Horrocks v. Lowe*, [1975] A.C. 152 (H.L.).
42 Supreme Court of Ontario, Toronto Court File No. 957/85; *Municipal World*, August 1986, p. 206.
43 (1993), 105 D.L.R. (4th) 37 (B.C.C.A.).

neer. In a letter to the provincial Minister of the Environment, the plaintiff opposed the proposed water source. In turn, the minister referred to the plaintiff's correspondence in a letter to the mayor. In replying to the minister, the mayor stated that, in his opinion, the plaintiff had misused his status as a professional engineer. The court held that, as the mayor was fulfilling his duty to ensure the adequacy of the district's water supply and the minister had a reciprocal interest in receiving the mayor's views, then the occasion of writing the letter was one of qualified privilege.

The limitations on the protection of qualified privilege must also be regarded. In *Peckham v. Mount Pearl (City)*, a municipal councillor, at a council meeting, said that an Assistant Deputy Minister of Municipal Affairs (ADM) had been inciting "sabotage" in the ranks of the senior civil service with respect to a regional services program. He also stated that the ADM was guilty of "deliberately lying" to the minister and the premier. The Newfoundland Supreme Court, Trial Division determined that none of the bases that the defendant councillor asserted as the foundation of these statements existed, and that the statement that a senior civil servant had deliberately lied to his minister was clearly defamation.

While acknowledging that the defence of qualified privilege is available at a council meeting, the court nevertheless found it to be inapplicable in the circumstances because "there must be an objective assessment of whether or not there was a legal, social or moral duty to communicate the information, erroneous though it may have been."[44] The Trial Judge went on to observe that "in my view, application of this test leads to the conclusion that no duty to communicate the information existed." The court further concluded that the defendant could not rely on the defence of fair comment, as it was not applicable to an action against the person making the statement, but rather applied to the publisher of the statement.

Many case examples exist where the courts have been called upon, with varying results, to assess the impact of strong language used both within and outside a council meeting, and the availability of the defence of qualified privilege:

---

44 *Peckham v. Mount Pearl (City)*, [1994] N.J. No. 302 at p. 8.

- an allegation at a council meeting that the plaintiff's actions in erecting a fence on the municipal road allowance was a "blatant disregard" for the by-laws was protected by qualified privilege;[45]
- a comment describing a contractor as "not reliable" during a council meeting was defamatory, but also protected by qualified privilege.[46]

Perhaps the most eloquent and colourful judgment regarding the defence of qualified privilege was that of Mr. Justice Spencer in the British Columbia case, *Ralston v. Fromich*.[47] During a city council debate, the defendant alderman called the plaintiff alderman a "sick son of a bitch." Although he apologized during the meeting, the defendant alderman later told reporters, "You can quote me that, in my personal opinion, Ralston is a sick son of a bitch." With respect to the comments made during the meeting, the court found the defendant alderman was protected by qualified privilege. However, the subsequent comments made outside the council chamber were not so protected. This left Mr. Justice Spencer with the duty to determine whether the defendant's comments were capable of being defamatory:

> In my opinion the words "son of a bitch" by themselves are not capable of any defamatory meaning. They are peculiar, in that they take their meaning either from the tone of voice used or from whatever adjective accompanies them. They are a translucent vessel waiting to be filled with colour by their immediate qualifier. Thus, one has sympathy for a poor son of a bitch, admiration for a brave son of a bitch, affection for a good old son of a bitch, envy for a rich son of a bitch and, perhaps incongruously, dislike for a proper son of a bitch. Why right-thinking people should dislike anything that is proper is rather a mystery unless proper is used to mean "real," but I am confident that is the colour that adjective gives to the expression. It is perhaps a throw-back to an earlier use of the expression when the mere words themselves carried an opprobrious meaning, see for example Kent's apostrophe to Oswald:

---

45 *Cardwell v. Hutchinson*, [1995] B.C.J. No. 1656.
46 *McKinnon v. Dauphin (Rural Municipality)* (1996), 31 M.P.L.R. (2d) 13 (Man. Q.B.); affirmed (1997), 41 M.P.L.R. (2d) 207 (Man. C.A.).
47 [1992] B.C.J. No. 463.

"(thou) art nothing but the composition of a knave, beggar, coward, panderer and the son and heir of a mongrel bitch." – (Shakespeare, King Lear, Act 2, Scene 2)

There are other early examples to be found of a stand alone meaning of the phrase, but in modern times the bare words are not capable of bearing a defamatory meaning. At most they insult. They are not likely to lower the object in the estimation of right-thinking people. More probably they will demean the speaker, depending upon the company and the occasion. As an example of the modern neutrality of the phrase, I refer to *The New Dictionary of American Slang* (Chapman, Harper and Row, 1986) where it means a person or thing that is remarkable, wonderful or superior, with a reference to the phrase, "Their new album is a son of a bitch I tell you." One imagines that was not said on the Saturday afternoon Metropolitan Opera program, but on some less formal occasion.[48]

Having said all that, Spencer J. ultimately determined that the use of the adjective "sick" in this case was defamatory given that its ordinary meanings included:

... that the plaintiff was either mentally ill, unstable or unbalanced, that he was perverted, unwholesome or morally corrupt, or that he was unfit to hold public office or to practice his profession as a barrister and solicitor.

While the judicial determination in these cases varied depending upon the particular circumstances, they all serve to illustrate that, despite the broad reasoning of Lord Diplock in *Horrocks v. Lowe* cited above, a prudent councillor would be wise to temper his or her language even though the member may speak "freely and frankly" in a council session protected by qualified privilege.

Finally, in the case of *New York Times v. Sullivan*,[49] the United States Supreme Court extended qualified privilege to publication of material about "public figures" that would otherwise have been considered defamatory. While this principle is not applicable in Canada, the close me-

---

48 *Ibid.*, at pp. 3-4.
49 (1964), 376 U.S. 254.

dia intercommunication with the United States sometimes gives rise to confusion on this point.[50]

Retraction

Ontario's *Libel and Slander Act* confers the defence of retraction upon a newspaper.[51] It states that in an action for libel, the defendant may plead in mitigation of damages that:

- the libel was inserted therein without actual malice and without gross negligence;
- before the commencement of the action, or at the earliest opportunity afterwards, the defendant inserted in such newspaper a full apology for the libel; or
- if the newspaper in which the libel appeared is one ordinarily published at intervals exceeding one week, the defendant offered to publish the apology in any newspaper to be selected by the plaintiff.

In an action for libel in a broadcast, the Act further provides that the defendant may plead in mitigation of damages that:

- the libel was broadcast without actual malice and without gross negligence; and
- before the commencement of the action, or at the earliest opportunity afterwards, the defendant will broadcast a full apology for the libel.[52]

Malice

Where a member makes a statement maliciously, the defences of qualified privilege and fair comment are not available. The Supreme Court of Canada has noted that "malice is commonly understood, in the popular sense, as spite or ill will." The court went on to observe that malice also includes:

---

50 *Hill v. Church of Scientology of Toronto* (1995), 126 D.L.R. (4th) 129 at 165-170.
51 *Libel and Slander Act*, R.S.O. 1990, c. L.12, s. 9 (1); "Newspaper" is defined in part as " ... being published ... at least 12 times a year."
52 *Ibid.*, s. 9 (2).

- any indirect motive or ulterior purpose that conflicts with the sense of duty or the mutual interest which the occasion created;
- speaking dishonestly; or
- speaking in knowing or reckless disregard for the truth.[53]

Establishing malice, however, may be difficult. In the case of *Baumann v. Turner*,[54] it was stated that "the only possibility of showing malice to have been present would be proof of personal spite on the part of the defendant," or that he was seeking "to obtain some private advantage unconnected with the duty or interest which constitutes the reason for the privilege."

Municipal Corporations

As creatures of statute, most municipalities in Canada are corporations with the legal capacity to sue or be sued. Do these rights extend to defamation lawsuits? In the late 19th century, an Ontario municipality was successfully sued by its own registrar of deeds when it published material that impugned the plaintiff's honesty.[55]

More recently, the courts have upheld the right of local government entities to sue for libel in two cases. In *Prince George (City) v. British Columbia Television Systems Limited*, the British Columbia Court of Appeal ruled that a municipality is a corporation and therefore has the right to sue. On finding that a municipal corporation can sue in libel, the court ruled that "a municipality may have a reputation, distinct from the reputation of its elected representatives and of its officials and servants." In summary, the court held:

> In my opinion, it is beyond question that municipal corporations have reputations. A cursory examination of the *Municipal Act* reveals the great diversity of matters in respect of which municipalities may legislate and the diversity of activities in which such corporations may engage. The way in which a municipality legislates and the way in which it administers the legislation it enacts and conducts itself in relation to activities which it lawfully undertakes cannot but create a municipal reputation, be it good, bad or

---

53 *Hill v. Church of Scientology of Toronto* (1995), 126 D.L.R. (4th) 129 at 171.
54 (1993), 16 M.P.L.R. (2d) 114 (B.C.C.A.); *Municipal World,* April 1992, p. 22.
55 *McLay v. The Corporation of the County of Bruce* (1887), 14 O.L.R. 398 (C.P.D.).

indifferent. I can see no basis in principle for holding that a municipal corporation, empowered by statute to sue in its corporate name, cannot maintain an action for libel. To hold otherwise would leave municipalities the helpless victims of all those who choose to publish untrue imputations which injure their reputations.[56]

In the 1984 case of *Windsor Roman Catholic School Board et al. v. Southam Inc.*, the court dismissed an application to have the board struck as a complainant. In rejecting the defendant newspaper's argument that the school board "had no reputation to protect," DuPont J. stated:

The board's reputation for honesty, probity, fairness and decency must, of necessity, play an important role in the performance of its duties and responsibilities. Libels on its reputation would not only interfere in the performance of these duties and responsibilities, but would act to deter people from taking part in the board itself.[57]

Despite these Canadian cases supporting a local government entity's right to sue in defamation, a recent House of Lords' ruling points toward the opposite conclusion in England. In the 1993 case of *Derbyshire County Council v. Times Newspaper Ltd., et al.*, the Law Lords found:

I regard it as a right for this House to lay down that not only is there no public interest favouring the right of organs of government, whether central or local, to sue for libel, but it is contrary to the public interest because to admit such actions would place an undesirable fetter on the freedom of speech.[58]

---

56 *Prince George (City) v. British Columbia Television Systems Limited* (1979), 95 D.L.R. (3d) 577; affirming 85 D.L.R. (3d) 755.

57 *Windsor Roman Catholic School Board et al. v. Southam Inc.* (1984), 46 O.R. (2d) 231 at 235.

58 *Derbyshire County Council v. Times Newspaper Ltd., et al.*, [1993] 1 All E.R. 1011 (H.L.).

Charter of Rights and Freedoms

With the growing influence of the *Canadian Charter of Rights and Freedoms*, the law of defamation is under active scrutiny as a prelude to change.[59] Returning to the 1995 decision of the Supreme Court of Canada in *Hill v. Church of Scientology of Toronto*, Mr. Justice Cory made the following general comments with respect to the dueling values of a good reputation versus the Charter right to freedom of expression:

> Although it is not specifically mentioned in the Charter, the good reputation of the individual represents and reflects the innate dignity of the individual, a concept which underlies all the Charter rights. It follows that the protection of the good reputation of an individual is of fundamental importance to our democratic society.[60]

Further, the Supreme Court ruling observed that there "can be no doubt that in libel cases, the twin values of reputation and freedom of expression will clash."

Nevertheless, the courts have also offered a caution to those who would speak in defamatory terms of persons holding public office. In *Mack v. North Hill News Ltd.*[61] in which a newspaper published false charges against members of a city council, Kirby, J. stated:

> The publication of defamatory words ... against people in public life, undermines and weakens the fabric of our democratic process. By imputing improper motives and a lack of good faith, people of high purpose and personal integrity are discouraged from entering public service.

Conclusions

Although new, omnibus legislation for municipalities has recently been enacted in Saskatchewan and Ontario, most statutes remain silent on the issue of privilege for elected representatives.[62] In fact, most provincial legislation ignores the fact that councillors and staff at the local level do not have the protection of absolute privilege accorded to members of ei-

---

59 *Constitution Act, 1982*, c. 11 (U.K.), Schedule B, Part I, Canadian Charter of Rights and Freedoms.
60 *Hill v. Church of Scientology of Toronto* (1995), 126 D.L.R. (4th) 129 at 163.
61 (1964), 44 D.L.R. (2d) 147.
62 See Ontario's *Municipal Act, 2001*, c. 25 and Saskatchewan's *Cities Act*, being Bill No. 75 of 2002, S.S. 2002.

ther the federal or provincial legislatures.[63] This omission to extend the definition of absolute privilege to local governments was one of the primary reasons for the holding of closed meetings in the past.

In Ontario, a strong recommendation was made to the legislative committee conducting public hearings on the changes to the *Municipal Act* in 1994. As an absolute minimum, it was recommended that the fundamental rules of qualified privilege should be codified in the *Municipal Act* so that members of council could place their new, open local government responsibilities in the proper context.[64] It was suggested that they be codified in the following form:

(1) A statement made by a member of council or local board, as the case may be, at a meeting shall not be construed as defamatory if made in accordance with the principles set out in subsection (2).

(2) What is said by a member at a meeting shall not be construed as defamatory where the member who makes the communication,

   (a) makes such statement without malice;

   (b) has an interest, or a duty, legal, social or moral, to make the communication;

   (c) to the person or persons to whom it is made; and

   (d) such person has a corresponding interest and duty to receive it.

(3) Despite subsection (2), the presence of members of the public or media at a meeting where such a statement is made shall not be construed as detracting from the qualified privilege conferred upon the members present.

Although this recommendation was not accepted, it remains a useful guide for members of council and local boards in exercising their right

---

63 See editorial, "Absolute privilege for municipal councils?" *Municipal World*, November 1994, p. 2.

64 This recommendation was included in a brief by Michael J. Smither, presented to the Standing Committee on the Administration of Justice at a public hearing on Bill 163 in London, Ontario, August 31, 1994.

to freedom of expression, as well as their duty to represent their constituents, without fear of repercussions.

As local governments across Canada move forward into the new millennium, it is obvious that they will continue to embrace various technological wonders, such as websites or portals, while seeking to promote new ideas like "e-democracy." It remains to be seen whether such advances will also introduce the troublesome legal concept of "cyber-libel" and whether or not the traditional defences available to municipal councillors (such as qualified privilege) will be extended to the outer reaches of the Internet.

Chapter 9
NEGLIGENT MISREPRESENTATION

> *No matter how uncomfortable it might have been for the other members of council, it was surely incumbent upon them to speak up if, as it turned out to be the case, the reeve did not represent their views. They must have known that the respondent was relying upon these statements and they could not simply leave the respondent with the impression that council had approved the immediate improvement of the Blind Line. The fact that there was no such commitment was highly pertinent information.*
>
> Mr. Justice M. Rosenberg (2000)

A distant second cousin to the tort of defamation is that of "negligent misrepresentation" – an action that may arise when incorrect information, provided by a local government official, is relied on by another person to his or her detriment. As the level of government most closely identified with providing fundamental services to constituents on a daily basis, municipalities and local boards are frequently required to respond to inquiries from members of the public. This is due to the vast array of services they provide, as well as the large number of records they maintain within their jurisdiction. As one authoritative source described it, "it has long been the law in Canada that negligently rendered information or advice, which proves to be false, misleading or inaccurate, can give rise to liability for damages suffered by a member of the public who receives such information and relies on it to his or her detriment."[1] While most negligent misrepresentation cases in the local government arena arise from the information or advice given by municipal staff, a number of recent cases have expanded that liability to the action taken by members of municipal councils.

---

1 David G. Boghosian and J. Murray Davison, *The Law of Municipal Liability in Canada*, Butterworths, at p. 8.1.

Common Law

The 1963 House of Lords decision in *Hedley-Byrne & Co. Ltd. v. Heller & Partner* is the seminal U.K. case on the law regarding negligent misrepresentation. The general summary of the law was offered by Lord Morris:

> My Lords, I consider that it follows and that it should now be regarded as settled, that if someone who possessed of a special skill undertakes, quite irrespective of contract, to apply that skill for the assistance of another person who relies on such skill, a duty of care will arise. The fact that the service is to be given by means of, or by the instrumentality of, words can make no difference. Furthermore, if, in a sphere in which a person is so placed that others can reasonably rely on his judgment or his skill or his ability to make careful inquiry, a person takes it upon himself to give information or advice to, or allows his information or advice to be passed onto, another person who, as he knows or should know, will place reliance on it, then a duty of care will arise.[2]

The so-called *Hedley-Byrne* principles were identified as being applicable to municipal corporations in 1971 following the Supreme Court of Canada ruling in the case of *Wellbridge Holdings Ltd. v. Greater Winnipeg (Metropolitan Corporation)*.[3]

In the case of *The Pas (Town) v. Porky Packers Ltd.*,[4] the Supreme Court of Canada directly considered a negligent misrepresentation involving a municipality in Manitoba. In that instance, a town councillor, who was also a businessman, asked the municipality's secretary-treasurer about the availability of properly zoned industrial land for a meat packing plant. After being referred to various town-owned lots, the councillor/businessman wrote to the mayor and council offering to purchase the lots for a meat packing operation. Although the council agreed to this offer, the resolution was quashed in a court application by residents who successfully argued that the operation of a slaughterhouse was prohibited on the lands in question. The councillor/businessman subsequently sued the town, alleging that it had misrepresented the permitted

---

2 *Hedley-Byrne & Co. Ltd. v. Heller & Partner*, [1963] 2 All. E.R. 575 at 578-579; [1964] A.C. 465 (H.L.).
3 [1971] S.C.R. 957, 22 D.L.R. (3d) 470.
4 *The Pas (Town) v. Porky Packers Ltd.*, [1977] 1 S.C.R. 51.

land use of the subject lots. Ultimately, the Supreme Court confirmed the application of the principles set out in *Hedley-Byrne*, although it dismissed the specific claims against the municipality.

Subsequently, in the *Queen v. Cognos Inc.*, the Supreme Court of Canada reiterated the five basic elements to establish a claim in negligent misrepresentation:

1. The existence of a duty of care based on a "special relationship" between the representor and the representee;

2. The representation in question must be untrue, inaccurate or misleading;

3. The representor must have acted negligently in making the representation;

4. The representee must have relied, in a reasonable manner, on the negligent misrepresentation; and

5. The reliance must have been detrimental to the representee in the sense that damages resulted from reliance on the misrepresentation.[5]

In order to better appreciate these five principles within the confines of a negligent misrepresentation action against elected municipal representatives, the remaining portion of this chapter will review these principles of law as discussed by the courts in four recent cases.

Hercules Management Ltd. v. Ernst & Young

In 1997, the Supreme Court of Canada had an opportunity to review the above-noted general requirements in the negligent misrepresentation case of *Hercules Management Ltd. v. Ernst & Young*.[6]

Mr. Justice La Forest used this case as an opportunity to emphasize that the existence of a duty of care in the tort of negligent misrepresentation required the application of the two-part test first enunciated in the House of Lords decision in *Anns v. Merton London Borough Council*[7] and later adopted by the Supreme Court in the decision of *Kamloops*

---

5 *Queen v. Cognos Inc.*, [1993] 1 S.C.R. 87.
6 [1997] 2 S.C.R. 165.
7 [1978] A.C. 278 (H.L.).

(City) v. Nielsen:[8]

> Is there a sufficiently close relationship between the parties (the [defendant] and the person who has suffered the damage) so that, in the reasonable contemplation of the [defendant], carelessness on its part might cause damage to that person? If so, are there any considerations which ought to negative or limit (a) the scope of the duty and (b) the class of persons to whom it is owed or (c) the damages to which a breach of it may give rise?

In adopting this approach, the court addressed the second part of the test regarding a duty of care in the following fashion:

> A *prima facie* duty of care will arise on the part of a defendant in a negligent misrepresentation action when it can be said (a) that the defendant ought reasonably to have foreseen that the plaintiff would rely on his representation, and (b) that reliance by the plaintiff, in the circumstances, would be reasonable.[9]

In setting out this principle, the Supreme Court clarified that no duty will arise where that duty imposes upon the defendant indeterminate liability to an indeterminate number of people.

Lakefield (Village) v. Black

In the 1998 case of *Lakefield (Village) v. Black*, the original property owners applied to the Ministry of Municipal Affairs for approval of a draft plan of subdivision of the property in 1986. The ministry then elicited responses to the draft plan from various agencies that might be affected by the plan, including the Village of Lakefield. The municipality advised the ministry that water service was available and that it was not premature to subdivide the property in question. This statement was false and made negligently; however, it was never shared directly with the property owners, only the Ministry of Municipal Affairs. The following year, the ministry approved the plan of subdivision, subject only to standard conditions that were unrelated to the water service for the property. In December 1988, the plaintiff purchased property after reviewing the plan of subdivision and the standard conditions. After the purchase, the plaintiff discovered the serious water service problem and sold the property at a significant loss. Subsequently, the plaintiff sued

---

8   [1984] 2 S.C.R. 2 at 10-11.
9   *Hercules Management Ltd. v. Ernst & Young*, [1997] 2 S.C.R. 165 at 200.

the Village of Lakefield for negligent misrepresentation. The action was successful at trial and the municipality appealed.

On October 9, 1998, the Ontario Court of Appeal dismissed the village's appeal.[10] The municipality argued that, under all the circumstances, the imposition of a legal duty would place the village in the position of owing a duty of care to an indeterminate number of people, such as the plaintiff purchasers, who are not directly known to the municipality. The Ontario Court of Appeal rejected this argument by applying the two-part *Anns/Kamloops* test in the following fashion:

> As to the first branch of the test, in my opinion, a *prima facie* duty of care arises on the facts of this case. Lakefield ought reasonably to have foreseen that Black would rely on its representation. Lakefield made the representation based on its special knowledge of the circumstances and as a formal response to a permanent evaluation of a request for approval of a plan to subdivide this property. It ought to have foreseen that its representation would be relied on by someone seeking to effect that very subdivision, particularly where its representation was reflected in the draft plan approval, which resulted from the representation.
>
> As to the second branch of the test, in my view it too is met. The class of those who might rely on the representation as the respondent [Black] did is strictly limited. It is those who could seek to proceed with the subdivision of the property. Given that Lakefield was fully aware that its representation was being made in the context of a proposed plan of subdivision, it must be taken to know of the class of those who could properly complain about its misrepresentation, namely those who would seek to subdivide the property. Moreover, the representation was made for the very purpose of facilitating the subdivision of the property. It was in just this context that the respondent used the representation. He relied on it to purchase the property for development. Hence, there is no risk of indeterminacy here. The scope of Lakefield's liability is readily circumscribed. There is no policy basis, therefore, for overriding the *prima facie* duty of care resting on the appellant [municipality].[11]

---

10 *Lakefield (Village) v. Black*, [1998] O.J. No. 4060.

11 Ibid., at p. 6.

Moin v. Blue Mountains (Town)

In this 2000 case, the plaintiff property owner intended to develop a subdivision. However, access to the land was by way of an unimproved road allowance owned by the defendant municipality, the Town of Blue Mountains. In May 1989, the plaintiff attended a council meeting and asked whether the road, known as the Blind Line, would be upgraded. The reeve responded by saying, "there is going to be a road this summer." This statement went unchallenged by any of the other four members of council who were present at the time, even though some did not agree with the reeve about when the road upgrade would actually occur. Although work began on the upgrade during the summer of 1989, delays forced the plaintiff to reappear before council in July of that year and again in March 1990. Each time, the plaintiff requested completion of the upgrade and each time he was told by the reeve, in the presence of other members of council, that the road would be upgraded shortly. Based on these comments, the plaintiff entered into a development agreement with the municipality in May 1990, wherein he was required to construct an interior road within one year. Unfortunately, completion of the interior road could not be done until the municipality first upgraded its road allowance, and that was not finished until September 1991. By that time, the plaintiff had run into financial difficulties.

In granting Moin's claim, the Trial Judge held the municipality liable for damages in excess of $187,000. On appeal, the municipality argued that it could not be held liable for the statements made by the reeve as these were, in effect, political promises, potentially involving the expenditure of public funds. In any event, it also argued that the elements of negligent misrepresentation had not been made out.

On August 22, 2000, the Ontario Court of Appeal affirmed the trial judgment against the defendant municipality for negligent misrepresentation.[12] The court agreed that it was open to the Trial Judge to find that the statements made by the reeve were in the municipality's operational or business capacity, rather than its legislative capacity. Furthermore, the Court of Appeal found that the council was assembled to answer questions of this very nature, an act which gave rise to a private duty of care and cited the case of *Black v. Lakefield (Village)* in support of this proposition. In a related fashion, the municipality also argued that the

---

12 *Moin v. Blue Mountains (Town)*, [2000] O.J. No. 3039.

tation.[12] The court agreed that it was open to the Trial Judge to find that the statements made by the reeve were in the municipality's operational or business capacity, rather than its legislative capacity. Furthermore, the Court of Appeal found that the council was assembled to answer questions of this very nature, an act which gave rise to a private duty of care and cited the case of *Black v. Lakefield (Village)* in support of this proposition. In a related fashion, the municipality also argued that the Trial Judge's finding of liability hinged on the silence of the members of council, other than the reeve. The municipality argued that silence could not be the basis of liability – absent a legal duty to make disclosure under all of the circumstances. On behalf of the Court of Appeal, Mr. Justice Rosenberg also rejected this argument in the following fashion:

> I am also of the view that this is not a case of the municipality being held liable for silence or non-disclosure. This was not a case where a statement or promise was made in private by a council member to a citizen. The council had assembled to deal with questions from citizens and organized itself to speak through the reeve. There was nothing in the circumstances to alert the plaintiff or any other citizen that the reeve was speaking only for himself or that he was anything other than the spokesperson for the municipality. The issue was not whether the appellant [municipality] was liable for non-disclosure, but whether it breached its duty to exercise reasonable care in its dealing with the respondent [landowner or purchaser].
>
> ...
>
> No matter how uncomfortable it might have been for the other members of council, it was surely incumbent upon them to speak up if, as it turned out to be the case, the reeve did not represent their views. They must have known that the respondent was relying upon the statements and they could not simply leave the respondent with the impression that council had approved the immediate improvement of the Blind Line. The fact that there was no such commitment was highly pertinent information.[13]

---

12 *Moin v. Blue Mountains (Town)*, [2000] O.J. No. 3039.

13 *Ibid.*, paras. 28-29.

The dismissal of the town's appeal in this instance means that the silence of councillors in a similar situation may constitute a failure on the part of the municipality to take reasonable care in its dealings with members of the public. It is interesting to note that, following this decision, the Ontario Regional Solicitors' Association recommended that the Minister of Municipal Affairs and Housing include a specific provision in Ontario's new *Municipal Act* to ensure that such statements made in the course of a public meeting by individual members of council are not binding on the municipality unless a resolution or by-law has been passed, confirming them as council's statement. This recommendation was not adopted by the province when it enacted the new *Municipal Act, 2001*.

Wozniak v. Erin (Town)

This 2001 case concerned the establishment of a lot created in 1987 as part of a plan of subdivision under an agreement between the town and a developer. Throughout the late 1980s and early 1990s, it was documented that there were some grading deficiencies, and that water was pooling near the foundation of the newly constructed house on the lot. As a result, the town's staff recommended that a grading security deposit of $500 not be released because of the ongoing drainage and grading problems. In 1992, the plaintiffs entered into an agreement to purchase the property, after the town responded that there were no outstanding infractions or work orders against the lot in question. Shortly thereafter, the plaintiffs began to experience significant pooling and flooding problems on their property and brought an action against the town alleging, among other things, negligent misrepresentation.[14]

At trial, the Town of Erin was held liable to the plaintiffs for more than $83,000 as a result of the municipality's failure to advise them of deficiencies in lot grading that caused the property in question to experience flooding. As one case comment concluded about this decision, "*Wozniak* is consistent with a multitude of decisions in which municipalities have been held to be responsible for representations which are inaccurate because they are incomplete and, thus, do not fully inform the inquiring party."[15]

---

14 *Wozniak v. Erin (Town)* (2001), 20 M.P.L.R. (3d) 9.
15 Frederick P. Crooks, "Municipal Liability for Negligent Misstatement: *Wozniak v. Erin (Town)*," *Municipal Liability Risk Management* (September 2001) 84 at 87.

David v. Halifax (Regional Municipality)

In August 2003, the Nova Scotia Supreme Court had an opportunity to consider the earlier ruling on negligent misstatements by the Ontario Court of Appeal in the *Moin v. Blue Mountains (Town)* case. The plaintiffs were municipal property owners who had solicited municipal, provincial and federal funding in order to extend municipal water services to their community in Nova Scotia. In the subsequent lawsuit, the plaintiffs sought damages against the following defendants: the Halifax Regional Water Commission (the commission); its general manager, Carl Yates; the Halifax Regional Municipality (HRM); as well as Reginald Rankin, the community's councillor. The plaintiffs alleged that the general manager and the councillor had informed them that their frontage charges would be reduced if the construction costs for the water infrastructure project were less than estimated. However, the area originally covered by the project was subsequently expanded after it was discovered that there were additional funds available because the tenders were less than estimated. Ultimately, the plaintiffs argued that they were entitled to damages because their frontage fees were not reduced, and based their claim on a number of actions, including negligent misrepresentation.

After citing both Supreme Court of Canada decisions in *Queen v. Cognos Inc.* and *Hercules Management Ltd. v. Ernst & Young*, Mr. Justice Hilroy S. Nathanson reviewed the Ontario Court of Appeal's ruling in *Moin v. Blue Mountains (Town)* and made the following findings of liability with respect to the commission's general manager, Carl Yates:

> Yates represented that there was an existing policy or practice of [the commission] or HRM, or both, that savings resulting from lower tenders would be returned to the community in the form of lower frontage charges. This representation led the ... community to accept the project. It was an unequivocal representation made in the exercise of his powers and duties.
>
> Yates had the implied actual authority of [the commission], deriving from his position as general manager of [it]. When he made his representation to the ... community, he was acting within the scope of his duties in dealing with the expansion of the municipal water infrastructure in general and, more particularly, extension of the water supply to [the community]. Yates' principal [the commission] is not a municipality. His misrepresentation is attribut-

able to his principal, which is vicariously liable for the negligent misstatement of its servant, Yates.[16]

Despite the trial judge's finding that the commission and its general manager were liable for latter's comments to the community, the court distinguished the statements made by a single councillor under all of the circumstances:

> Liability for negligent misrepresentation does not extend to Rankin, nor do his statements serve as a basis to attribute liability to HRM. He was only one of many municipal councillors, and had no power to speak on behalf of, or bind, HRM. Since HRM is a municipality, Rankin did not have ostensible authority to speak or act on its behalf.
>
> In the result, I find no direct liability in negligence for HRM. But do find liability against Yates for innocent but negligent misrepresentation and, on an agency basis, such liability extends to [the Commission] and, in turn, to HRM.[17]

Ultimately, Nathanson J. awarded damages to the plaintiffs in excess of $267,000.

Conclusions

Due to the advent of email and voicemail, the number of inquiries to local government staff has likely increased exponentially over the last decade. Therefore, it is not surprising that most negligent misrepresentation claims arise as a result of erroneous information being dispersed by staff in busy operational areas (such as building or zoning departments) and then relied upon by the public. Having said that, the judicial rulings in this chapter should serve as a stark reminder that the individual and collective actions of members of council or local boards are also vulnerable to such negligent misrepresentation claims.

---

16 *David v. Halifax (Regional Municipality)*, [2003] N.S.J. No. 289 at paras. 150-151.
17 *Ibid.*, at paras. 153-154.

Chapter 10
MEMBERS' CODE OF CONDUCT

> *I believe that there is an expectation today on the part of the public that there be clear and definite guidelines regarding the conduct of their elected officials. Other levels of government have established similar codes, and I believe that Halifax Regional Municipality, as the largest municipality in the Province, should be taking the lead at the local government level.*[1]
>
> Mayor Peter Kelly
> October 18, 2002

An in-depth discussion focusing on the appropriate standard of conduct for an elected or appointed representative of local government is likely to be too philosophical or far-ranging to be contained within the pages of this text. Furthermore, a detailed examination of the current statutory requirements that govern various aspects of this behaviour – often contained in provincial conflict of interest legislation – is neither practical nor helpful due to the various differences found in each province across Canada. In light of these limitations, this chapter will provide a brief overview of the conflict of interest legislation as it has evolved in Ontario and identify similar statutes for local government representatives in other Canadian jurisdictions. More particularly, this chapter will focus on the ability of local government bodies themselves to enact codes of conduct to govern the behaviour of councillors or members of local boards, as well as identifying some fundamental elements often included in those codes.

---

1 "Mayor Proposes Code of Ethics and Conduct," Halifax Regional Municipality Press Release (October 18, 2002).

Ontario's Legislative Experience

Conflict of Interest

Thirty years ago, Ontario enacted the first *Municipal Conflict of Interest Act* in Canada to govern the behaviour of members of council and local boards. At that time, the 19th century concept of "disqualification" – where an individual who received a municipal allowance or had an interest in a contract with a municipality was statutorily disqualified from sitting on the council – was replaced by the new, dual principles of "disclosure and abstention."[2] In 1983, the legislation was revised, ensuring that, when a member had a pecuniary interest in a matter under consideration by a municipal council or local board, he or she would be required to publicly disclose the general nature of this pecuniary interest and abstain from participating any further in the matter.[3]

On November 28, 1994, Bill 163 received Third Reading in the Ontario Legislature. Known as the *Planning and Municipal Statute Law Amendment Act, 1994*, this piece of omnibus legislation amended numerous municipal statutes. Significantly, it also purported to repeal the *Municipal Conflict of Interest Act*, and replace it with a new statute, entitled the *Local Government Disclosure of Interest Act, 1994*.[4] While the focus of this chapter does not permit a detailed review of this legislation, it will suffice to highlight some of the unique provisions of the 1994 statute that differed from its predecessor:

- the requirement that a member "shall not, either directly or through another person, accept a fee, gift or personal benefit;"

- where the member did accept such a gift or personal benefit "as an incident of the protocol or social obligations that normally accompany the responsibilities of office," the member would then be required to complete a disclosure statement, which would be filed with the clerk of the municipality or local board and made available to the public;

---

2 *Municipal Conflict of Interest Act, 1972*, S.O. 1972, c. 142; some statutes continue to disqualify certain persons from holding municipal office. For example, see: *City of St. John's Act*, R.S.N. 1990, c. C-17, s. 10.

3 *Municipal Conflict of Interest Act, 1983*, S.O. 1983, c. 8; now R.S.O. 1990, c. M.50, as amended.

4 S.O. 1994, c. 23, Schedule B.

- the requirement that municipal councillors file detailed financial disclosure statements (similar to the ones completed by members of provincial parliament), describing their personal assets and liabilities as set out by the regulations;
- the establishment of a commissioner, to be appointed by the minister, who would investigate and prosecute any members for alleged breaches under the Act; and
- finally, while deleting the traditional saving provisions of inadvertence or error in judgment, the proposed legislation set out a variety of judicially-imposed penalties for breaching the Act, including suspension and restitution.

Despite being given an implementation date of April 15, 1995, the provincial government of then Premier Bob Rae opted not to proclaim the *Local Government Disclosure of Interest Act, 1994* in effect. On April 13, 1995, the Minister of Municipal Affairs made the following announcement:

> The Guidelines Committee has impressed on me that there is a level of discomfort by some local government members with their understanding of what will be required of them. I am convinced that more work needs to be done. Until I am satisfied this work is done, the legislation won't be proclaimed.[5]

In the absence of this proclamation, the *Municipal Conflict of Interest Act, 1983* remained the relevant ethics law for councillors and local board members in Ontario. However, this was not the end of the ongoing conflict of interest saga.[6] Subsequently, the next provincial government indicated a desire to revise the *Municipal Conflict of Interest Act*. In fact, when the Ministry of Municipal Affairs and Housing released a consultation document called "A Proposed New Municipal Act" in the spring of 1998, an explanatory note provided the following rationale for the complete omission of the *Municipal Conflict of Interest Act* from the proposals:

---

5 "Government to delay proclamation of disclosure of interest legislation," Provincial press release (April 13, 1995); M. Rick O'Connor was a member of the Guidelines Committee that submitted its report to the minister on April 7, 1995.

6 For an example, see "Local Government Pecuniary Interest Act: A Proposal by the Municipal World Conflict of Interest Advisory Team," *Municipal World*, September 1995, at p. 9.

Nor does the draft Act incorporate the provisions of the *Municipal Conflict of Interest Act*. Instead, the intention is to review that statute with the goal of bringing it more into conformity with the provincial conflict of interest and integrity principles.[7]

On the surface, this appeared to be a rather unusual comment, since many believed that the *Local Government Disclosure of Interest Act, 1994* had already been modelled after the MPP's integrity legislation. In fact, in December 1999, one provincial government member described the *Local Government Disclosure of Interest Act* as "basically like the *Integrity Act* for MPPs, but for municipal councillors."[8] Despite the government's express intention to review the legislation in 1998, and the fact that the *Members' Integrity Act* was itself subsequently amended in 1998 and 1999, no new conflict of interest provisions for municipal councillors or local board members ever materialized.[9] In the absence of any official government action, the provincial legislature, on April 20, 2000, surprisingly (albeit narrowly), passed a motion requesting that the government proclaim the *Local Government Disclosure of Interest Act, 1994* in force.[10] Perhaps *not* surprisingly, that request was not acted upon. To the contrary, buried deep within the numerous clauses contained in the *Municipal Act, 2001* is section 484, which repeals the *Local Government Disclosure of Interest Act, 1994*, thereby formally ending its stunted legislative existence at last.

Nepotism

Despite the Government of Ontario's seeming disinterest in generally reviewing the *Municipal Conflict of Interest Act*, the *Municipal Act, 2001* does expressly require every municipality and local board to adopt a specific policy "with respect to the hiring of its employees" prior to January 1, 2005. In particular, section 270 of the Act provides that this requirement must include a policy with respect to "the hiring of relatives of a member of council or local board."[11] In addition, the clause endows the minister with the ability to require the time within which the

---

7 "A Proposed New Municipal Act," Ministry of Municipal Affairs and Housing (Spring 1998), p. xv.

8 Legislative Assembly of Ontario, *Official Report of Debates (Hansard)*, December 15, 1999, Brad Clark, MPP Stoney Creek.

9 S.O. 1994, c. 38, as amended.

10 Legislative Assembly of Ontario, *Official Report of Debates (Hansard)*, April 20, 2000.

11 *Municipal Act, 2001*, S.O. 2001, c. 25, s. 270 (1) (a).

hiring policy must be adopted, as well as the power to prescribe other matters for which municipalities and local boards must adopt such policies.

The sudden appearance of this nepotism concern in the *Municipal Act, 2001* is somewhat conspicuous, as it was neither mentioned in the 1998 draft Act proposals or even in the 1996 Who Does What Panel recommendations. It is suggested that the negative media coverage of this issue at the City of Toronto in early 2000 may have been the catalyst for including this unique provision in the *Municipal Act, 2001*. It was in February 2000 when a member requested council adopt a hiring policy with respect to city councillors and their families.[12] In June 2000, Toronto city council adopted a policy with respect to "Council Office Support Staff," which effectively prohibited the hiring of relatives in the mayor's or councillors' offices.[13]

As troublesome as it is to discover the origins of this particular provision, it is also difficult to accurately determine the precise behavioural evil it is designed to combat. The underlying intent of most traditional "nepotism" policies would be to eliminate the perceived, unfair practice of favouring relatives in employment matters. For example, a comprehensive nepotism policy will usually prohibit an existing employee or elected representative from improperly influencing the appointment, advancement, promotion, transfer or any other employment benefit of a family member.

These nepotism policies often go far beyond the limited "hiring" policy required by the *Municipal Act, 2001*. Ironically, due to the rather open-ended drafting of section 270, a local government body would appear to meet the statutory requirements of having a policy regarding "the hiring of relatives of a member of council or local board" by merely passing a resolution stating that it is permissible to hire the relatives of such members. Clearly, such a jaded approach would do nothing to increase the level of openness and accountability in local government and could attract an uninvited ministerial regulation.

---

12 "Council queries practice of hiring family members," *Toronto Star*, February 7, 2000; "Province leaves it up to council to end all-in-the-family hiring," *Scarborough Mirror*, February 11, 2000.

13 City of Toronto, "Council Office Support Staff" (June 7, 8 and 9, 2000).

The broad legislative drafting set out in this particular provision also raises a host of related questions. For example, what is the consequence of a local government body not complying with section 270? Obviously, the municipality or local board could be forced to abide by the legislation pursuant to a court order. Furthermore, what is the precise penalty if a local government enacts but does not comply with its own hiring policy?

Looking ahead, it is suggested that the hiring requirement under section 270 of the *Municipal Act, 2001* will be largely ineffective if its intent is to ameliorate all of the traditional problems associated with nepotism in the workplace. Nevertheless, it is a statutory requirement that must be addressed by all municipalities and local boards in Ontario before January 1, 2005, and its insertion into a more comprehensive code of conduct for members of council or local boards is likely appropriate.

Municipal Initiatives

In Ontario, the province's inability over the last two decades to provide any meaningful reform measures with regard to municipal conflict of interest legislation prompted various councils to adopt their own codes of conduct. As noted previously, section 102 of the former *Municipal Act* provided municipal councils with a broad authority to enact by-laws directly addressing the conduct of their members:

> Every council may pass such by-laws and make such regulations for the health, safety, morality and welfare of the inhabitants of the municipality in matters not specifically provided for by this Act and for governing the conduct of its members as may be deemed expedient and are not contrary to law.[14]

In some instances, municipalities would append these local codes of conduct to their respective procedure by-laws.[15] However, the passage of the *Municipal Act, 2001* only requires the enactment of a by-law that governs "the calling, place and proceedings of meetings," thereby re-

---

14 *Municipal Act*, R.S.O. 1990, c. M.45, s. 102; local boards would have to seek a similar provision within the confines of their respective enabling statutes; for example, see "School board drawing up code of ethics," *Thunder Bay Chronicle-Journal*, March 6, 2003.

15 For example, see: Appendix 'C' attached to the City of Windsor's Procedural By-law, being By-law No. 420-2001, is entitled "Code of Conduct for Members of Council"; or Schedule 'D' attached to the City of Greater Sudbury's Rules of Procedure, being By-law No. 2002-202, entitled "Code of Ethics and Conduct."

Chapter 10
MEMBERS' CODE OF CONDUCT

moving the express ability of a municipal council to pass a procedure by-law to regulate "the conduct of its members."

Despite the absence of any unequivocal authority for municipalities in Ontario to impose codes of conduct on their members, the *Municipal Act, 2001* seems to have resolved some of this uncertainty with the introduction of natural person powers. Section 8 of the Act provides as follows:

> A municipality has the capacity, rights, powers and privileges of a natural person for the purpose of exercising its authority under this or any other Act.

Although, in the years immediately preceding the introduction of the statute, there was a great deal of "pre-legislative hype" surrounding the potential breadth of these particular powers,[16] much of this excitement subsided with the introduction of "New Directions – A New Municipal Act for Ontario" by the Minister of Municipal Affairs in August of 2001. The rather subdued description of natural person powers contained therein clarified that these powers were not "magical," but rather "practical," and meant to deal with routine administrative matters:

> As in the 1998 draft Act, new provisions would propose that municipalities have powers of a natural person. This would enable municipalities to conduct their day-to-day business without the need for specific legislative authority. They could enter into agreements, purchase land and equipment, hire employees, and delegate administrative responsibilities to committees, staff members or other bodies, such as boards of management. Municipalities would not be allowed to provide service for which they do not have legislative authority.[17]

However, as observed in Chapter 1, powers under section 8 of the *Municipal Act, 2001* expressly limit a municipality to "exercising" its authority under this or any other Act." As such, the so-called "natural person power" appears less like a substantive right and more a means to implement other powers. In the absence of a clear, judicial interpreta-

---

16 See George H. Rust-D'Eye, "Section 8 of Ontario's New Municipal Act – Entering the Magical World of Natural Persons" (April 11-12, 2002), Insight Information Co., pp. 1-4.

17 "New Directions – A New Municipal Act for Ontario" (August 2001), Ministry of Municipal Affairs and Housing, at p. 7.

tion, the broad wording of section 8 and the brief ministerial explanation above may provide a municipality with the authority necessary to enact a code of conduct for its members of council. Should a municipal council decide to enact a code of conduct pursuant to section 8, the *Municipal Act, 2001* further mandates that the use of such a power "shall be exercised by by-law."[18]

Members' Code of Conduct

Developing a Code

Other than the express hiring policies to be enacted by municipalities and local boards in Ontario by January 1, 2005, local governments would appear to have a great deal of flexibility with regard to the development of a code of conduct for their members.[19] Set out below is a brief overview of how, and by whom, such policies are traditionally prepared by:

- local government staff (usually the human resources department);
- a semi-autonomous committee (eg. "blue ribbon panel") comprised of residents from the jurisdiction;
- a professional consultant;
- an external public body (eg. a Royal Commission); or
- any combination of the above methods.

When deciding which approach to take, it will be prudent to appreciate that acceptance or "buy-in" by both the elected or appointed officials on a code affecting them is crucial. By way of example, the City of Edmonton recently undertook revisions to its staff code of conduct and employed the rather unique methodology described below:

> The process used to develop the code of conduct included the participation by every city department, union representatives, and those with subject-matter expertise on an inter-departmental team

---

18 *Municipal Act, 2001*, S.O. 2001, c. 25, s. 5 (3).

19 This discussion was derived from "All in the Family: A Human Resources Guide to the Municipal Act, 2001," presented on January 28, 2003 at the Insight Information Co. in Toronto, Ontario.

Chapter 10
MEMBERS' CODE OF CONDUCT

and focus groups with employees from all parts of the organization. Substantial work was done in researching best practices and legal requirements and attempting to incorporate them into a document that is designed to meet the needs of city employees. The following steps were undertaken:

- A cross-departmental project team was established in spring of 2001.
- The team redrafted the [existing] code based on initial feedback from department management teams.
- City staff reviewed this draft in focus group sessions held throughout the organization. A cross-section of all unions, employees and management staff were consulted with over 150 individuals participating in total.
- Comments from the focus group sessions and department management teams were then categorized into themes and incorporated into the policy document by project team members.[20]

While such approaches can be a useful reference in the creation of a code of conduct, it is strongly recommended that each local government attempt to develop a policy based on its own unique needs.

---

20 City of Edmonton, "Code of Conduct Development," Office of the City Auditor (September 18, 2002), at pp. 2-3.

Elements of a Code

What elements should be in a code of conduct for members of municipal councils or local boards? In drafting such a code, and for the reasons previously set out in Chapter 5, Procedure By-law on the procedure by-law, municipal councils and local boards need not duplicate existing statutory provisions with regard to members' conduct. Therefore, matters with respect to direct, indirect or deemed pecuniary interests under the relevant provincial conflict of interest legislation,[21] as well as those of municipal corruption or breach of trust under the federal *Criminal Code* need not be included in a local government's code of conduct. The basic framework for a comprehensive code of conduct could include the following distinct sections:

- Preamble
- Application
- Authority
- Definitions
- Specific Policy Statements
- Implementation and Enforcement

In exploring the specific policy areas that may be included in a code of conduct for elected or appointed officials, reference should be had to those existing ethical rules or expectations for both senior levels of government and other local government entities. For example, on October 23, 2002, the Prime Minister of Canada tabled a draft document in both the House of Commons and the Senate entitled "Code of Conduct for Parliamentarians."

Among the various guidelines and requirements set out in this draft code were the following matters: provisions on insider information

---

21 See: Alberta: *Municipal Government Act, 1994*, c. M-26; British Columbia: *Financial Disclosure Act*, R.S.B.C. 1996, c. 139; Manitoba: *Municipal Council Conflict of Interest Act*, C.C.S.M., c. M255; New Brunswick: *Municipalities Act*, R.S.N.B. 1973, c. M-22; Newfoundland: *Municipalities Act*, R.S.N. 1990, c. M-23; Nova Scotia: *Municipal Conflict of Interest Act*, R.S.N.S. 1989, c. 299; Prince Edward Island: *Municipalities Act*, R.S.P.E.I. 1988, c. M-13; Quebec: Elections and Referendums in *Municipalities Act*, R.S.Q. 1988, E-2.2; Saskatchewan: *Urban Municipality Act, 1984*, S.S. 1984, c. U-11, *Rural Municipality Act, 1999*, S.S. 1989-90, c. R-26.1; *Northern Municipalities Act*, S.S. 1983, c. N-5.1; *Cities Act*, S.S. 2002, c. C-11.1; and Yukon: *Municipal Act*, R.S.Y. 1986, c. 119.

(section 13); a prohibition on receiving gifts and personal benefits (section 16); as well as a variety of sections clearly aimed at combatting nepotism. In a similar fashion, these same types of issues are addressed in various provincial statutes concerning the behaviour and expectations of members of a Legislative Assembly. In Ontario, the *Members' Integrity Act, 1994* sets out similar rules with respect to insider information (section 3), gifts (section 6) and various other sections concerning matters arising from nepotism.[22]

In addition to these types of rules for senior levels of government reference may also be had to such matters as the provincial rules of conduct for members of various local government entities. By way of legislative example, reference can be had to various provincial statutes across Canada. In Manitoba, the *Municipal Council Conflict of Interest Act* establishes detailed disclosure requirements concerning the receipt of gifts by councillors (sections 9 to 13), as well as rules prohibiting the use of insider information (section 14), and influence (section 16).[23] Similarly, the *Community Charter* in British Columbia has proposed restrictions against members of council accepting gifts (section 105), disclosure requirements when a gift is accepted (section 106), and a ban on the use of insider information (section 108).[24] In Ontario, the enactment of Ontario Regulation 421/97, made pursuant to the *Police Services Act*, is entitled "Members of Police Services Boards – Code of Conduct."[25] As in the previous citations noted above, this regulation establishes uniform rules with regard to the confidentiality requirements of police board members (section 4), as well as provisions regarding nepotism (sections 11 and 12).

The last few examples demonstrate the existence of such legislated behavioural requirements in at least three provinces. Based upon these examples, the remainder of this chapter will examine the following four policy areas that are often found in codes of conduct for elected or appointed representatives:

- gifts and benefits;

---

22 *Members' Integrity Act, 1994*, S.O. 1994, c. 38.

23 *Municipal Council Conflict of Interest Act*, C.C.S.M., c. M255.

24 *Community Charter*, S.B.C. 2003, c. 26, Bill 14 (Third Reading May 8, 2003), British Columbia Legislative Session: 4th Session, 37th Parliament.

25 Ontario Regulation 421/97, as amended to O.Reg. 277/00.

- nepotism;
- insider/confidential information; and
- use of local government property.

Gifts and Benefits

In examining the underlying rationale for regulating gifts, it is worth recalling the old axiom that "in politics, perception is reality." Regrettably, adherence to such an inherently flawed concept does little to explain the necessity for imposing a scheme to regulate the receipt of gifts and benefits on local government officials.

In his 1993 report on Ontario's former *Members' Conflict of Interest Act*, the Integrity Commissioner, the Honourable Gregory T. Evans, described this maxim as "a false and fraudulent statement ... that the general public in the past has been brainwashed into believing." He further stated that "opinion polls show that the electorate is not prepared to be ignored and that politicians will be judged by their actual contribution to public office, rather than some fanciful appearance standard which varies with the subjective viewpoint of the individual electorate."[26] In light of this assessment, it is arguable that the general public may not be prepared to automatically brand a member who receives a gift as a paid lobbyist for a particular interest group.

In attempting to address this subject within the confines of a local government code of conduct, it is crucial to appreciate that there is no definitive, royal commission-style report that accurately, logically and objectively depicts the reasons for restricting or banning the receipt of gifts and benefits. In the absence of such an identifiable source, it is suggested that any code or policy that seeks to regulate the receipt of gifts and personal benefits may originate from any number of sources. In Ontario, one need look no further than the comments set out in the 1991 report of the Municipal Conflict of Interest Consultation Committee.

After having toured the province and received more than 200 submissions, the committee's report drew the following conclusions concerning the receipt of gifts and benefits by councillors and local board members:

---

26 Commissioner on Conflict of Interest Annual Report 1992-93 (June 1993), at p. 2.

The majority of submissions to the committee recommended that the acceptance of gifts, benefits and other gratuities by members should be subject to some type of regulation. There was consensus that it is inappropriate for members to accept these items from those who carry on business with or make representations before municipal councils, school boards or local boards. Some people felt that accepting gifts or benefits of a modest value should be permissible, especially in the cases where gifts are given in relation to protocol and official duties. Others, however, felt strongly that accepting any gift or benefit, regardless of the scope or value, could potentially compromise or obligate the member.[27]

The committee's official recommendation that "the *Municipal Act*, the *Education Act*, and other appropriate statutes related to local boards and commissions be amended to regulate the acceptance of gifts and benefits in the same manner as the *Members' Conflict of Interest Act,*"[28] ultimately found its way into the never-proclaimed *Local Government Disclosure of Interest Act, 1994*, in the following fashion:

> 5 (1)   A member shall not, either directly or through another person, accept a fee, gift or personal benefit except compensation authorized by law that is connected with the performance of his or her duties of office.[29]

Several observations can be made with respect to this short clause. First, the principle that "a member" shall not accept gifts or benefits related to their public office is extended to encompass the indirect receipt of gifts or benefits "through another person." As the term "another person" was not specifically defined in the Act, it is suggested that it could be given the widest possible interpretation, thus including spouses, same-sex partners, siblings, parents and children, as well as other relatives, friends, employees and acquaintances of the member and perhaps even corporations.

Second, the prohibition is directed against a member accepting a "fee, gift or personal benefit." None of these terms, however, was defined in

---

27   Report of the Municipal Conflict of Interest Consultation Committee (July 1991), p. 82.
28   *Ibid.*
29   *Local Government Disclosure of Interest Act, 1994*, S.O. 1994, c. 23, Schedule B, s. 5 (1); see the almost identical language found in subsection 105 (1) of British Columbia's *Community Charter*.

the legislation, despite requests to do so during the consultation process.[30] In addition to the lack of definitions to clarify this clause, the existence of similarly undefined terms in the Act, such as "financial benefit," further extended the appearance of inconsistent terminology.[31]

In addition to these observations, subsection 5 (1) contained two preliminary exceptions to the rule against receiving gifts. First, a member was entitled to receive a "fee, gift or personal benefit" that constituted "compensation authorized by law." Most enabling statutes for local governments across Canada authorize councils to pass by-laws to pay remuneration and expenses for members of council or local boards. Therefore, any fees or personal benefits attributable to such statutory compensation would be acceptable.[32] Furthermore, while members of council need not file individual disclosure statements on such matters, Ontario's *Municipal Act, 2001* does require councils and local boards to file annually itemized statements of the remuneration and expenses paid to members in the preceding year.[33]

Second, the regulatory scheme previously established in subsection 5 (1) of the Act only prohibited a member from receiving a "fee, gift or personal benefit ... that is connected with the performance of his or her duties of office." For example, the receipt of a birthday present or an anniversary gift from a family relation would not be connected with the performance of a member's public responsibilities and, thus, need not constitute a breach of the provision.

In addition to these two exceptions, subsection 5 (2) of the Act exempted the application of the prohibition provision in the following circumstances:

5 (2) Subsection (1) does not apply to,

    (a) a gift or personal benefit that is received as an incident of the protocol or social obligations that normally accompany the responsibilities of office; or

---

30 Association of Municipalities of Ontario, " Developing New Decision-Making Practices for Councils and Councillors" (August 1994), p. 9.
31 *Local Government Disclosure of Interest Act, 1994*, S.O. 1994, c. 23, Schedule B, s. 3 (k).
32 In Ontario, see *Municipal Act, 2001*, S.O. 2001, c. 25, s. 283.
33 *Ibid.*, s. 284.

(b) a contribution that is authorized under the *Municipal Elections Act* made to a member who is a registered candidate under that Act.

Beginning with clause 5 (2) (a), it is suggested that such an exemption expressly recognizes the fact that receiving gifts or personal benefits of a social or protocol nature is a valid aspect of being a member of a municipal council or local board. Broadly speaking, the term "protocol" is said to encompass "the ceremonial forms accepted as correct in official dealings."[34] Furthermore, the addition of the phrase "social obligations" to this provision would appear to expand this exception even more, thus including social events that may be less official in nature. Alternatively, to automatically refuse to accept such formality-driven gratuities could produce potentially embarrassing results for both the member as well as the group offering the gift, and may even reflect badly upon the respective municipal council or local board.

The second exception, in clause 5 (2) (b), is more limited in that it must constitute a contribution to a registered candidate pursuant to Ontario's *Municipal Elections Act, 1996*. It is important to recall that a "contribution" under this legislation includes "money, goods and services given to and accepted by or on behalf of a person for his or her election campaign." Furthermore, the *Municipal Elections Act, 1996* has its own detailed disclosure provisions making it unnecessary to require the filing of the receipt of such a contribution elsewhere in legislation.[35]

Some other exemptions that may be considered appropriate when seeking to regulate the receipt of gifts and benefits include the following:

(a) personal gifts, benefits, rewards, commissions or advantages from any person or organization not connected directly or indirectly with the performance of duties of office;

(b) political contributions that are otherwise offered, accepted and reported in accordance with applicable law;

(c) food and beverages at banquets, receptions, ceremonies or similar events;

---

34 *Webster's New Dictionary and Thesaurus* (New York, N.Y. Windsor Court: 1989).
35 *Municipal Elections Act, 1996*, S.O. 1996, c. 32, Schedule, ss. 66-82.1.

(d) services provided without compensation by persons volunteering their time;

(e) food, lodging, transportation and entertainment provided by other levels of governments or by other local governments, boards or commissions;

(f) a reimbursement of reasonable expenses incurred in the performance of office;

(g) meeting allowances received from the conservation authority;

(h) a reimbursement of reasonable expenses incurred and honorariums received in the performance of activities connected with municipal associations;

(i) token gifts such as souvenirs, mementoes and commemorative gifts that are given in recognition of service on a committee, for speaking at an event or representing the corporation at an event; and

(j) gifts that are received as an incident of protocol or social obligation that normally and reasonably accompany the responsibility of office.[36]

Where a member decides that it is appropriate to accept a gift or personal benefit as an incident of protocol or social obligation, the code should require written disclosure of this acceptance. Once again, the former, never-proclaimed *Local Government Disclosure of Interest Act, 1994* provided for the following disclosure process:

5 (3) A member shall complete and file a disclosure statement with the clerk of the municipality or secretary of the board as soon as possible after receiving a gift or personal benefit described under clause (2) (a) if,

(a) the value of the gift or benefit exceeds the lower of the amount prescribed or provided by by-law or resolution; or

---

[36] This list, as modified, was derived from section 2 of Schedule 'A' to By-law A-13 of the City of London, being "A by-law to adopt a code of conduct for members of council" (October 20, 1997).

(b) the total value received directly or indirectly from one source in one calendar year exceeds the lower of the amount prescribed or provided by by-law or resolution.

Inherent in clause 5 (3) (a), and expressly set out in section 19 of the former Act, was the opportunity for a municipal council or local board to prescribe, by by-law or resolution, a dollar value for such gifts and benefits. By contrast, British Columbia's *Community Charter* sets a statutory limit of $250 for such gifts or personal benefits.[37]

Clause 5 (3) (b) also acted as a cumulative total clause, whereby a member was required to disclose the source of a number of gifts and personal benefits, the total value of which exceeded the limit established by either the province, municipal council or local board in the calendar year. In such circumstances, it would be crucial for members to keep an ongoing tally of all gifts or benefits from any single source. Once the total exceeded the established limit, written disclosure would be required. The more cautious alternative would, of course, be to disclose and file all gifts and personal benefits received, no matter how small the dollar value.[38] Although more administratively onerous, this conservative approach would likely preclude any unwelcome debate about the precise moment at which the gifts or benefits received from a single source exceeded the limit and triggered the member's obligation to file a disclosure statement.

Finally, reference should be had to subsection 5 (4) of the former Act, which provided that the disclosure statement "shall state the nature of the gift or benefit, its source and the circumstances under which it was given or accepted." By specifically setting out these mandatory details in the statute, the province seemed to be emphasizing the importance of such particulars. The underlying rationale for requiring such detailed information about each gift or benefit received is probably two-fold.

First, and hopefully foremost, it is suggested that such a requirement could motivate each member to contemplate – beforehand – various is-

---

37 *Community Charter*, SBC 2003, c. 26, Bill 14, s. 106 (1).
38 This approach has been adopted in Manitoba, where clause 10 (h) of the *Municipal Council Conflict of Interest Act*, C.C.S.M. c. M255 requires all councillors to disclose "the nature, and the identity of the donor, of every gift given to the councillor or any of his dependents at any time after the coming into force of this Act."

sues, including the nature of the gift, its source and the circumstances in which it was given. This basic analysis could assist the member in determining the preliminary question of whether or not the gift is truly a matter of protocol or social obligation that normally accompanies the responsibilities of public office. As a disclosure register would likely be maintained by the municipal clerk or secretary of the board, and open to the public, it is possible that similar analysis could also be done by the member's constituency, the media and political rivals.[39]

Second, it is possible that the disclosure details may be of assistance in subsequently identifying an apparent breach of the Act, or local code of conduct, by the member. Therefore, such an administrative tool could prove to be a double-edged sword.

The following are different gift and benefit provisions taken from various existing codes of conduct for members of council:

- Members shall not accept fees, gifts, hospitality or personal benefits that are connected directly or indirectly with the performance of duties as city councillors, except compensation authorized by law.[40]

- No member shall accept a fee, advance, gift or personal benefit that is connected directly or indirectly with the performance of his or her duties of office. One example would be that no member should act as a paid agent before council, or a committee of council, or any agency, board, or commission of the city. Another example would be that no member should refer third parties to a person, partnership, or corporation in exchange for payment or other personal benefit.[41]

- Members should not directly or indirectly solicit any gift or accept or receive any gift – whether it be money, services, loan, travel, entertainment, hospitality, promise, or any other form – under the following circumstances: (1) it could be reasonably inferred or expected that the gift was intended to influence them in

---

39 *Local Government Disclosure of Interest Act, 1994*, S.O. 1994, c. 23, Schedule B, s. 15.

40 By-law No. 01-300, a City of Hamilton by-law to adopt rules for procedures of council and committees thereof (December 11, 2001), at Appendix B, "Code of Conduct for Members of Council."

41 City of Toronto, "Code of Conduct for Members of Council" (September 28-29, 1999), as amended.

the performance of their official duties; or (2) the gift was intended to serve as a reward for any official action on their part.

...

This section does not apply to tokens, mementos, souvenirs, or such gifts or benefits up to and including an annual amount of $200 that are received as an incident of protocol or social obligation that normally accompanies the responsibilities of office. Tokens, mementos, souvenirs or gifts with a value of greater than $200 shall be the property of the municipality, and should be reported and turned over to the clerk.[42]

Nepotism

In preparing to develop a nepotism or hiring policy, including provisions with respect to the hiring of relatives, a municipality or a local board should receive legal advice to ensure that its requirements are drafted in accordance with the relevant provincial human rights legislation, as well as the *Canadian Charter of Rights and Freedoms*. For example, subsection 5 (1) of the *Ontario Human Rights Code* provides as follows:

> 5 (1) Every person has a right to equal treatment with respect to employment without discrimination because of race, ancestry, place of origin, colour, ethnic origin, citizenship, creed, sex, sexual orientation, age, record of offences, marital status, same-sex partnership status, family status, or handicap.

At first glance, one might conclude that a local government's policy in accordance with section 270 of the *Municipal Act, 2001* could be contrary to the *Human Rights Code* should it be found to constitute "discrimination" as a result of one's marital, same-sex partnership or family status. However, this provision must be read in conjunction with clause 24 (1) (d) of the Code:

> 24 (1) The right under section 5 to equal treatment with respect to employment is not infringed where,

...

---

[42] By-law No. 420–2001, a by-law to provide rules governing the proceedings of the council of the City of Windsor and the conduct of its members (November 19, 2001), at Appendix C, "Code of Conduct for Members of Council."

(d) An employer grants or withholds employment or advancement in employment to a person who is the spouse, same-sex partner, child or parent of the employer or an employee.[43]

In light of these legal parameters, in Ontario at least, it would seem wise to consider only including a member's spouse, same-sex partner, child or parent within the terms of a hiring policy like the one required by section 270 of the *Municipal Act, 2001*.[44]

Whether the exclusion of such nepotism policies from the ambit of provincial human rights legislation may, itself, be unconstitutional is unclear, particularly given the judicial treatment the issue has recently received. To begin with, a number of lower courts and human rights tribunals across Canada have produced varying decisions with respect to the nepotism policies of local government employers.[45] Despite these decisions, the Supreme Court of Canada reviewed a municipality's nepotism policy in light of the relevant human rights statute in the 1988 decision, *Brossard (Ville) v. Quebec (Commission des Droits de la Personne)*.[46]

In the *Brossard* case, the municipality refused to hire a young woman as a lifeguard in the summer because its anti-nepotism policy precluded the hiring of immediate family of existing staff. The applicant's mother was employed full-time as a typist at the municipal police station. The town argued that the policy was intended to avoid favouritism or any appearance thereof in its hiring practices. The applicant responded that the policy discriminated against her based on her "civil status," in contravention of Quebec's *Charter of Human Rights and Freedoms*.[47] In the unanimous decision, the Supreme Court of Canada rejected the town's

---

43 *Human Rights Code*, R.S.O. 1990, c. H.19, s. 24 (1) (d).

44 See also s. 11 of "Members of Police Services Boards - Code of Conduct," O.Reg. 421/97 as amended, which prohibits board members from using "their office to obtain employment with the board or the police force for themselves, their family member or their same-sex partner." This provision further defines "family member" to mean "the parent, spouse or child of the person as defined in s.1 of the *Municipal Conflict of Interest Act*."

45 See, for example, *Bosi v. Michipicoten (Twp.)* (1983), 4 C.H.R.R. D/1252 (Ont. Bd. of Inquiry); *Mark v. Porcupine General Hospital* (1984), 6 C.H.R.R. D/2538 (Ont. Bd. of Inquiry); and *Quebec (Commission des Droits de la Personne) v. Lachine (Ville)* (1988), 34 C.H.R.R. D/287.

46 (1988), 53 D.L.R. (4th) 609.

47 R.S.Q. 1977, c. C-12, s. 10.

position. In fact, in a concurring judgment, Madam Justice Wilson concluded that the municipality's broad anti-nepotism policy could not constitute a valid *bona fide* occupational qualification if other "less drastic means" existed to accomplish the same objectives:

> It seems to me that the hiring of relatives may well pose a threat or be perceived as a threat to the integrity of the town's administration ... The extent of the threat such a hiring practice poses is obviously a matter of degree and should be established by evidence. Were the hiring of relatives to become common practice, it could obviously constitute a serious threat. This being so, is it "reasonably necessary" in this case to ban the hiring of relatives entirely, or would it adequately serve the purpose if a watchful eye were kept on the situation and discretion exercised in order to keep the hiring of relatives (assuming their ability to do the job concerned) within reasonable proportions?
>
> It seems to me that, having regard to the nature of the right which is violated by an anti-nepotism policy, i.e. the right under s. 10 not to be discriminated against, the adoption of a total ban is not "reasonably necessary" in order to avoid a threat to the integrity of the town's administration. The town can avoid the threat by the less drastic means I have suggested.[48]

The decision in *Brossard* suggests that any nepotism policy that equates to a total ban on hiring relatives will not escape judicial review.

Additional steps in the development of a hiring policy would likely include scrutinizing any existing policies of the local government (including collective agreements), identifying any omissions, reviewing sample rules from other municipalities or local boards, consulting with relevant stakeholders, and then drafting the policy. While a hiring policy under Ontario's *Municipal Act, 2001* must be in place by January 1, 2005, the more strategic date of when to prepare one remains open to the municipality or local board to determine. A media frenzy publicizing an alleged nepotism scandal in a community may demonstrate the need for a hiring policy concerning relatives, but it is also likely a poor time to develop such a policy. As is often the case, a policy prepared in the

---

48 See *Brossard (Ville) v. Quebec (Comission des Droits de la Personne)* (1988), 53 D.L.R. (4th) 655; see also the most recent decision of the Supreme Court of Canada in *B. v. Ontario (Human Rights Commission)*, [2002] S.C.J. No. 67.

shadow of such a crisis may be perceived as a stop-gap measure aimed at the solitary incident, and not necessarily useful in the more general sense.[49]

For more than a decade, the City of Fredericton, New Brunswick has had a rather broad nepotism policy directed at the city's elected officials:

12.0 Nepotism

12.1 All applicants for city positions shall have an equal opportunity to obtain employment with the City of Fredericton. No elected official shall unduly use their position to promote the hiring of specific individuals.

12.2 No elected official shall use their position to promote the hiring of relatives. "Relative" is defined as brother, sister, mother, father, son, daughter, son-in-law, daughter-in-law, mother-in-law, father-in-law, niece, nephew or any other member of the immediate family.[50]

A more recent example of a hiring or nepotism policy established for municipal councillors was the June 2000 proposal adopted in Toronto with respect to council office support staff:

(1) No employment of relatives of members of council shall be permitted within councillors' offices and the mayor's offices;

(2) Relatives, for the purpose of this policy, shall be defined as:

(i) spouse, including common-law and same-sex spouse;

(ii) parent, including step-parent and legal guardian;

(iii) child, including step-child;

(iv) sibling; and

---

[49] See, for example, "Evidence lacking on nepotism allegations: Councillor," *Sudbury Star*, January 31, 1996, p. A3, and "Nepotism report rejected," *Sudbury Star*, February 1, 1996, p. A1.

[50] City of Fredericton, "City Council Code of Ethics," (April 13, 1992), s. 12.

(v) any person who lives with the employee on a permanent basis; and

(3) Implementation of this policy shall take effect with the new term of city council, on December 1, 2000.[51]

Insider/Confidential Information

As previously noted in Chapter 5, Procedure By-law, provincial enabling legislation generally permits municipal councils and local boards to hold closed meetings where the subject-matter to be considered falls within one of the grounds listed in the legislation. Where such an *in camera* meeting has occurred and the council or committee has not arisen and reported on the issue, many procedure by-laws will require that members not disclose any of the information discussed at the closed session. One example of such a provision is as follows:

> Members of council shall ... hold in strict confidence all information concerning matters dealt with *in camera*. The member shall not release, make public, or in any way divulge any such confidential information or any aspect of the *in camera* deliberations, unless expressly authorized or required by law.[52]

While it may be of critical importance that members not "leak" any confidential information to the media, the public, or indeed to other parties interested in a particular matter being considered by the council or local board, the fundamental problem surrounding such a disclosure ban lies in the absence of a straightforward enforcement mechanism.[53]

For example, where the confidentiality requirement is included in a procedure by-law, it is suggested that, in breaching such a provision, the member is merely not in compliance with that by-law. Therefore, whatever disciplinary mechanisms exist within the rules of procedure (eg. calling the member to order, requiring an apology for or a withdrawal of the comments, censuring him or her, or ordering the member to vacate his or her seat for the remainder of a particular meeting) are often ineffective in preventing such leaks from re-occurring.

---

51 City of Toronto, "Council Office Support Staff Policy," (June 7, 8 and 9, 2000).
52 City of Burlington, By-law No. 117-2002 (December 16, 2002) at s. 24.1(h).
53 These comments exclude those situations where the disclosure of confidential (e.g. personal) information may be a breach of a statute such as the *Municipal Freedom of Information and Protection of Privacy Act*, R.S.O. 1990, c. M.56, as discussed in Chapter 13.

Taken one step further, some municipal councils and local boards have pondered the possibility of attaching an offence provision to such by-laws, thereby incurring a penalty under the respective provincial offences legislation. Despite the possibility of a fine, or even incarceration, the practical matter of enforcement remains a difficult issue, since such a charge could require a trial between a municipality or local board and a sitting member. For example, should a councillor be suspected of "leaking" a confidential document to the press, it would likely be a member of staff (i.e. a senior manager, auditor or solicitor) who would be required to undertake an investigation on behalf of the municipality. On the one hand, it is suggested that none of these local government officials has the necessary and relevant expertise in investigative techniques in order to carry out such a sensitive task. On the other hand, the use of staff in this particular fashion will likely do little to improve their relationship with any of the members of council.

An example that shows the legal difficulties inherent in attempting to regulate the use of insider/confidential information are set out in a report before the City of Toronto council in 2001, entitled "Review of Computer Leasing Contract Between City of Toronto and MFP Financial Services." In essence, while approving a host of recommendations with regard to this specific matter, city council moved the following two motions, which directly addressed the more general issue of leaking of confidential information:

(7)   The following motion be adopted in principle and referred to the Ethics Steering Committee for detailed review and report thereon to council, through the Administration Committee:

Moved by Mayor Lastman:

It is further recommended that, given the consequences to the City of Toronto when confidential information is released without authorization:

    (a)   A by-law be enacted, substantially in the form of the attached by-law, that provides for an offence for breach of confidentiality by members of council;

    (b)   The acting chief financial officer and acting treasurer be instructed to renegotiate the city's insurance policies to delete coverage for members of council who disclose confidential information to the public, including the media;

Chapter 10
MEMBERS' CODE OF CONDUCT

(c) The issues of implementation and enforcement of the by-law be referred to the ethics steering committee ... and the ethics steering committee be requested to report back to the first regular meeting of city council in 2002; and

(d) The city solicitor be requested to submit a report to the ethics steering committee on the issue of breaches of confidentiality by council staff, city staff and consultants; and

(8) The ethics steering committee be requested to review the following processes used by the board of education for the former City of Etobicoke, during its consideration of the mechanics of the implementation of the by-law related to confidentiality:

Members of the board shall observe their duty to respect the confidentiality of the committee of the whole board (private). In this regard, the board sought and received legal counsel on the matter of a breach of confidentiality by a member of the board and the following sanctions are available to the board in such cases:

(a) An action for damages would lie against any member who fails to observe the duty to maintain confidentiality and the board would not indemnify a member for legal costs incurred in defending such an action;

(b) A member could, by resolution, be publicly censured for failing to observe the duty to maintain confidentiality; and

(c) A member who fails or refuses to observe the duty to maintain confidentiality could be excluded from confidential meetings; be refused confidential reports; and be required to undertake, in writing, to observe the duty to maintain confidentiality in future, before being allowed back into such meetings.[54]

In addition to the type of concerns noted above, some municipal polices go beyond restricting the mere disclosure of information discussed at

---

54 City of Toronto, "Review of Computer Leasing Contract Between City of Toronto and MFP Financial Services," (December 4, 5 and 6, 2001) at pp. 89-90.

closed meetings, to prohibit the use of such information that could benefit the member's personal or private interests. An example of this broader provision is as follows:

> No elected official shall, without proper legal authorization, disclose confidential information concerning the property, government or affairs of the city, nor shall he/she use such information to advance the financial or other private interest of himself/herself or others.[55]

Finally, one more succinct approach to this type of prohibition would be as follows:

> Members of council shall not ... use any information gained in the execution of office that is not available to the general public for any purpose other than for official duties.[56]

Use of Local Government Property

Although the *Criminal Code of Canada* addresses the issue of theft and other matters related to property, its application and severe consequences are generally not appropriate when seeking to regulate the use of public property by a member of council or local board. In light of this concern, some local governments have incorporated general provisions regulating the use of municipal or local board property by their members. Two examples will suffice to better appreciate these issues:

> Where a member makes use of any city property, equipment, supplies, or services of consequence other than for purposes connected with the discharge of city duties, it is incumbent upon the member to make restitution for any additional expenses which are incurred by the city for the use of said equipment, supplies or services.

> No member shall obtain financial gain from the use of city-developed intellectual property, computer programs, technological innovations, or other patentable items, while an elected official or thereafter. All such property remains the exclusive property of the city.

---

55 City of Fredericton, "City Council Code of Ethics," (April 13, 1992), section 13.1.

56 City of London, Code of Conduct By-law A-13, (October 20, 1997), Schedule 'A' – A By-law to Adopt a Code of Conduct for Members of Council – Part 1 – Ethical Behaviour, s. 3 (d).

Chapter 10
MEMBERS' CODE OF CONDUCT

> No member shall use information gained in the execution of his or her duties that is not available to the general public, for any purposes other than his or her official duties.[57]

Alternatively:

> No elected official shall request or permit the use of municipal-owned vehicles, equipment, materials, or property for personal convenience or profit, except when such services are available to the public generally or are provided as municipal policy for the use of such elected official in the conduct of official business.[58]

In addition to the above provisions, some larger municipalities – usually where councillors are provided with their own budget to operate their city hall or ward offices – have enacted rules regarding the appropriate use of corporate resources during an election period.[59] Such guidelines are undertaken for a variety of reasons, including to protect both the legal interests of the municipality and its elected representatives, as well as to foster the perception of a level playing field in the municipal electoral process. One such policy includes the following provision:

> In a municipal election year, corporate resources and members' budgets are not to be used to sponsor any advertisements, flyers, newsletters or householders from the day after nomination day up to and including voting day. This prohibition also applies to the use of any city equipment, facilities or websites if the access is city-sponsored.[60]

If a council or local board seeks to implement such a ban on corporate resources during an election period, it is important to note that consideration may be given to an exemption for emergency situations and for those instances where the municipality's equipment or facilities are available for use by the public, generally, and the member would not receive any special preference with respect to its particular use.

---

57 By-law No. 420-2001, A by-law to provide rules governing the proceedings of the council of the City of Windsor and the conduct of its members (November 19, 2001), Appendix 'C' – Code of Conduct for Members of Council.

58 City of Fredericton, City Council Code of Ethics (April 13, 1992), s. 8.

59 City of Toronto, Use of Corporate Resources for Election Purposes Especially During a Municipal Election Year (October 29, 30 and 31, 2002).

60 City of Ottawa, Election-Related Resources Policy (February 12, 2003).

Implementation/Enforcement

In developing a code of conduct for municipal councillors or local board members, it must be remembered that, unless specific enabling legislation exists with respect to a particular penalty (fine, suspension with or without pay for a period of time, or that the member vacate his or her seat), it is unlikely that a municipality or local board will have the legal authority necessary to impose such harsh consequences for non-compliance. Alternatively, such penalties may be accessible if the code's enforcement has been made subject to a provincial offences statute. Having said that, it is most likely that adherence to such a code of conduct will largely be through voluntary compliance by individual members, aided by sufficient orientation of the code's expectation and peer pressure. Therefore, the traditional penalties that result from a breach of the procedure by-law may suffice.

Finally, reference should be made to the City of Toronto's integrity initiatives in the midst of two judicial inquiries.[61] In 1999, city council adopted "a very basic code of conduct" for councillors that required any suspected violations to be brought before the full council. The main disadvantage of this approach and the proposed solution to it was candidly described by Toronto Councillor Joe Mihevc, chair of the city's ethics steering committee, as follows:

> Councillors are understandably reticent to openly judge their peers, which greatly compromises council's ability to act. The [judicial] inquiry needs to address how this basic code can be strengthened to prevent a recurrence of MFP-type impropriety, cronyism and uncontrolled spending.
>
> What Toronto needs is an arm's-length integrity commissioner.[62]

In November 2002, Toronto city council approved an immediate, interim protocol for handling complaints about councillors. The complaint protocol established both informal and formal procedures – the latter approach even contemplates investigations by external legal counsel. In addition, the city is to seek private enabling legislation from the province to "establish a city integrity commissioner similar to the

---

61 See the Toronto Computer Leasing Inquiry and the Toronto External Contracts Inquiry at: www.torontoinquiry.ca.

62 Joe Mihevc, "Keeping Council Honest: MFP scandal shows that City of Toronto urgently needs an integrity commissioner," *Toronto Star* (January 31, 2003).

provincial model."[63] If enacted, only time will tell if these proposals result in a more effective enforcement mechanism for addressing complaints under Toronto city council's code of conduct.

Conclusions

It is important to appreciate that the passage of a code of conduct by a municipal council or a local board is not merely meant to enforce a local government's behavioural expectations on its respective members. One of the main advantages of a local code is to fill the regulatory vacuum that exists with respect to many matters affecting a member's role and to remove any doubt surrounding the ethical standards they are expected to meet. Furthermore, a code of conduct for municipal councillors or local board members clearly demonstrates a local government's commitment to promoting those ethical rules most respected by the community they serve.

---

63 City of Toronto, Approval of a Complaint Protocol for Council's Code of Conduct (November 26, 27 and 28, 2002).

Chapter 11
CRIMINAL CODE

On Monday, February 19th, 2001, at 5:45 p.m., Peel Regional Police Intelligence and Fraud Bureau officers concluded a month-long intensive probe, which culminated in the arrest of a Region of Peel and City of Mississauga Councillor.

The investigation was initiated as a result of a complaint from a local businessman with respect to an allegation that he had been approached and requested to provide a sum of money, in exchange for political influence and consideration on a pending property zoning application.

Peel Regional Police Press Release
(February 20, 2001)[1]

It is a chilling reality that not every person seeking election to municipal office in Canada does so solely with the public interest in mind. While those with self-serving intent are few and far between, high profile cases in the media over the last decade have evoked strong public concern.

Beginning in April 1991, Project 80 was a special police task force established by the provincial government to investigate complaints of corruption involving municipalities and land developers in Ontario.[2] Once the public learned of its existence, the project began to receive a

---

1   On June 25, 2003, Madam Justice B. Wein found Mississauga Councillor Clifford Gyles guilty of breach of trust and municipal corruption charges: see *R. v. Gyles*, [2003] O.J. No. 3188.
2   Project 80 evolved from what was originally known as Project 50, which investigated the so-called Patti Starr Affair in the early 1990s. Subsequently re-named Project 80, the task force was comprised of investigators from municipal and provincial police services across the Greater Toronto Area.

stream of complaints – more than it had resources to examine.[3] Project 80 was subsequently enlarged and the scope of its investigations widely extended. This particular development only served to emphasize the negative perception of some local governments, and raise the simmering distrust of certain members of the public to a boiling point. It is important for all elected and appointed members of municipal councils and local boards to be fully aware of the specific constraints imposed by the *Criminal Code of Canada* to ensure that they do not inadvertently infringe upon them. This chapter will review the relevant sections of the *Criminal Code* that local government officials should be familiar with when performing public duties. Most of these provisions are found in Part IV of the Code, aptly entitled "Offences Against the Administration of Law and Justice."

Breach of Trust

Section 122 of the *Criminal Code* establishes the offence of "breach of trust by [a] public officer:"

> 122. Every official who, in connection with the duties of his office, commits fraud or a breach of trust is guilty of an indictable offence and liable to imprisonment for a term not exceeding five years, whether or not the fraud or breach of trust would be an offence if it were committed in relation to a private person.[4]

The phrase "indictable offence" is generally considered to be the more serious kind under the *Criminal Code*. For example, "summary conviction offences" will likely include most minor offences under the Code and, unless otherwise stated, are punishable by a fine of up to $2,000 or six months in jail or both. Conversely, conviction of an indictable offence will usually expose the guilty parties to more severe penalties, as set out in the *Criminal Code*.

In attempting to determine the scope of this provision, section 118 of the Code defines an "official" to mean a person who "holds an office" or is "appointed to discharge a public duty." This provision further defines the word "office" to include "an office or appointment under the government."

---

3 Jock Ferguson, "Special force tracking allegations" *Globe and Mail*, December 2, 1993, p. A12.

4 *Criminal Code*, R.S.C. 1985, c. C-46, s. 122.

The following case examples may assist in clarifying the breadth and impact of the offence of breach of trust. Of significance was the 1992 case of *R. v. Perreault*, wherein the Quebec Court of Appeal held that an offence under section 122 requires proof that:

- the accused is an official;
- the impugned acts were committed in the general context of the execution of the official's duties;
- the acts constituted a fraud or a breach of trust.[5]

These three prerequisites form a suitable framework from which to examine this particular offence.

Accused is an official – application to local government – In the case of *R. v. Sheets*, the accused, a member of a municipal council, was charged with breach of trust by causing payment to be made out of county funds for work done on his land to his personal benefit.[6] An initial decision quashed the indictment on the ground that it did not disclose any offence known to law. In effect, the defence argued that the accused was a municipal officer and not an "official" as defined in sections 103 and 99 of the former *Criminal Code*. An appeal to the Alberta Court of Appeal by the Crown was dismissed. On a further appeal to the Supreme Court of Canada, however, Chief Justice Fauteux, delivering the unanimous judgment for the court, held that an elected municipal official was an "official" holding an office within the meaning of section 103 of the *Criminal Code* [now section 122 cited above] and as such was subject to the provisions of that section. The Supreme Court held further that such a person holds a position of duty, trust or authority in the public service and may be held to be an "official" within the meaning of the *Criminal Code*.

Appointed official – execution of duties – In *R. v. Vandenbussche*, the accused was the chief zoning planner for the City of Toronto.[7] It was alleged that, during the years 1973 to 1977, being a public official, he committed a breach of trust by "advising, consulting, and giving preferential considerations to building applications made by [K] or his agents

---

5   *R. v. Perreault* (1992), 75 C.C.C. (3d) 425, 48 Q.A.C. 303 (C.A.); refused leave to appeal [1993] 1 S.C.R. at p. viii.

6   *R. v. Sheets* (1971), 1 C.C.C. (2d) 508, 16 D.L.R. (3d) 221 (S.C.C.).

7   *R. v. Vandenbussche* (1980), 50 C.C.C. (2d) 15.

in return for considerations." It was further argued that the chief zoning planner unlawfully accepted "benefits or rewards" as consideration for performing his official acts or duties. The benefits alleged included the employment by K of the accused's son and son-in-law in drafting plans; the installation by K's company of siding on the accused's house at no charge; and the receipt of a Christmas gift ($500 gift certificate) from K and his associate.

The charges against the accused were dismissed. The Trial Judge held that the evidence failed to show anything untoward in the processing of K's application. As to the alleged indirect benefits from employment, the evidence showed that the accused's son-in-law was employed by K even before he was related to the accused and that he was unaware of K's plans to illegally convert the premises involved. The accused's son became involved with K only when his, by then, brother-in-law was too busy to do K's work. The court further held that, on the evidence, it "strained credibility to conclude that the alleged gift in 1972 somehow related to the performance of the accused's duties in 1976."

The court also ruled that, where the allegation is that the acts constituted a breach of trust, while it is not necessary to prove corruption, it must be shown that the accused did an act or failed to do an act contrary to the duty imposed upon him by statute, regulation, his contract of employment or directive in connection with his office, and that the act gave him some personal benefit either directly or indirectly. Finally, the court held that the criminal law should not be used as a sanction to punish mere technical breaches of conduct or acts of administrative discipline or administrative fault.

In the 1967 case of *R. v. Campbell*, the Ontario Court of Appeal determined that a breach of trust under this section was not to be confused with any necessary breach of trust in respect of trust property, as it merely relates to an abuse of public trust.[8]

Fraud or breach of trust – In the *Perreault* case, discussed earlier, the Quebec Court of Appeal issued the following instructive comments with respect to the final factor necessary for the offence of breach of trust:

---

8   *R. v. Campbell*, [1967] 3 C.C.C. 250, 50 C.R. 270 (Ont. C.A.), affirmed 2 C.R.N.S. 403 (S.C.C.).

Now, to identify the necessary conditions for this third constituent element in the case of a breach of trust, it appears that the following conditions must be met:

1. The accused did an act or failed to do an act contrary to the duties imposed on him by statute, regulation, his contract of employment or directive in connection with his office.

2. The act done must give him a personal benefit directly (for example: pecuniary compensation, an advantage in kind, in services, etc.) or indirectly (for example: an advantage to his spouse, member of his family, or even in certain cases, a third person). This benefit may be direct (for example: the payment of an amount of money) or indirect (for example: the hope of promotion, the desire to please a superior).[9]

The court went on to emphasize that, although the offence of breach of trust does not necessarily involve the concept of corruption, it does include the receipt of some benefit.[10]

In the case of *R. v. McKitka*, the accused, the town's mayor was charged with allegedly misleading a constituent as to the value of land and endeavouring to procure the constituent's land for himself for personal profit.[11] The British Columbia Court of Appeal found that the mayor had been convicted by a judge and jury on four counts of breach of trust in connection with the duties of his office; two counts of demanding a benefit; and one count of attempting to influence the municipal officer. In dismissing the appeal, the court referred to the 19th century decision of Chancellor Boyd in *R. v. Arnoldi*, where he stated of the official before him:

The defendant was tempted to do what he did by the prospect of gain – he profited by his own dereliction of duty, and to accomplish his purpose it was necessary to conceal the actual transac-

---

9 *R. v. Perrault* (1992), 75 C.C.C. (3d) 425 at 442, 48 Q.A.C. 303 (C.A.); refused leave to appeal [1993] 1 S.C.R. at p. viii.

10 See also *R. v. Pomeroy*, [1995] O.J. No. 590 at paragraph 25, where this decision was recently cited with approval.

11 *R. v. McKitka* (1982), 66 C.C.C. (2d) 164, 35 B.C.L.R. 116 (C.A.).

tion. This was misbehaviour in office, which is an indictable offence at common law.[12]

The Court of Appeal expressed agreement with the comments of the learned Chancellor, and stated further that:

> The work of a public servant must be a real service in which no concealed pecuniary self-interest should bias the judgment of the officer, and in which the substantial truth of every transaction should be made to appear.

In the 1995 decision of *R. v. Pomeroy*, an Ontario Trial Judge dismissed a charge of breach of trust leveled against the defendant, a former town mayor and regional chair.[13] The facts, which are somewhat complex, surround an amendment to the town's official plan, which incorporated a substantial rural property as part of the municipality's expanded urban area. The Crown alleged that the member had accepted an undeclared secret benefit, being 50 common shares or one-half of a company's interest in the subject property. In dismissing the charges, the Trial Judge found no evidence that the accused knew of or accepted the transfer of 50 common shares, nor was there any evidence that he abused his elected office or favoured any person in the performance of his duties.

Municipal Corruption

The *Criminal Code* is explicit in prohibiting any covert action that may exert criminal influence upon a municipal official. In effect, there is a specific clause meant to prohibit bribery at the local government level. Section 123 of the Code, subtitled, "Municipal Corruption," addresses this in the following manner:

123 (1) Every one who

  (a) gives, offers or agrees to give or offer to a municipal official, or

  (b) being a municipal official, demands, accepts or offers or agrees to accept from any person,

a loan, reward, advantage or benefit of any kind as consideration for the official

---

12 *R. v. Arnoldi* (1892), 23 O.R. 201 (H.C.J.); it is important to note that this case was decided before the passage of Canada's first *Criminal Code* in 1892.

13 *R. v. Pomeroy*, [1995] O.J. No. 590.

(c) to abstain from voting at a meeting of the municipal council or a committee thereof,

(d) to vote in favour of or against a measure, motion or resolution,

(e) to aid in procuring or preventing the adoption of a measure, motion or resolution, or

(f) to perform or fail to perform an official act,

is guilty of an indictable offence and liable to imprisonment for a term not exceeding five years.

123 (2) Every one who

(a) by suppression of the truth, in the case of a person who is under a duty to disclose the truth,

(b) by threats or deceit, or

(c) by any unlawful means,

influences or attempts to influence a municipal official to do anything mentioned in paragraphs (1) (c) to (f) is guilty of an indictable offence and liable to imprisonment for a term not exceeding five years.

123 (3) In this section, "municipal official" means a member of a municipal council or a person who holds an office under a municipal government.

In the recent case of *R. v. Gyles*, the Trial Judge provided the following instructive comments regarding an offence under section 123 of the *Criminal Code*:

> The offence of municipal corruption is rarely prosecuted. In order to prove a violation of subsection 123 (1), as set out in this case, the Crown must establish beyond a reasonable doubt that Mr. Gyles is:
>
> 1. a municipal official;
> 2. that he demanded or accepted a benefit as consideration;

3. and that he accepted this consideration for voting or procuring the adoption of a municipal motion.[14]

The following points are of relevance with respect to understanding the offence of municipal corruption.

Office – The courts have held that the definition of "office" under section 118 of the *Criminal Code* does not apply to an office under a municipal government so as to determine liability for an offence contrary to section 123.[15] Therefore, in *Belzberg v. The Queen*, the Alberta Court of Appeal applied the dictionary definition of "office" as being:

> A position to which certain duties are attached, especially a place of trust, authority, or service under constituted authority.[16]

In that case, the accused was charged with offering a bribe to a "municipal official ... to perform or fail to perform an official act." The chief building inspector, a municipal official of the City of Calgary, testified at the trial, without contradiction, that he was offered money to rescind orders condemning and requiring structural corrections in certain buildings in which the accused had an interest.

At the trial, the accused was acquitted on the ground that the appointment of the witness as chief building inspector had not been proved by by-law or resolution and that there was no evidence that he held an office under a municipal government. Upon appeal, the Alberta Court of Appeal set aside the acquittal and directed a verdict of guilty on the grounds that "there was no conflict of evidence as to the fact that Walker was the chief building inspector." Ultimately, the Supreme Court of Canada upheld the appellate ruling and found the Court of Appeal was "entirely justified in referring to the definitions of 'office' in the New Century and Shorter Oxford English dictionaries."

Municipal official – As will be noted from subsection 123 (3), cited above, the words "municipal official" expressly include "a member of a municipal council or a person who holds an office under a municipal government." This broad definition could include both a member ap-

---

14 *R. v. Gyles*, [2003] O.J. No. 3188, at para. 137.

15 Section 118 states that "office" includes, (a) an office or appointment under the government; (b) a civil or military commission; and (c) a position or an employment in a public department.

16 *Belzberg v. The Queen* (1961), 131 C.C.C. 281, 36 C.R. 368 (S.C.C.).

pointed to a local board and an officer or member of the staff of a council or local board. For example, in the case of *R. v. St. Pierre*, a police officer, within the *Criminal Code* definition of "peace officer," was held to be a municipal official.[17] Furthermore, in *R. v. Krupich*, the Alberta Provincial Court found a supervisor of the property standards section for the City of Calgary to be a municipal official under section 123 of the Code.[18]

In the 1918 decision of *R. v. Legault*, the accused, members of a school commission, were convicted of illegally asking a person for a sum of money in consideration for the passing of a by-law for payment of a claim due to the person by the commission.[19] The appellate court held that the conviction could not be supported under section 161 (now section 123), which related to the bribery of members or officers of municipal councils, and not to members of school commissions. The facts shown in the evidence, however, did constitute it an offence under section 69 (now subsection 21 (1)) referring to aiding or abetting or procuring the commission of an offence, and under section 72 (now subsection 24 (1)) where a person does or omits to do anything for the purpose of carrying out their intention to commit the offence.

Nature of the offence – The following cases provide an indication of the scope of an offence under section 123.

In the earlier Ontario case of *R. v. Milani*, the Trial Judge made the following general observations with respect to this provision:

> The present section 112 [now subsection 123(1)] appears to me to aim broadly, with a much wider shot pattern, at the elimination of the practice of procuring a favourable vote or abstention. The present section, it seems to me, was passed in its present form to prevent the bribing of municipal officials. If this is the case, then the section must mean this crime may be committed by three different vehicles:
>
> - a motion;
> - a resolution;

---

17 *R. v. St. Pierre*, [1971] Que. C.A. 758 (C.A.).
18 *R. v. Krupich*, [1991] A.J. No. 497.
19 *R. v. Legault*, [1918] 27 Que. K.B. 516, 33 C.C.C. 116 (C.A.).

- a measure, or by a combination of the three.[20]

Similarly, in *Haineault v. The Queen*, a city alderman was convicted on a charge of bribery and corruption, by accepting money from a hospital's director of works, to vote in favour of a zoning by-law beneficial to the hospital.[21]

Furthermore, in the 1982 case of *R. v. Leblanc*, a municipal treasurer accepted $1,125 from an urban planner. The treasurer was not to perform or fail to perform any of his official duties; rather, the money was in exchange for greater cooperation with a developer. This transaction was later held by the Quebec Court of Appeal and the Supreme Court of Canada to be preferential treatment sufficient to constitute a criminal offence.[22]

Finally, in *R. v. Chrétien*, it was held that the municipality's superintendent of public works had received a gift from a contractor when the entrance to his home was paved in asphalt. As no compensation was rendered, the Quebec Court of Appeal found that the gift constituted a breach of an appropriate standard of conduct:

> The fact of him accepting a gift and, a substantial gift, from a contractor whose work he had to supervise and, what is more, a gift directly connected with that work, appears to me to be in and of itself a breach of the appropriate standard of conduct prohibited by section 111 [now section 123] of the *Criminal Code*.[23]

Selling or Purchasing Office

Section 124 of the *Criminal Code* provides that:

124. Every one who

(a) purports to sell or agrees to sell an appointment to or a resignation from an office, or a consent to any such appointment or resignation, or receives or agrees to receive a reward or profit from the purported sale thereof, or

---

20 *R. v. Milani* (1980), 57 C.C.C. (2d) 417.
21 *Haineault v. The Queen* (1964), 44 C.R. 131.
22 *R. v. Leblanc* (1982), 44 N.R. 150 (S.C.C.); cited with approval in *R. v. Gyles*, [2003] O.J. No. 3188, at para. 139.
23 *R. v. Chrétien* (1988), 40 M.P.L.R. 306, [1988] R.L. 267, 26 Q.A.C. 241.

(b) purports to purchase or gives a reward or profit for the purported purchase of any such appointment, resignation or consent, or agrees or promises to do so,

is guilty of an indictable offence and liable to imprisonment for a term not exceeding five years.[24]

Succinctly, this section of the Code creates the related criminal offences of:

- agreeing to sell; or
- agreeing to purchase,

a public office.

It also includes the arrangement of a resignation from, or appointment to, such office.

In examining this particular provision, *Martin's Annual Criminal Code* states, in part:

> No sale need take place; the agreement to carry out one side of transaction of the proposed buying, selling, purchasing, etc., establishes the criminal liability. This indictable offence carries a five-year maximum punishment.[25]

Furthermore, the term "office," referred to in this provision, is defined in section 118 of the Code.

Influencing or Negotiating Appointments

The *Criminal Code* further establishes the offence of "influencing or negotiating appointments or dealing in offices" as follows:

125. Every one who

(a) receives, agrees to receive, gives or procures to be given, directly or indirectly, a reward, advantage or benefit of any kind as consideration for cooperation, assistance or exercise of influence to secure the appointment of any person to an office,

---

24 *Criminal Code*, R.S.C. 1985, c. C-46, s. 124.
25 *Martin's Annual Criminal Code, 2003*, p. 241.

(b) solicits, recommends or negotiates in any manner with respect to an appointment to or resignation from an office, in expectation of a direct or indirect reward, advantage or benefit, or

(c) keeps without lawful authority, the proof of which lies on him, a place for transacting or negotiating any business relating to

  (i) the filling of vacancies in offices,

  (ii) the sale or purchase of offices, or

  (iii) appointments to or resignations from offices,

is guilty of an indictable offence and liable to imprisonment for a term not exceeding five years.[26]

Once again, *Martin's Annual Criminal Code* provides the following guidance with respect to this provision:

> Section 125 prohibits attempts to influence or negotiate appointments to, or resignations from, office. Paragraphs (a) and (b) create criminal liability for a person who agrees to receive any benefit and the person who offers such benefit, respectively. The expansive language includes indirect benefits of any kind.
>
> Paragraph (c) prohibits keeping a place for the purpose of business relating to the resignation from or appointments to offices or sales or purchases of offices. This paragraph permits the defence of lawful authority, but the accused has the burden of proof of establishing it. This indictable offence has a maximum punishment of five years imprisonment.[27]

In the 1942 case of *R. v. Auger*, it was held that the receipt of money by a municipal employee in return for using his influence to procure the appointment of those paying the money to minor positions in a munitions factory of the federal government constituted an offence under this section.[28] The Quebec court held that the term "office" was not limited to offices of high responsibility, but extended to every kind of employment

---

26 *Criminal Code*, R.S.C. 1985, c. C-46, s. 125.
27 *Martin's Annual Criminal Code, 2003*, p. 242.
28 *R. v. Auger* (1942), 78 C.C.C. 136 (Que. C.S.P.).

or occupation in a public department. This analysis, therefore, included the position of a day labourer in a munitions factory of the federal government and the position of a day labourer in a municipal sewage plant. In addition, the court found that proof of corrupt intent was not a necessary element of this office.

However, in the earlier case of *R. v. Melnyk*, an Alberta court took an opposite position and argued that proof of a corrupt intent was a necessary element of this particular offence.[29] In that 1938 case, the daughter of the accused was a schoolteacher who no longer desired the position. The accused, who held no public office, received a payment of $80 to intercede with the school trustees on behalf of the daughter of the person making the payment. The Trial Judge held that, in the absence of some corrupt act, such as bribing the trustee, the accused was not committing an offence. The payment was merely one for services to be rendered.

Secret Commissions

One of the few provisions *not* found in Part IV of the *Criminal Code*, but that local government officials should still be aware of, is the offence critically entitled "Secret Commissions."

Section 426 of the Code provides as follows:

426 (1) Every one commits an offence who

    (a)   corruptly

        (i) gives, offers or agrees to give or offer to an agent, or

        (ii) being an agent, demands, accepts or offers or agrees to accept from any person,

        any reward, advantage or benefit of any kind as consideration for doing or forbearing to do, or for having done or forborne to do, any act relating to the affairs or business of his principal or for showing or forbearing to show favour or disfavour to any person with relation to the affairs or business of his principal; or

    (b)   with intent to deceive a principal, gives to an agent of that principal, or, being an agent, uses with intent to de-

---

29   *R. v. Melnyk*, [1938] 3 W.W.R. 425, 71 C.C.C. 362, [1939] 1 D.L.R. 270 (Alta. T.D.).

ceive his principal, a receipt, an account, or other writing

> (i) in which the principal has an interest,
>
> (ii) that contains any statement that is false or erroneous or defective in any material particular, and
>
> (iii) that is intended to mislead the principal.

(2) Every one commits an offence who is knowingly privy to the commission of an offence under subsection (1).

(3) A person who commits an offence under this section is guilty of an indictable offence and liable to imprisonment for a term not exceeding five years.

(4) In this section "agent" includes an employee, and "principal" includes an employer.[30]

Briefly, this provision makes it an offence for an agent to corruptly accept a benefit of any kind as consideration for doing or forbearing any act in relation to the affairs or business of the principal. In the 1992 case of *R. v. Kelly*, the Supreme Court of Canada drew the following conclusions with respect to the elements necessary for the offence of secret commissions under section 426 of the *Criminal Code*:

> There are then three elements to the *actus reus* [the action part] of the offence set out in s. 426 (1) (a) (ii) as they apply to an accused agent/taker with regard to the acceptance of a commission:
>
> (1) The existence of an agency relationship;
>
> (2) The accepting by an agent of a benefit as consideration for doing or forbearing to do any act in relation to the affairs of the agent's principle; and
>
> (3) The failure by the agent to make adequate and timely disclosure of the source, amount and nature of the benefit.[31]

---

30 *Criminal Code*, R.S.C. 1985, C-46, s. 426.
31 *R. v. Kelly* (1992), 73 C.C.C. (3d) 385 at 406.

Chapter 11
CRIMINAL CODE

The most recent judicial analysis on the offence of secret commissions as it may apply to local government officials is the 1993 decision of *R. v. Gentile*.[32] In that instance, a host of criminal charges were brought against a City of Toronto councillor for breach of trust and municipal corruption, as well as nine counts of accepting secret commissions in breach of section 426 of the Code. As a preliminary matter, the defendant argued that the relationship between a member of council and his or her municipal corporation was not that of "agent" and "principal" within the meaning of the Code's secret commission provisions. After reviewing the *Kelly* decision, the Provincial Court Judge held that the relationship between an elected member of municipal council and the municipal corporation was one of agent and principal within the meaning of section 426 of the *Criminal Code*.

In responding to a submission that section 426 was not intended to apply to the relationship between municipal councillors and municipal corporations, MacDonnell P.D.J. stated as follows:

> I do not believe that the affairs of a municipal corporation can be characterized as being removed from the world of trade and commerce. Municipal corporations have an extensive jurisdiction to administer. They are active participants in the commercial life of the company. They become engaged in matters of undertaking with private parties. They enter into contracts committing themselves to the expenditure of substantial sums of taxpayers' money. As with any other corporation, they can only act through agents. There is no persuasive reason why municipal corporations should be excluded from the protection which the *Criminal Code* provides against faithless agents just because those agents happen to be elected officials.[33]

The decision in this case further clarified that, even where the agent can only exercise the principal's powers in combination with other persons (i.e. the city council), this arrangement is not inconsistent with the existence of the agency relationship for the purposes of section 426. Thus, the fact that a municipal councillor casts only one vote and cannot contract alone on behalf of the municipality does not mean that he or she is not an "agent" within the meaning of the *Criminal Code*. In effect, a sin-

---

32 *R. v. Gentile* (1993), 81 C.C.C. (3d) 541.
33 *R. v. Gentile* (1993), 81 C.C.C. (3d) 556.

gle councillor may be in a position to influence the decision-making process of the entire municipal council.[34]

Theft and Fraud

There are two other criminal charges that could apply to elected or appointed officials in local government. One concerns an offence "resembling theft" and a second one pertains to the "falsification of books and documents." In the former instance, section 337 of the *Criminal Code*, subtitled "Public servant refusing to deliver property," provides as follows:

> Every one who, being or having been employed in the service of Her Majesty in Right of Canada or a province, or in the service of a municipality, and entrusted by virtue of that employment with the receipt, custody, management or control of anything, refuses or fails to deliver it to a person who is authorized to demand it and does demand it is guilty of an indictable offence and liable to imprisonment for a term not exceeding fourteen years.

In order for this provision to apply to a municipal councillor or local board member, the court would have to conclude that the accused was "employed ... in the service of the municipality" and refused or failed to deliver the property requested.

In the latter case, section 399 of the Code sets out the following offence:

> Every one who, being entrusted with the receipt, custody or management of any part of the public revenues, knowingly furnishes a false statement or return of any sum of money collected by him or entrusted to his care, or any balance of money in his hands or under his control, is guilty of an indictable offence and liable to imprisonment for a term not exceeding five years.

In effect, a member who "knowingly furnishes a false statement or return" in connection with public monies is liable, upon conviction, to five years in prison.

Penalties

In each of the *Criminal Code* provisions described above, there are specific penalties set out therein. However, as none of these offences prescribe a *minimum* punishment, a Trial Judge could impose an alternate

---

34 *Ibid.*, see the headnote.

order or penalty, such as a conditional discharge or a fine.[35] An example of this type of alternative sentence can be found in the 1994 case of *R. v. Currie*, in which two long-standing members of the local hydro commission pleaded guilty to breach of trust charges. After reviewing the discharge provision of the *Criminal Code*, especially the requirements that it be "in the best interests of the accused and not contrary to the public interest," the Trial Judge drew the following conclusions:

> They have been exemplary citizens who have made significant contribution to the life of this community. Until this matter arose, their honesty and integrity had never been called into question.
>
> ...
>
> All counsel acknowledge that, having regard to the unquestionable qualities of both accused as long-standing good citizens of this community, specific deterrence, rehabilitation and protection of the public are not the governing considerations in this sentencing. The main sentencing principle is general deterrence.[36]

Based on this legal analysis, the Trial Judge granted a conditional discharge upon both accused completing a 12-month probation order and making a $2,500 cash contribution to the local United Way organization.

Criminal Conviction

In accordance with section 750 of the *Criminal Code*, a member of council who is convicted of an indictable offence and sentenced to two years or more of imprisonment and, at the time, holds an office under the Crown or other federal public employment, the office or employment becomes vacant immediately. Similarly, if a sitting member is sentenced to a term of imprisonment, he or she may be disqualified from holding office as a member of a council during the sentence.[37]

However, the Supreme Court of Canada recently issued its seminal ruling in *Sauvé v. Canada's Chief Electoral Officer*, on the right of prison-

---

35 See *Criminal Code*, R.S.C. 1985, c. C-46, Section XXIII, "Sentencing."

36 *R. v. Currie*, [1994] O.J. No. 1440.

37 For example, in Ontario, see *Municipal Act, 2001*, S.O. 2001, c. 25, s. 258 and *Municipal Elections Act, 1996*, S.O. 1996, c. 32, Schedule, s. 17.

ers to vote in federal elections.[38] On October 31, 2002, the court ruled that the section in the *Canada Elections Act* (which prohibits persons in jail for sentences of two years or more from voting in a federal election), violated the appellant's Charter rights to vote and to equality under the law. Local governments across Canada will want to review this decision with respect to how it may affect them or their electoral process.

Despite these concerns, there are very few statutory restrictions preventing candidates who have previously served a term of imprisonment from running for local government office. For example, after being convicted in 1994 on eight criminal counts, Mr. Mario Gentile served eight months of a two-year jail term. In 1997, he registered as a candidate for the municipal election in Toronto, but later withdrew his name from the electoral process. However, his subsequent registration to run for municipal office in 2000 brought a sharp response from the Toronto city council. In a 40-10 vote, the council urged the province to amend the *Municipal Elections Act, 1996* in order to prohibit ex-convicts from being allowed to run for municipal office. The province declined to legislate such a ban for the following fundamental reason cited by the Minister of Municipal Affairs: "Our position, quite frankly, is that the electors are the best people to make that decision, not city council."[39]

Although the Province of Ontario expressed an unwillingness to legislate in the Gentile affair, media disclosure of a candidate's past criminal record may produce the same result in some cases. For example, in a related situation in Alberta, a candidate running for the position of alderman was publicly identified as having been convicted on two counts of sexual assault involving children. Noting that it was too late to take his name off the ballot, the candidate declared that he'd step down if elected, because "the publicity about his past [was] putting too much pressure on him and his family."[40]

Finally, as discussed earlier, reference should also be had to the recent appellate decision in this area of the law concerning Clifford Gyles. In September 2003, the court of appeal had an opportunity to review those few instances when a candidate may be prohibited from running for mu-

---

38 [2002] S.C.C. 68.

39 Paul Maloney, "Breach of trust won't bar politicians: convicted can take second run at council, province tells city," Toronto Star, February 10, 2000, at p. D.3.

40 Canadian Press, "Sex offender won't take elected post," *Ottawa Sun*, December 2, 2002.

nicipal office in Ontario. In *R. v. Gyles*, the defendant applicant, a city councillor convicted of municipal corruption and breach of trust under the Criminal Code, was released on bail pending his appeal. Although the release order prohibited Mr. Gyles from performing any duties as a councillor for the balance of the current term, the appellate court declined the Crown's request that he also be prohibited from running in the pending municipal election. Associate Chief Justice Dennis O'Connor's succinct analysis reviewed both the legislation and policy reasons for denying this request:

> There is no statutory bar to a person in the applicant's circumstances from standing for election to municipal office. The only legislative prohibition is found in subsection 91 (1) of the *Municipal Elections Act, 1996*, c. 32. The Act prohibits individuals from standing for election when they have been convicted of either a corrupt practice as set out in sections 89 and 90 of the Act or of an offence under the *Criminal Code*, R.S.C. 1985, c. C-46 in connection with a municipal election. The offences of which the applicant stands convicted fall under neither head and as such do not attract the subsection 91 (1) prohibition.
>
> The policy underlying the legislative scheme would seem to be that it is up to the electorate to decide whether it wishes someone with a criminal record, other than a record referred to in the *Municipal Elections Act, 1996*, to represent it.[41]

In light of the court of appeal's comments, it is interesting to note that the results of the November 2003 municipal election revealed that Mr. Gyles placed sixth and garnered less than fix percent of the votes cast.[42]

Related Offences

In closing this chapter, it is important for local government officials to appreciate that offences under the *Criminal Code* are not the only ones they could face should they decide to act for their personal gain, as opposed to the public good. On the one hand, elected or appointed representatives could be subject to court challenges based on respective provincial conflict of interest legislation. On the other hand, municipal councillors or local board members who argue that they have merely re-

---

41 *R. v. Gyles*, [2003] O.J. No. 3724, at paras. 3-4.
42 See City of Mississauga's election website: www5.mississauga.ca/vote2003 (accessed December 17, 2003).

ceived "gifts," could find themselves charged with failing to declare income and tax evasion under the federal *Income Tax Act*. In the 1994 case of *R. v. Gentile*, the accused received over $196,000 during a three-year period, from Mr. Louis Charles, which he characterized as a gift based on their "father-son" relationship. In finding the accused guilty, the court made the following observations with respect to the so-called "father-son" defence:

> The accused and Charles may refer to each other in public as father and son, and may well appear close socially. The enormity of the funds, however, and their often abusive disbursement, causes me to conclude that in the hands of the accused, these monies were not a gift, but were in fact income resulting from his office or employment as an elected politician and consisted of salary, wages, or other remuneration including gratuities, or benefits received or enjoyed by him by virtue of his office. Surely, the fact that Charles wrote off all sums in question on his income tax return as business expenses, at least in his mind, accords with his comment that the gift-giving to the accused was a cost of doing business. If it was not a cost of doing business, and was meant purely as a gift or gifts to a friend, and not given to secure a service in the past, present or future, it is questionable whether he would have attempted to write them off as income tax deductions.[43]

Conclusions

In concluding this chapter, local government representatives across Canada would do well to heed the following sound advice found in a 1998 editorial of *Municipal World* by Michael J. Smither:

> It is irrefutable that by far the majority of members of council are indeed the "cream of the crop." While it is highly unlikely that they will, unintentionally or otherwise, contravene the *Criminal Code*, it is nevertheless advisable that they take a few moments to contemplate the serious consequences that can arise when the foregoing provisions are not regarded.[44]

---

43 *R. v. Gentile*, [1994] O.J. No. 2664.
44 Michael J. Smither, "Council Members and the Criminal Code," *Municipal World*, January 1998, p. 11.

Chapter 12
FREEDOM OF INFORMATION

Why do democratically elected politicians and well-paid civil servants need so many rules about allowing the people who elect and pay them access to information? Shouldn't it merely be a question asked and the information received? Unfortunately, it doesn't work that way, right from Ottawa down to municipal governments.

First there are no regulations on what the public could access and what it couldn't, and that was a reason to deny the information. Now there are probably too many rules and that's the reason to say no.

Editorial, Barrie Examiner
July 28, 2001

For many years, the courts across Canada consistently followed the early ruling in *Journal Printing Co. v. McVeity*, in which it was held that no right of access to municipal meetings existed, "except as expressly or by implication given by statute."[1] This narrow position was subsequently applied to restrict access to local government records in Ontario by Mr. Justice Steele in 1976. In *Re Simpson and Henderson*, His Honour held that "the applicant has no right to disclosure of the information to him other than that which can be found in the statute."[2] Therefore, in the absence of a legislated right, the common law was of little assistance to members of the public seeking to access information held by their local government.

In 1982, the Province of Quebec became the first provincial jurisdiction in Canada to enact a cohesive statutory regime to govern the rights of those persons seeking to access information held by public bodies. That legislation, called *An Act respecting access to documents held by public*

---

1 *Journal Printing Co. v. McVeity* (1915), 3 O.L.R. 166.
2 *Re Simpson and Henderson* (1976), 13 O.R.(2d) 322; 71 D.L.R. (3d) 24; *Municipal World*, August 1976, p. 206.

bodies and the protection of personal information, also encompassed local governments.[3] In the years following, most provinces either enacted such legislation for municipal authorities or included them in their provincial access to information schemes.[4] For the purposes of this chapter, the Ontario experience represents a typical approach to the issue of freedom of information in the local government realm and is examined below in greater detail.

Ontario's Legislation

Prior to the adoption of the recommendations of the Commission on Freedom of Information and Individual Privacy, public access to government information in Ontario was regarded as a matter of privilege, and one that could be easily denied.[5]

Based on the commission's report in 1980, legislation affecting both the provincial and municipal levels of government was subsequently adopted, making access to government-held information a statutory right. On January 1, 1988, the *Freedom of Information and Protection of Privacy Act, 1987* came into force, embracing Ontario government ministries and numerous provincial agencies, boards, commissions and corporations.[6] Shortly thereafter, on January 1, 1991, the *Municipal Free-*

---

3 R.S.Q., c. A-2.1; this statute was based on the recommendations found in a report tabled by the Paré Commission in May 1981, entitled "Information et liberté."

4 Alberta: *Freedom of Information and Protection of Privacy Act*, S.A. 1994, c. F-18.5; (now R.S.A. 2000, c. F-25); British Columbia: *Freedom of Information and Protection of Privacy Act*, S.B.C. 1992, c. 61, as amended; (now R.S.B.C. 1996, c. 165); Manitoba: *Freedom of Information and Protection of Privacy Act*, C.C.S.M., c. F175; New Brunswick: *Protection of Personal Information Act*, c. P-19.1; Newfoundland: *Freedom of Information Act*, R.S.N.L. 1990, c. F-25; Nova Scotia: *Freedom of Information and Protection of Privacy Act*, 1993, c. 5; P.E.I.: *Freedom of Information and Protection of Privacy Act*, R.S.P.E.I. 1988, c. F-15.01; Saskatchewan: *Freedom of Information and Protection of Privacy Act*, S.S. 1990-91, c. F-20.01; Yukon: *Access to Information and Protection of Privacy Act*, S.Y. 1995, c. 1; Northwest Territories and Nunavut: *Access to Information and Protection of Privacy Act*, S.N.W.T. 1994, c. 20; Privacy Commissioner of Canada: *Privacy Act*, R.S. 1985, c. P-21; Information Commissioner of Canada, *Access to Information Act*, R.S. 1985, c. A-1.

5 "Public Government for Private People: Report of the Commission on Freedom of Information and Individual Privacy," August 4, 1980.

6 *Freedom of Information and Protection of Privacy Act, 1987*, S.O. 1987, c. 25 (Now R.S.O. 1990, c. F.31).

dom of Information and Protection of Privacy Act, 1989 came into effect.[7]

Modelled on the provincial statute, it nevertheless had been modified to take into account some of the particular circumstances of municipal corporations and local boards. The Act extended the freedom of information and protection of privacy provisions to thousands of local government "institutions," including:

- municipalities;
- school boards;
- municipal service boards;
- transit commissions;
- local roads boards;
- public library boards;
- boards of health;
- police services boards;
- conservation authorities;
- district social services administration boards;
- local services boards;
- planning boards;
- police villages; and
- joint committees of management or joint boards of management established under the *Municipal Act, 2001*.[8]

In addition, the Act provides the provincial government with the power to enact a regulation to designate "any agency, board, commission, corporation or other body" as an institution pursuant to the legislation. In this respect, reference should be had to Ontario Regulation 372/91 concerning "institutions." This regulation provides a list of other specific

---

[7] *Municipal Freedom of Information and Protection of Privacy Act, 1989*, S.O.1989, c. 63 (now R.S.O. 1990, c. M.56).

[8] *Municipal Freedom of Information and Protection of Privacy Act*, R.S.O. 1990, c. M.56, s. 2 (1).

bodies that are designated as institutions under the *Municipal Freedom of Information and Protection of Privacy Act*, including such entities as the Board of Governors of Exhibition Place, the Municipal Property Assessment Corporation and every local housing corporation incorporated under Part III of the *Social Housing Reform Act, 2002*.[9]

In addition to the regulations, reference should also be had to subsection 2 (3) of the *Municipal Freedom of Information and Protection of Privacy Act*, which establishes a legislative approach to determine whether or not other bodies are "deemed" to be part of a municipal corporation for the purposes of this statute:

> 2 (3) Every agency, board, commission, corporation or other body not mentioned in clause (b) of the definition of "institution" in subsection (1) or designated under clause (c) of the definition of "institution" in subsection (1) is deemed to be part of the municipal corporation for the purposes of this Act if all of its members or officers are appointed or chosen by or under the authority of the council of the municipal corporation.

For example, one such case concerned the status of the Renfrew Industrial Commission, from whom the appellant had requested certain information. In particular, the appellant sought a list of the local businesses assisted by the commission, as well as the manner of assistance, whether by loan or guarantee. The commission maintained that it was not subject to the *Municipal Freedom of Information and Protection of Privacy Act*.

After reviewing subsection 2 (3) of the legislation, and the relevant corporate history of the commission, as well as its officers, directors and members, the inquiry officer agreed with the commission:

> I have found above that as of the dates of the request and the appeal, neither the "members" nor the "officers" of the commission were "appointed or chosen by or under the authority of" the town council pursuant to subsection 2 (3) of the Act.

> Accordingly, I find that the commission cannot be deemed to be a part of the municipal corporation of the town by virtue of subsection 2 (3) of the Act. Therefore, the commission does not qualify

---

[9] Ontario Regulation 372/91, "Institutions," amended to O.Reg. 162/03.

as an institution under subsection 2 (1) of the Act, and the Act does not apply to the commission.[10]

Purposes of the Act - An Interesting Balancing Routine

Introducing the Act in the Ontario Legislature in 1989, the Honourable Murray J. Elston, Chairman of the Management Board of Cabinet and Minister of Financial Institutions, acknowledged that the legislation "builds upon the tradition of openness at the local level, while also ensuring the privacy of people's own information."[11]

The minister, referring to provincial practices, further stressed the following important points:

> The legislation is shortened in its popular name to "freedom of information," and it leads to the impression that everyone can get any information about any person that he cares to. That is not so. It is an *interesting balancing routine* that is managed by the people who are administering this Act provincially to ensure the protection of privacy is given a deliberation that is necessary to ensure that no one is disadvantaged.[12]

Appearing to reflect these sentiments, the statute sets out express purposes in section 1:

The purposes of this Act are,

(a) to provide a right of access to information under the control of institutions in accordance with the principles that,

(i) information should be available to the public,

(ii) necessary exemptions from the right of access should be limited and specific, and

(iii) decisions on the disclosure of information should be reviewed independently of the institution controlling the information; and

---

10 *Renfrew Industrial Commission*, Order M-343 (July 11, 1994) at p. 4; see also *Ottawa-Carleton Regional Transit Commission*, Order M-13 (May 4, 1992); and *Township of Temagami*, Order M-415 (November 2, 1994).

11 Legislative Assembly of Ontario, *Official Report of Debates (Hansard)*, October 10, 1989, p. 2772 (emphasis added).

12 *Ibid.*

(b) to protect the privacy of individuals with respect to personal information about themselves held by institutions and to provide individuals with a right of access to that information.[13]

Designation of Head

In order to manage this "interesting balancing routine," the Act provides for the creation of a position known as the "head" of the municipality.[14] Alternative methods to determine how this position *may* be filled are permitted:

- the members of the council may, by by-law, designate from amongst themselves an individual, or committee of council to act as the head; and

- the members elected or appointed to a board, commission or other body may, in writing, designate from amongst themselves, an individual or committee of the board, commission or other body, to act as head.

If no such designation is made, the Act provides that the head *shall* be:

- the council, in the case of the municipality; and

- the members elected or appointed to the board, commission or other body in the case of an institution other than a municipality.

The practical aspects of how this provision operates were discussed in a 1998 decision involving the Town of Amherstburg and the Amherstburg Police Services Board. Briefly, the appellant submitted a request under the legislation to the Town of Amherstburg for information pertaining to delivery of police services in the municipality. More particularly, the request sought copies of correspondence from the police services board and the town to the Ontario Civilian Commission on Police Services and the Ministry of the Solicitor General and Correctional Services.

Prior to the town's decision, the appellant received a notice from the police services board indicating that they considered her request for re-

---

13 *Municipal Freedom of Information and Protection of Privacy Act*, R.S.O. 1990, c. M.56, s. 1.

14 *Ibid.*, s. 3.

cords to be frivolous and vexatious. On December 4, 1998, the town subsequently issued its decision and the appellant appealed both of these rulings. In subsequent representations, the appellant raised at least two new issues, including the propriety of the decision of the mayor to transfer the request to the police services board, of which he was also the chair.

The appellant argued that, as the mayor had not yet been duly appointed as "head" of the institution, his unilateral decision to transfer the request was invalid. The town acknowledged that it did not have a designation of "head" until after the response had been issued to the appellant on December 4, 1998. Conceding that the town council was the "head" at that time, the municipality argued that, even though the mayor had not been officially delegated at the time the decision was issued, he was speaking on their behalf as the "head of council."

In rejecting the town's decision in this instance, the adjudicator made the following pertinent observations:

> In objectively assessing the content and intent of this letter, the only conclusion that I am able to draw is that the mayor has treated this matter as though he were the "head" of the institution. In my view, it is not sufficient that he simply be "head" of council and therefore able to respond on its behalf to an access request without the requisite and evident authority of council to do so. It also appears to me, although I acknowledge that this may be more in appearance than in fact, that the town has attempted to rectify the validity of the mayor's December 4, 1998 decision by very quickly enacting the by-law. While this action deals with any request of the authority of the "head" for future requests, in my view it cannot save a decision which was invalid at the time it was made.
>
> Consequently, at the time the mayor issued his decision transferring the appellant's request to the police, he was not properly delegated as "head" of the town council and his decision is invalid. Consequently, any decisions flowing from that initial decision cannot stand, and I find that they are null and void.[15]

---

15 *Town of Amherstburg and the Amherstburg Police Services Board*, Order MO-1221 (June 29, 1999) at p. 4.

Delegation of Powers

A head may, in writing, delegate a power or duty granted or vested in it to an officer or officers of the institution or another institution. This delegation may be subject to such limitations, restrictions, conditions and requirements as the head may set out in the delegation.[16] It is important to note that, in this provision, it is the *power* or *duty* that is delegated, not the position of "head." Even though the officer appointed will usually assume the primary responsibility for the discharge of the statutory functions, the position of "head" remains vested in the person or body designated by the council or local board in accordance with the requirements under the Act.

In a case involving the former City of Etobicoke, an appellant requested access to the cellular telephone billing for a named city councillor respecting each call made to 911 or the Metropolitan Toronto Police. Upon appeal, the councillor consented to the disclosure, and the city issued a new decision letter providing the requested information to the appellant. However, the appellant also alleged that "three named city employees do not have valid delegations to permit them to make decisions under the Act."

In addressing the delegation of authority in question, the inquiry officer reviewed various by-laws and documentation from the municipality, as well as other statutory references to the *Municipal Act* in order to support the validity of the delegation of authority to the city employee who signed the decision letters in that instance. After agreeing with the municipality, however, the inquiry officer made the following practical comments to assist other municipalities or local boards facing similar circumstances in the future:

> However, the analysis required to reach this conclusion was complicated. In my view, a council resolution or by-law delegating the head's powers under the Act by reference to specific (and current) position titles would make it much easier to determine that the incumbent of such a position had a valid delegation. It would also provide a much simpler answer when a city employee's authority

---

16 *Municipal Freedom of Information and Protection of Privacy Act*, R.S.O. 1990, c. M.56, s. 49 (1).

to make decisions under the Act is scrutinized by a member of the public such as the appellant.[17]

Access to Records

With respect to a requester's ability to access an institution's "records," section 4 of the Act specifically provides that:

Every person has a right of access to a record or a part of a record in the custody or under the control of an institution unless,

- (a) the record or part of the record falls within one of the exemptions under sections 6 to 15; or

- (b) the head is of the opinion on reasonable grounds that the request for access is frivolous or vexatious.[18]

Such exemptions, and the role of the "head" in determining access to the records, are discussed more fully in the next chapter. The obligations of an elected or appointed member are discussed later in Chapter 14, Obligations of a Member.

Importantly, the Act confirms the continuation of a past practice of access in section 50:

This Act shall not be applied to preclude access to information that is not *personal information* and to which access by the public was available by *statute, custom* or *practice* immediately before the 1st day of January 1991.[19]

Furthermore, the statute does not impose any limitation on the information otherwise available by law to a party to litigation, nor does it affect the power of a court or tribunal to compel a witness to testify or compel the production of a document.[20]

For the purposes of the Act, the word "record" is expressly, albeit broadly, defined in subsection 2 (1) as follows:

---

17 *City of Etobicoke*, Order M-971 (July 18, 1997), at p. 2; see also *Metropolitan Toronto Police Services Board*, Order M-116 (March 31, 1993).

18 *Municipal Freedom of Information and Protection of Privacy Act*, R.S.O. 1990, c. M.56, s. 4 (1); see also sections 24 and 25.

19 *Ibid.*, s. 50 (2) (emphasis added).

20 *Ibid.*, ss. 51 (1) and (2).

"record" means any record of information however recorded, whether in printed form, on film, by electronic means or otherwise, and includes,

(a) correspondence, a memorandum, a book, a plan, a map, a drawing, a diagram, a pictorial or graphic work, a photograph, a film, a microfilm, a sound recording, a videotape, a machine readable record, any other documentary material, regardless of physical form or characteristics, and any copy thereof, and

(b) subject to the regulations, any record that is capable of being produced from a machine readable record under the control of an institution by means of computer hardware and software or any other information storage equipment and technical expertise normally used by the institution.[21]

Two brief comments on the issue of accessible "records" will suffice in assisting to better understand the broad application of these terms. In a decision involving the City of Stoney Creek, the appeal concerned a request for access to documentation regarding communications between the mayor and certain named individuals. During the mediation of the appeal, the city located a copy of one of the records identified in the request, being a one-page draft letter prepared by legal counsel and addressed to a named individual other than the appellant. The city subsequently advised the appellant that it would not release the correspondence for a number of reasons, including the fact that the document was only a draft and, as it was not sent or communicated to anyone, it did not constitute a "record" for the purposes of subsection 2 (1) of the Act. In examining that provision of the Act, the inquiry officer drew the following conclusions:

> In my opinion, the use of the word "includes" means that the types of documents described [in the definition of the word "record"] are not exhaustive; they merely provide examples of things that constitute records for the purposes of the Act. Therefore, the fact that the draft may not be correspondence because it was not sent is not germane to this discussion.

---

21 *Ibid.*, s. 2 (1).

Moreover, there is no dispute that the document constitutes "recorded information." In my view, whether the recorded information is a draft or otherwise of some document is likewise irrelevant to the determination of whether it is a "record." Once something is "recorded information," it is, in my opinion, a "record" within the above-mentioned definition.

Accordingly, I find that Record 1 is a "record" for the purposes of the Act.[22]

While an institution is required to consider whether or not to disclose a record to a requester, the case law is clear that it is not required to create a record. In a recent appeal, the North Bay Police Service had received a request for access to information pertaining to an assault against the requester in 2001, as well as "all information respecting any criminal record checks (CPIC) on me since 1991 – require who performed the check and for what reasons." Although the police initially responded to the first part of the request by granting access to portions of the requested records, they subsequently issued a second decision letter with respect to the latter portion of the request indicating that the record was known as an "off-line search" performed through CPIC and the response indicated that "this record [was] not in existence."

In reviewing this matter, the adjudicator referred to Order No. 17 in which Commissioner Linden quoted with approval the following portion of the Williams Report, "Public Government for Private People," which provided as follows:

A common feature of the freedom of information schemes in place in other jurisdictions is that the type of "information" to which access is given is material which is already recorded in the custody or control of the government institution. Thus, a right to "information" does not embrace the right to require the government institution to provide an answer to a specific question; rather, it is generally interpreted as requiring that access be given to an existing document on which information has been recorded.

In upholding the decision of the police, the adjudicator went on to note these observations:

---

22 *City of Stoney Creek*, Order M-839 (January 31, 1997), at p. 3.

> The appellant is of the view that I have the authority to order the police to comply with the procedures set out in the CPIC manual for requesting an off-line search. In my view, this would be tantamount to ordering the police to create a record. It is well established in previous orders of this office that I have no such authority.[23]

The statute further provides that it applies to any record in the custody or under the control of the institution regardless of whether it was recorded before or after the first day of January, 1991. However, it does *not* apply to records placed in the archives of an institution by or on behalf of a person or organization other than the institution.[24]

Furthermore, the confidentiality provisions in any other Act are also overridden by the freedom of information legislation, unless this Act or the provisions in the other statute provide otherwise.[25]

In this respect, Ontario's legislation expressly states that the confidentiality provisions in the following two Acts will take precedence over it:

- the protection afforded to the contents of a ballot box at a municipal election, pursuant to subsection 88 (6) of the *Municipal Elections Act, 1996*;[26] and

- the prohibition against disclosure of information obtained by an assessment commissioner, assessor or other person when making an assessment, in accordance with subsection 53 (1) of the *Assessment Act*.[27]

Obligation to Disclose

There is a specific provision in the freedom of information legislation that requires a head to disclose any record that reveals a grave environmental, health or safety hazard to the public and where it is in the public interest to do so. Specifically, subsection 5 (1) of the Act provides as follows:

---

23 *North Bay Police*, Order MO-1596 (December 5, 2002), at p. 4.

24 *Municipal Freedom of Information and Protection of Privacy Act*, R.S.O. 1990, c. M.56, ss. 52 (1) and (2).

25 *Ibid.*, ss. 53 (1) and (2).

26 *Municipal Elections Act, 1996*, S.O. 1996, c. 32, Schedule, s. 88 (6).

27 *Assessment Act*, R.S.O. 1990, c. A.31, s. 53 (1).

Chapter 12
FREEDOM OF INFORMATION

Despite any other provision of this Act, a head shall, as soon as practicable, disclose any record to the public or persons affected if the head has reasonable and probable grounds to believe that it is in the public interest to do so and that the record reveals a grave environmental, health or safety hazard to the public.

Therefore, if these statutory conditions are met, and the head has reasonable and probable grounds to believe that such a hazard exists, the record must be disclosed as soon as possible, and there is no requirement that a request under the statute must be made before the head is required to act. However, before disclosing such a record, the head "shall cause notice to be given to any person to whom the information in the record relates, if it is practicable to do so."[28]

The notice must indicate that the head intends to release the record or part of a record that may affect the interests of the person, as well as a description of the record or part relating to that person. The notice must also state that the person may make representations forthwith to the head as to why the record or part of the record should not be disclosed.

In a 1994 appeal order concerning the City of Peterborough, the municipality received separate requests from three related individuals for access to any records that contained their personal information. Although the city originally denied that it held any files containing such personal information, that decision was successfully appealed and the municipality was ordered "to conduct a further search for responsive records." Upon completing the further search, the city identified a number of records that were responsive to the request; however, access was denied to portions of these records. Upon appeal, the issue arose as to whether or not section 5 applied to the circumstances of the appeal. In searching the previous case law on this matter, the inquiry officer reviewed an earlier decision pursuant to section 11 of the *Freedom of Information and Protection of Privacy Act*, a provision identical to section 5 of the municipal legislation:

> In Order P-482, Inquiry Officer Holly Big Canoe addressed the application of section 11 of the *Freedom of Information and Protection of Privacy Act*, which corresponds to section 5 of the *Mu-*

---

28 *Municipal Freedom of Information and Protection of Privacy Act*, R.S.O. 1990, c. M.56, s. 5 (2).

nicipal Freedom of Information and Protection of Privacy Act. She stated that:

> Section 11 of the Act is a mandatory provision which requires the head to disclose records in certain circumstances. The duties and responsibilities set out in section 11 of the Act belong to the head alone. As a result, the Information and Privacy Commissioner, or his delegate, do not have the power to make an order pursuant to section 11 of the Act.

I agree with this interpretation and adopt it for the purposes of this appeal. In my view, as a delegate of the commissioner, I do not have the power to make an order pursuant to subsection 5 (1) of the Act. In addition, I find that records of the sort sought by the appellant would not reveal a grave environmental, health or safety hazard to the public. Rather, such records would pertain to the appellant's compliance with certain fire regulations and his dispute with the city over its interpretation of those regulations. Accordingly, I find that this section has no application in the circumstances of this appeal.[29]

Compelling Public Interest

In a manner similar to the obligation to disclose provision set out in section 5 above, section 16 of the Act states that, even where certain statutory exemptions apply to a record, disclosure may still be required if a compelling public interest in the disclosure of the records clearly outweighs the purpose of the exemption. Briefly, section 16 provides as follows:

> An exemption from disclosure of a record under section 7 [Advice or recommendations], section 9 [relations with governments], section 10 [third party information], section 11 [economic and other interests], section 13 [danger to safety or health] and section 14 [personal privacy] does *not* apply if a *compelling public interest* in the disclosure of the record clearly outweighs the purpose of the exemption.

In order for section 16 to apply, two requirements must be met. First, there must be a compelling public interest in the disclosure of the re-

---

29 *City of Peterborough*, Order M-401 (October 13, 1994), at p. 2.

spective records. Secondly, this interest must clearly outweigh the purpose of the respective exemption.[30] With respect to the first requirement, the following comments by Adjudicator Holly Big Canoe are often cited as a rather definitive analysis when determining the existence of a "compelling public interest:"

> "Compelling" is defined as "arousing strong interest or attention" (Oxford). In my view, the public interest in disclosure of a record should be measured in terms of the relationship of the record to the Act's central purpose of shedding light on the operations of government. In order to find that there is a compelling public interest in disclosure, the information contained in a record must serve the purpose of informing the citizenry about the activities of their government, adding in some way to the information the public has to make effective use of the means of expressing public opinion, or to make political choices.[31]

In another case involving the Town of Ajax, the municipality had participated in a regional cooperative tender for garbage collection services. Ultimately, the town withdrew from the regional tender and put out its own tender for garbage collection. Subsequently, a request was received under the legislation for copies of the tender bids submitted by the two lowest bidders. The town provided the appellant with a blank copy of the contract, the names of the two lowest bidders, and the total amount submitted by each. The town denied access to any other information regarding the bids, relying on the exemption in section 10 (third party information) of the freedom of information legislation.

On appeal, the appellant argued that there was a "public policy objective" in "ensuring that the public and resident [sic] of the town in particular have confidence and faith that the process [of public tenders] is being administered fairly and in their best interests." In interpreting section 16 of the legislation, the adjudicator examined the requirements that there first exists a compelling public interest in the disclosure of records, and secondly, that the interest must clearly outweigh the purpose

---

30 *Ministry of Finance,* Order P-1398 (May 27, 1997), upheld on judicial review in *Ontario (Ministry of Finance) v. Ontario (Information and Privacy Commissioner)* (1999), 118 O.A.C. 108 (C.A.), leave to appeal refused [1999] S.C.C.A. No. 134 (note).

31 *Ministry of the Attorney General,* Order P-984 (August 28, 1995).

of the exemption. In doing so, the adjudicator made the following significant observations:

> A compelling public interest has been found, for example, in situations questioning the propriety of the disposal of billions of dollars of public property (Order PO-1804), the safety and reliability of the operations of Ontario's nuclear power plans (PO-1805), and in situations that raised allegations of improper conduct on the part of elected officials (M-710).

> The appellant in this appeal questions the town's bidding process in a single tender. While there is a public interest in scrutinizing records relating to tender bids, the town has gone some way in meeting its obligation through its disclosure of the total bid amounts of the two lowest bidders and its subsequent explanation of the discrepancy between the bid amount submitted by the lowest bidder and the final offer that was accepted. In these circumstances, it cannot be said that the public interest in disclosure of the unit prices is compelling. Accordingly, since the first requirement of section 16 has not been satisfied, I find that the section 16 exemption does not apply.[32]

A recent decision involving the Waterloo Regional Police Services Board set out the analysis used when determining whether a record's disclosure outweighs the purpose of the exemption. This appeal arose with respect to a request for access to a copy of the transcription of an interview conducted by two named police officers with an affected person in regard to a murder-suicide involving the requester's daughter (the deceased) and granddaughter. The police services board denied access under a variety of provisions, including those under various provisions in section 14 (invasion of privacy). One of the issues to be decided upon in the appeal was whether or not there was a compelling public interest in the disclosure of the records which outweighed the stated exemptions.

The following comments of the adjudicator are instructive for the purposes of interpreting the second requirement of an application under section 16:

> I find that the circumstances surrounding this case raise issues that are public in nature, including public awareness about unlicensed

---

32 *Town of Ajax*, Order MO-1471 (October 11, 2001).

therapy and therapeutic practices. However, this appeal arises out of the appellant's wish for access to records that document matters relating to a private therapeutic relationship between the deceased and an affected person. The appellant has not demonstrated that a sufficiently strong relationship between the disclosure of *these particular* records and the advancement of the public interest she identifies, in this case exposing unlicensed therapy and therapeutic practices. Given the particular sensitivity of the information contained in these records, I find that the public interest in disclosure does not clearly outweigh the purpose of the subsection 38 (b)/14 exemption. I therefore conclude that section 16 does not apply in the circumstances of this case.

I am not without sympathy for the predicament of the appellant. I have considered her arguments carefully. Although they raise some important issues, I am satisfied that in this case, the exemption applies and it is not overridden by section 16 of the Act.[33]

Access Procedure

The Act requires a person seeking access to make a request in writing, with the prescribed fee, including sufficient detail to enable an experienced employee of the institution, upon a reasonable effort, to identify the record. Where the request does not "sufficiently describe the record sought," then the institution is required to "inform the applicant of the defect and shall offer assistance in reformulating the request."[34] A number of previous orders have identified the requirements in "reasonable search appeals." In an appeal involving the Township of Stone Mills, the requester sought "a copy of the record of the council members present at the meeting on the afternoon/evening of January 22, 2001" as well as the minutes for this meeting. Although the municipality provided a list of names and partial access to the minutes, an appeal was launched to determine "whether the township has conducted a reasonable search for responsive records." In dismissing the appeal, the adjudicator provided the following helpful comments regarding a reasonable search:

---

33 *Waterloo Regional Police Services Board*, Order MO-1563 (August 9, 2002).
34 *Municipal Freedom of Information and Protection of Privacy Act*, R.S.O. 1990, c. M.56, s. 17. See also sections 18 and 19 as to forwarding of requests to another institution.

A number of previous orders have identified the requirements in reasonable search appeals (see, for example, Orders M-282, P-458, P-535, M-909, PO-1744 and PO-1920). In Order PO-1744, acting Adjudicator Mumtz Jiwan made the following statements with respect to the requirements of reasonable search appeals:

> ... the Act does not require the ministry to prove with absolute certainty that records do not exist. The ministry must, however, provide me with sufficient evidence to show that it has made a reasonable effort to identify and locate responsive records. A reasonable search is one in which an experienced employee expends a **reasonable** effort to locate records which are reasonably related to the request (Order M-909).

I agree with acting Adjudicator Jiwan's statements.

Where a requester provides sufficient detail about the records that he/she is seeking and the institution indicates that records or further records do not exist, it is my responsibility to ensure that the institution has made a reasonable search to identify any records that are responsive to the request. The Act does not require the institution to prove with absolute certainty that records or further records do not exist. However, in my view, in order to properly discharge its obligations under the Act, the institution must provide me with sufficient evidence to show that it has made a reasonable effort to identify and locate records responsive to the request.[35]

A notice of refusal to give access shall be given:

- where there is no such record; or
- where there is such a record, but access is being refused pursuant to the statute.[36]

---

35 Township of Stone Mills, Order MO-1662 (June 26, 2003).

36 *Municipal Freedom of Information and Protection of Privacy Act*, R.S.O. 1990, c. M.56, s. 22.

Duty of the Head

Upon receipt of a request for access to a record, the head or person to whom the responsibilities have been delegated, must not only perform certain routine duties but also be prepared to respond to extraordinary circumstances.

Subject to a permitted time extension,[37] the head shall, within 30 days:

- give written notice to the applicant as to whether or not access to the record or part of it will be given; and
- if access is to be given, give the applicant access to the record or part, and, if necessary, cause the record to be produced.[38]

Where a request is received for access to a record that contains exempted information, the Act requires the head to disclose "as much of the record as can reasonably be severed without disclosing the information that falls under one of the exemptions."[39] For a full discussion of such exemptions, see Chapter 13, Protection of Privacy.

Frivolous or Vexatious Requests

In accordance with subsection 4 (1) of the legislation, "every person has a right of access to a record or part of a record in the custody or under the control of an institution" unless,

(a) the record or part of the record falls within one of the exemptions under sections 6 to 15; or

(b) the head is of the opinion on reasonable grounds that the request for access is *frivolous or vexatious*.

In addition, section 5.1 of the general regulation to the Act provides as follows:

A head of an institution that receives a request for access to a record or personal information shall include that the request is frivolous or vexatious if,

(a) the head is of the opinion on reasonable grounds that the request is part of a *pattern of conduct* that amounts

---

37 *Ibid.*, ss. 20 and 21.

38 *Ibid.*, ss. 19 (a) and (b). See also s. 23 as to a copy of the record.

39 *Ibid.*, s. 4 (2).

to an abuse of the right of access or would interfere with the operations of the institution; or

(b) the head is of the opinion on reasonable grounds that the request is made in *bad faith* or for a purpose other than to obtain access.[40]

Furthermore, section 20.1 of the Act sets out the written notice that must be given by a head who has refused to grant access to a record or part of a record because he or she is of the opinion that the request is frivolous or vexatious. As such, the notice given shall include:

(a) that the request is refused because the head is of the opinion that the request is frivolous or vexatious;

(b) the reasons for which the head is of the opinion that the request is frivolous or vexatious; and

(c) that the person who made the request may appeal to the commissioner under subsection 39 (1) for a review of the decision.

In Ontario, the *Corporate Freedom of Information and Privacy Office Manual* provides the following insightful comments with respect to frivolous or vexatious requests:

Under the regulations, a frivolous or vexatious request occurs where the request is part of a pattern of conduct that amounts to an abuse of the right of access or where responding to the request would interfere with the operations of the institution. Examples of the meaning of "abuse" in the legal context include:

- proceedings instituted without any reasonable ground;
- proceedings whose purpose is not legitimate, but is rather designed to harass, or to accomplish some other objective unrelated to the process being used;
- situations where a process is used more than once, for the purpose of revisiting an issue previously addressed.

In addition, the regulations provide that a request meets the definition of frivolous or vexatious if it is made in bad faith. Bad faith

---

[40] R.R.O. 1990, Regulation 823, amended to O.Reg. 480/97 (emphasis added).

is not simply bad judgment or negligence, but rather it implies the conscious doing of a wrong because of dishonest purpose. It contemplates a state of mind which views the access process with contempt and for the nuisance it creates, rather than a valid means of obtaining information.[41]

With respect to an allegation under clause 5.1 (a) of the regulation, the phrase "pattern of conduct" has been analyzed in light of previous cases in a 2002 decision affecting the City of Mississauga:

> In Order M-850, Assistant Commissioner Mitchinson defined the term "pattern of conduct." He stated that, for such a pattern to exist, one must find "recurring incidents of related or similar *requests* on the part of the requester (or with which the requester is connected in some material way)." He also pointed out that, in determining whether a pattern of conduct has been established, the time over which the behaviour occurs is a relevant consideration. Further, in Order P-1534, he determined that a distinction must be made between formal requests for access under the Act and informal contact between a member of the public and an institution outside the formal context of the Act. I agree with these approaches and adopt them for the purposes of this appeal.

> In Order M-947, former Adjudicator Fineberg considered whether the appellant's 14 requests submitted to the institution over an 11-month period constituted a "pattern of conduct." In that case, the appellant had submitted numerous previous requests. In determining that the city had established a pattern of conduct in the circumstances of that appeal, the former adjudicator noted that "the fact that previous requests may overlap with each other will not, on its own, establish that *these requests* are part of such a pattern" (emphasis in the original). She concluded, however, that:

>> What is most striking about the pattern of these requests is that the city has identified each of the ten parts comprising the August 7 request alone as being duplicates of previous requests. In addition, two parts of the November 10, 1995 request duplicate previous requests, and

---

41 *Corporate Freedom of Information and Privacy Office Manual*, Chapter 1, "Introduction to the Act," p. 6.

two are duplicated within this one request. Because of the application in the August 7 request, I have concluded that, by themselves, these 14 requests constitute "recurring incidents of related or similar requests" and, hence, a pattern of conduct for the purposes of clause 5.1 (a) of the regulation.[42]

With respect to a frivolous or vexatious ruling under the "bad faith" provision in clause 5.1 (b) of the regulation, a recent lengthy decision involving the Regional Municipality of Niagara is instructive in this respect:

> Under clause 5.1 (b), a request will be defined as "frivolous" or "vexatious" where the head of an institution is of the opinion, on reasonable grounds, that the request is made in bad faith, or that it was made for a purpose other than to obtain access. There are no further requirements to be met. In particular, no "pattern of conduct" is required.

The adjudicator then quoted, with approval, the reasons from an appeal involving a school board in 1998:

> In Order MO-1168-I, Adjudicator Laurel Cropley made the following findings with respect to a determination of whether a request was made in bad faith. She found that:
>
>> In Order M-864, former Assistant Commissioner Glasberg found that, in the situation where the appellant used information to assist his wife with her legal proceeding against the institution, the access request was filed for legitimate reasons. Having found that the objects of the appellant's request were genuine, and that they were not designed to harass the board, he concluded:
>>
>>> I find that the appellant filed his access requests for a legitimate, as opposed to a dishonest, purpose and that he was not operating with an obvious secret design or ill will.

---

42 *City of Mississauga*, Order MO-1519 (February 28, 2002), at pp. 13-14.

With these comments in mind, I have considered the board's representations. I will begin by saying that I am not persuaded that the board has demonstrated that the appellant's request was made in "bad faith." The Act provides a legislative scheme for the public to seek access to government-held information. In doing so, the Act establishes the procedures by which a party may submit a request for access and the manner in which a party may seek review of a decision of the head. It is the responsibility of the head and then the commissioner's office to apply the provisions of the Act in responding to issues relating to an access request. In my view, the fact that there is some history between the board and the appellant, or that records may, after examination, be found to fall outside the ambit of the Act, or that the appellant may have obtained access to some confidential information outside of the access process, in and of itself is an insufficient basis for finding that the appellant's request was made in bad faith. The question to ask is whether the appellant had some illegitimate objective in seeking access under the Act. I am not persuaded that because the appellant may not have "clean hands" in its dealing with the board, that its reasons for requesting the access to the records are not genuine.[43]

Appeal Procedure

A person may appeal, in writing, any decision of a head under the Act to the information and privacy commissioner if:

- the person has made a request for access to a record under subsection 17 (1);
- the person has made a request for access to personal information under subsection 37 (1);

---

43 *Regional Municipality of Niagara*, Order MO-1575 (September 30, 2002), at pp. 6-7.

- the person has made a request for correction of personal information under subsection 36 (2); or

- the "affected" person is given notice of a request under subsection 21 (1).[44]

The appeal must be made within 30 days after notice was given of the decision, accompanied by the prescribed fee. Full details of the right of an applicant to appeal to the Information and Privacy Commissioner/Ontario are set out in Part III of the Act.[45]

The commissioner may also authorize a mediator to investigate the circumstances and to try to effect a settlement of the matter under appeal.[46] If a settlement is not achieved, the commissioner shall conduct an inquiry to review the decision of the head.[47] In such circumstances, the burden of proof that the record or part falls within one of the exceptions in the Act lies with the head.[48]

Conclusions

Municipal elected members and appointed officials designated as the "head" continue to make good judgment calls concerning access to information on a daily basis. Unfortunately, these cases are not widely reported and cannot be referred to for guidance. However, the decisions made upon appeals to the information and privacy commissioner are available, both in printed copies and online, and constitute an excellent source for those seeking to better understand this important legislation.

---

44 *Municipal Freedom of Information and Protection of Privacy Act*, R.S.O. 1990, c.M.56, s. 39 (1).

45 *Ibid.*, s. 39; see also, "Code of Procedure," Information and Privacy Commissioner/Ontario (April 2002), a comprehensive set of rules concerning appeals under Ontario's privacy legislation.

46 *Ibid.*, s. 40.

47 *Ibid.*, s. 41.

48 *Ibid.*, s. 42.

Chapter 13
PROTECTION OF PRIVACY

Within government, privacy needs to be part of the foundation of new programs, rather than an add-on, said the Commissioner, stressing that there is a real need for Ontario to have a dedicated privacy champion within government itself.

In her annual report, she is urging government to appoint a chief privacy officer. "Increasingly," said Commissioner Cavoukian, "the personal information of citizens is being collected, stored and used in electronic form. The need for the government to address privacy as an issue that is distinct from security is greater than ever." She is recommending that the government appoint a senior public servant as chief privacy officer "to help ensure that its programs are designed and delivered in a manner that both protects and enhances the privacy of Ontarians." This would be a first in Canada, with the Ontario government taking the lead.

Information and Privacy Commissioner/Ontario
Press Release, June 12, 2002

For a person requesting access to information, the response will fall into one of two clearly distinguishable categories – the request is either accepted or denied. For the official discharging the responsibilities of the "head" or the Information and Privacy Commission (IPC), however, the interpretation of the legislation is far more precise. This is especially true with respect to the reason for denials, which are based on either:

- the applicability of a mandatory or discretionary exemption, explicitly provided by statute; or
- the request falling within the nebulous equation set out in Part II of the Act, which provides for protection of individual privacy.

While the head and the IPC must carefully weigh the relevance of these two factors, the difference may not always be apparent to the person making the request. It is this subtle distinction that sometimes leads to confusion. In an effort to clarify such matters, the 2001 Annual Report from the IPC provided the following insights on mandatory/discretionary exemptions in the face of a request for a general record versus a requester's own personal information:

> When a government institution receives a request for access to general records, the institution must deny access to the information if a mandatory exemption applies, but may disclose the information even if it qualifies for one or more discretionary exemptions.
>
> In contrast, when an institution receives a request for access to the requester's own personal information, it must disclose this information unless one or more discretionary exemptions apply.
>
> It is important to note that exemptions considered mandatory when requesting general records (for example, third party commercial information, cabinet records, or another individual's personal information) are discretionary when the request is for a requester's own personal information.[1]

Not surprisingly, the main exemptions under most freedom of information legislation may be classified as either:

- mandatory; or
- discretionary, being subject to a determination made by the head.

Case Law Review

In Ontario, local decisions with respect to the protection of privacy are not widely disseminated. Conversely, many rulings by the IPC are available to the general public.[2] In their detailed evaluation, these decisions clearly reflect the distinction made between an exemption and the protection of individual privacy.

The following examples provide a guide to the application of the Act by identifying those circumstances where an applicable exemption, or the protection of privacy, has been an issue. For convenience, the cases be-

---

[1] 2001 Annual Report from the Information and Privacy Commissioner/Ontario (June 2002).

[2] Copies of decisions of the commissioner may be obtained on the IPC website, www.ipc.on.ca or from Publications Ontario, 1-800-668-9938.

low are subdivided into the two categories of "mandatory" and "discretionary" exemptions that are most relevant to local government authorities.

Mandatory Exemptions

Subject to specific exceptions, Ontario's *Municipal Freedom of Information and Protection of Privacy Act* affords mandatory protection to the following records:

- confidential information received from the Government of Canada, the government of a province or territory in Canada, the government of a foreign country or state, or an agency of one of the foregoing governments;[3] and

- third party information that reveals a trade secret or scientific, technical, commercial, financial or labour relations information, supplied in confidence, implicitly or explicitly.[4]

These two mandatory exemptions, discussed below, require that the information requested be withheld in most instances.

Relations with Governments – ss. 9 (1) and 9 (2)

Subsection 9 (1) of the legislation requires that a head "shall refuse to disclose a record" if that disclosure could reasonably be expected to reveal information the institution has received "in confidence" from the following governments:

(a)   Government of Canada;

(b)   Government of Ontario, or the government of a province or territory in Canada;

(c)   government of a foreign country or state;

(d)   agency of a government referred to in either clause (a), (b) or (c) above; or

(e)   international organization of states or a body of such an organization.

---

3   *Municipal Freedom of Information and Protection of Privacy Act*, R.S.O. 1990, c. M.56, s. 9 (1).

4   *Ibid.*, s. 10 (1).

Despite this mandatory exemption, subsection 9 (2) mandates that a head "shall disclose a record to which subsection (1) applies" if the government, agency or organization from which the information was received "consents to the disclosure."

In a 1999 appeal involving the Toronto Police Services Board, a request was made for access to "all records concerning the appellant, including records related to an assault charge and investigation which took place in January of 1998." The police granted partial access to the records identified as responsive to the request. However, they relied on a number of exemptions, including the one found in clause 9 (1) (d), to deny access to other records. In addressing the appeal, the adjudicator stated that the "only issues remaining in this appeal are the application of clause 9 (1) (d) to Record 60," the latter being the Toronto Police Confidential Crown Envelope prepared for the assault charge laid against the appellant. In reviewing the legislation, the adjudicator set out the following two-part test with regard to section 9 of the *Municipal Freedom of Information and Protection of Privacy Act:*

> In order to deny access to a record under subsection 9 (1), the police must demonstrate that the disclosure of the record could reasonably be expected to reveal information which the police received from one of the governments, agencies or organizations listed in the section and that this information was received by the police in confidence.[5]

In an effort to demonstrate that it met this two-part test, the police indicated that the information on Record 60 was recorded on behalf of a Crown Attorney with the Ontario Ministry of the Attorney General. Furthermore, it was argued that there existed an expectation of confidentiality with respect to the exchange of comments, questions and/or instructions between the Crown Attorney and the police during the prosecution of this particular matter. Furthermore, the police submitted that the Ministry of the Attorney General did not consent to the disclosure of the information based on the confidential nature of the record and the expectation that the communication would remain private.

In reviewing these submissions, the adjudicator reviewed the relevant portions of the comments from the Williams Commission concerning

---

5   *Toronto Police Services Board*, Order MO-1202 (April 7, 1999).

the rationale for an exemption for information received in confidence from other governments in the provincial access to information scheme:

> It is our view that an Ontario freedom of information law should expressly exempt from access material or information obtained on this basis from another government. Failure to do so might result in the unwillingness of other governments to supply information that would be of assistance to the Government of Ontario in the conduct of public affairs. An illustration may be useful. It is possible to conceive of a situation in which environmental studies (conducted by a neighbouring province) would be of significant interest to the Government of Ontario. If the government of the neighbouring province had, for reasons of its own, determined that it would not release the information to the public, it might be unwilling to share this information with the Ontario government, unless it could be assured that access to the document could not be secured under the provisions of Ontario's freedom of information law. A study of this kind would not be protected under any of the other exemptions ... and accordingly, could only be protected on the basis of an exemption permitting the Government of Ontario to honour such understanding of confidentiality.[6]

Based on these reasons, the adjudicator was satisfied that the information was prepared or obtained for the dominant purpose of existing or reasonably contemplated litigation and with an intention that it be confidential in the course of that litigation. Ultimately, the adjudicator upheld the decision of the police not to disclose the relevant information on Record 60.

Third Party Information – ss. 10 (1) and 10 (2)

The second mandatory exemption in the *Municipal Freedom of Information and Protection of Privacy Act* relates to specific types of information that are obtained from a third party. In particular, subsection 10 (1) of the statute provides that a head "shall refuse to disclose a record that reveals a trade secret or scientific, technical, commercial, financial or labour relations information, supplied in confidence, implicitly or explicitly," if the disclosure could reasonably be expected to:

---

6 *Ibid.*

(a) prejudice significantly the competitive position or interfere significantly with the contractual or other negotiations of a person, group of persons, or organization;

(b) result in similar information no longer being supplied to the institution where it is in the public interest that similar information continue to be so supplied;

(c) result in undue loss or gain to any person, group, committee or financial institution or agency; or

(d) reveal information supplied to or the report of a conciliation officer, mediator, labour relations officer or other person appointed to resolve a labour relations dispute.

In wording almost identical to that found in subsection 9 (2) above, subsection 10 (2) also provides that a head may disclose a record if the person to whom the information relates has consented to that disclosure.

A recent example of how the IPC interprets the provisions under subsection 10 (1) of the legislation can be found in the case concerning the Regional Municipality of Peel. In that instance, the region received a request under the legislation for access to all files relating to two municipal infrastructure projects concerning sanitary trunk sewers. The records at issue consisted of a large number of invoices, payment certificates, cost breakdowns, change orders, minutes of meetings and other documents related to the sewer projects. Although the region provided access to many of the relevant records, it also denied access to other records based on a number of exemptions in the Act, including the mandatory exemption found in subsection 10 (1) related to third party information. The adjudicator confirmed that, in order for a record to qualify for exemption under clause 10 (1) (a), (b) or (c), the affected parties and/or the region would have to satisfy each component of the following three-part test:

1. The record must reveal information that is a trade secret or scientific, technical, commercial, financial or labour relations information; and

2. The information must have been supplied to the region in confidence, either implicitly or explicitly; and

3. The prospect of disclosure of the record must give rise to a reasonable expectation that one of the harms specified in (a), (b) or (c) of subsection 10 (1) will occur.

In addressing the first part of the tripartite test, the adjudicator observed that the affected parties were resisting disclosure on the basis that the records contained documents that qualified as either "financial" or "commercial" information for the purposes of subsection 10 (1). The adjudicator went on to note that those two terms have been defined in a number of previous IPC decisions in the following fashion:

> The term [financial information] refers to information relating to money and its use or distribution and must contain or refer to specific data. Examples include cost accounting methods, pricing practices, profit and loss data, overhead and operating costs.
>
> Commercial information is information which relates solely to the buying, selling or exchange of merchandise or services. The term "commercial" information can apply to both profit-making enterprises and non-profit organizations, and has equal application to both large and small enterprises.[7]

With respect to the second part of the test, the adjudicator found that, in order to establish the confidentiality component, the affected parties and/or the region must demonstrate that an expectation of confidentiality existed "at the time the records were submitted, and that this expectation was reasonable and had an objective basis." The decision goes on to note that all factors would be considered in determining whether an expectation of confidentiality was reasonable, including whether the information was:

1. Communicated to the region on the basis that it was confidential and that it was to be kept confidential.

2. Treated consistently in a manner that indicates a concern for its protection from disclosure by the affected parties prior to being communicated to the region.

3. Not otherwise disclosed or available from sources to which the public has access.

4. Prepared for a purpose which would not entail disclosure.

With respect to the two construction projects at the heart of this particular appeal, the adjudicator drew the following conclusions:

---

[7] *Region of Peel*, Final Order MO-1536-F (May 8, 2002).

I find further that, in the context of the normal practices of the construction industry, information pertaining to hourly rates and unit prices are submitted with a reasonably-held expectation that they will be treated in a confidential manner by the project managers and property owners. This finding is in keeping with a number of previous orders which have held that pricing information is generally considered to have been submitted on a confidential basis when determining whether it is properly exempt from disclosure under subsection 10 (1) or its provincial equivalent.[8]

Finally, in order to meet the third component of this tripartite test, the affected parties and/or the region must demonstrate that one or more of the harms enumerated in subsection 10 (1) could reasonably be expected to result from the disclosure of the records. In upholding the region's decision to deny access to certain pricing information contained in the records, the adjudicator found as follows:

In my view, the affected party has provided me with the kind of detailed and convincing evidence required to establish its position that harm to its competitive position could reasonably be expected to result from the disclosure of the pricing information contained in the records. The affected parties operate in a competitive industry where pricing practices are closely guarded and are not generally publicly disclosed. In my view, the third part of the test under subsection 10 (1) has been satisfied with respect to the pricing information contained in the invoices reflected in [various specific records].

Discretionary Exemptions

In contrast to the two mandatory provisions discussed above, and subject to specific exceptions and explicit evaluation criteria, the head is also granted discretionary authority under the statute and may refuse to disclose a record involving:

- a draft by-law or draft private bill;[9]

---

8   *Ibid.*

9   *Municipal Freedom of Information and Protection of Privacy Act*, R.S.O. 1990, c. M.56, s. 6 (1) (a).

- a record that reveals the substance of a closed meeting, "if the statute authorizes holding that meeting in the absence of the public;"[10]
- advice or recommendations of an officer or employee of an institution or a consultant retained by an institution;[11]
- a law enforcement matter;[12]
- matters related to proceedings under the *Remedies for Organized Crime and Other Unlawful Activities Act, 2001*, as well as those pursuant to the *Prohibiting Profiting from Recounting Crimes Act, 2002;*.[13]
- economic and other interests;[14]
- solicitor-client privilege;[15]
- danger to safety or health;[16] and
- information already published or available, or soon to be published.[17]

In its 2001 Annual Report, IPC addressed a growing concern with respect to this authority by suggesting that the "use of discretionary exemptions should never be automatic." The report emphasized that "just because a record or information satisfies the requirements of [a discretionary] exemption, that does not necessarily mean the record cannot be disclosed." The IPC further suggested that institutions must take the additional steps of assessing the particular circumstances surrounding the request and the record prior to deciding if it should be disclosed. The report summarized the basic criteria surrounding a proper and improper exercise of discretion in the following terms:

---

10 *Ibid.*, s. 6 (1) (b).
11 *Ibid.*,s. 7 (1).
12 *Ibid.*,s. 8 (1).
13 *Ibid.*,s. 8.1.
14 *Ibid.*,s. 11.
15 *Ibid.*,s. 12.
16 *Ibid.*,s. 13.
17 *Ibid.*,s. 15.

What is a proper exercise of discretion? In making a decision in response to an access request, institutions must consider the individual circumstances of the request, including factors personal to the requester, while also ensuring that decisions regarding access conform to the policies and provisions of the Acts. While the same factors are not relevant in every circumstance, it is important that all factors that are relevant receive careful consideration.

What is an improper exercise of discretion? It is improper for an institution to adopt a fixed rule or policy and apply it in all situations. To do so would constitute a fettering of discretion and would represent non-compliance with the institution's statutory obligations. Individual circumstances must be considered.[18]

Set out below are some cases that have interpreted the various discretionary exemptions to disclosure within the local government context in Ontario.

Draft By-laws or Draft Private Bills – ss. 6 (1) (a) and 6 (2) (a)

Clause 6 (1) (a) of the statute provides a head with the discretion to refuse to disclose a record "that contains a draft of a by-law or a draft of a private bill." Conversely, clause 6 (2) (a) states that "despite subsection (1), a head shall not refuse to disclose a record if the draft has been considered in a meeting open to the public." In a recent decision, an adjudicator made the following general comments with respect to the exemption regarding draft by-laws:

> In my view, the legislature's intention in including the exemption in clause 6 (1) (a) is to protect a particular type of record, a draft by-law, which relates to the "works in progress" of the city's law-making powers. In my view, the rationale for this exemption is to enable the city to fulfill its law-making mandate unencumbered. Where the city chooses to consider drafts in a public forum, or where it reaches a point at which public debate is desirable or required, the legislation dictates that confidentiality of the draft

---

[18] 2001 Annual Report from the Information and Privacy Commissioner/Ontario (June 2002) at p. 10.

by-law is lost, but only if the particular draft has been considered at a meeting open to the public.[19]

In an earlier decision, a municipality received a request from a former employee for copies of records pertaining to the position of city manager and, in particular, to a named individual. In denying access with respect to some of these records, the city relied upon the discretionary exemptions found in clause 6 (1) (a) of the Act. At appeal, the adjudicator quickly found that, as the drafts of the by-law to create the position of city manager were never considered at an open meeting, he deemed them to be exempt under this provision. However, with respect to other documents related to that by-law, he found in favour of the appellant:

> Records 35 and 43 do not contain drafts of the by-law per se; rather, they contain comments made by the city clerk pertaining to the draft by-law.
>
> With respect to these records, the city's position is that, if the city is not required to release a draft by-law, then it is not required to release the comments made by staff on the by-law. It maintains that to do so would indirectly disclose the contents of the by-law or some of its provisions. The city raised this argument in Appeal No. M9400197, which was resolved by Order M394. In that order, Inquiry Officer Anita Fineberg stated:
>
> > The wording of the draft by-law exemption in clause 6 (1) (a) may be usefully contrasted with that of the "closed meeting" exemption in clause 6 (1) (b) which states:
> >
> > > A head may refuse to disclose a record that reveals the substance of deliberations of a meeting of a council, board, commission or other body or a committee of one of them, if a statute authorizes holding that meeting in the absence of the public.
> >
> > ...
> >
> > In ... these instances, the wording of the exemption [in clause 6 (1) (b)], by the inclusion of the word "reveal," is broader than that in clause 6 (1) (a) of the Act. In my view, the use of the term "reveal" means that the exemp-

---

19 *City of Oshawa*, Order MO-1374 (December 7, 2000).

tion in which it appears will apply to the two records from which accurate inferences can be drawn about the types of information described in these sections. By contrast, the wording of clause 6 (1) (a) applies to records which actually contain a draft by-law.

In my view, subclause 1 (a) (ii) of the Act is also a relevant factor in the interpretation of the clause 6 (1) (a) exemption. That section sets out one of the main purposes of the Act and states that necessary exemptions from the right of access should be limited and specific. Accordingly, I find that the wording of the draft by-law exemption is not broad enough to bear the meaning which the city would ascribe to it. Rather, I am of the view that it only applies to records which actually contain the draft by-law.

I agree with Inquiry Officer Fineberg's analysis. Accordingly, I find that Records 35 and 43 are not exempt under clause 6 (1) (a).[20]

In light of these decisions, it seems clear that the scope of records that may be exempt from disclosure under clause 6 (1) (a) is rather narrow and limited to those that actually contain a draft by-law or private bill.

Record that Reveals Substance of Closed Meeting – ss. 6 (1) (b) and 6 (2) (b)

As noted earlier, clause 6 (1) (b), as well as clause 6 (2) (b) and (c) of the Act, provide:

6 (1)   A head may refuse to disclose a record,

...

(b)   that reveals the substance of deliberations of a meeting of a council, board, commission or other body or a committee of one of them if a statute authorizes holding that meeting in the absence of the public.

...

---

20   *City of Oshawa,* Order M-521 (May 10, 1995).

6 (2)   Despite subsection (1), a head shall not refuse under subsection (1) to disclose a record if,

...

(b)   in the case of a record under clause (1) (b), the subject-matter of the deliberations has been considered in a meeting open to the public; or

(c)   the record is more than twenty years old.

In order for a municipal council or local board to qualify for an exemption under clause 6 (1) (b), they must be able to establish that:

- a meeting of a council, board, commission or other body or a committee of one of them took place; and
- a statute authorizes the holding of this meeting in the absence of the public; and
- disclosure of the record at issue would reveal the actual substance of the deliberations of this meeting.

With respect to the first two parts of this test, a local government body must present clear and tangible evidence that the meeting, or a portion of the meeting, took place in the absence of the public and that a statute authorized such a closed session to occur. In the context of a municipal council meeting, such evidence would likely include a reference to the relevant provisions of the *Municipal Act, 2001*, as well as the actual resolution moved and voted upon to close the meeting pursuant to subsection 239 (4). In addition, reliance would be had on the official minutes reflecting the council's compliance with this statutory procedure.[21] However, various IPC decisions reveal a number of problems that can arise in attempting to meet these two components of the test, such as:

- The fact that the agenda of a meeting indicated that certain matters were "private" does not mean that they were dealt with in the absence of the public.

---

21   *Municipal Act, 2001*, S.O. 2001, c. 25, s. 239; other statutory examples include: subsection 35 (4) of the *Police Services Act*, R.S.O. 1990, c. P.15; subsection 807 (2) of the *Education Act*, R.S.O. 1990, c. E.2; and subsection 16.1 (4) of the *Public Libraries Act*, R.S.O. 1990, c. P.44.

- The fact that records were stamped *in camera* was not sufficient to establish that the matters were dealt with in the absence of the public.

- A general council resolution under the *Municipal Act* to discuss "legal and property matters" that failed to describe "the general nature of the matter" meant that the municipality had not established that it was authorized by the statute to hold a closed meeting.

In determining the third and final component of the three-part test of the closed meeting exemption, various decisions have discussed and attempted to interpret the phrase "that disclosure of the record at issue would reveal the actual substance of the deliberations of the meeting." In Order M-184, former Assistant Commissioner Irwin Glasberg made the following comments with respect to the word "deliberations:"

> In order for me to address the third part of the test (the disclosure of the record at issue would reveal the actual substance of deliberations of this meeting), I will need to define the term "deliberations." In my view, deliberations in the context of section 6 (1) (b) refer to discussions which were conducted with a view towards making a decision. Having carefully reviewed the contents of the minutes of settlement, I am satisfied that the disclosure of this document would reveal the actual substance of the discussions conducted by the Board, hence its deliberations, or would permit the drawing of accurate inferences about the substance of those discussions. On this basis, I find that the institution has established that the third part of the clause 6 (1) (b) test applies in this case.[22]

Shortly thereafter, in Order M-196, former Assistant Commissioner Glasberg expanded on his interpretation of clause 6 (1) (b) by reviewing the word "substance:"

> The *Concise Oxford Dictionary, 8th Edition*, defines "substance" as the "theme or subject" of a thing. Having reviewed the contents of the agreement and the representations provided to me, it is my view that the "theme or subject" of the *in camera* meeting was

---

22 *Leeds and Grenville County Board of Education*, Order M-184 (September 10, 1993).

whether the terms of the retirement agreement were appropriate and whether they should be endorsed.[23]

In a 1999 appeal involving the deliberations of a public utilities commission meeting in closed session, the adjudicator cited the two previous cases in determining whether the third test under clause 6(1)(b) had been met:

> "Substance" has been defined in previous orders as "the 'theme or subject' of a thing" (Order M-196). "Deliberations" has been interpreted as meaning "... discussions which were conducted with a view towards making a decision" (Order M-184). I adopt these interpretations for the purposes of this appeal. I find that the records contain the very information which was discussed during the commission's deliberations with respect to the matters raised by the appellant and that their disclosure would reveal the substance of deliberations of the commission during these meetings. Therefore, I find that all three parts of the clause 6(1)(b) test have been met.[24]

In order to meet the last component of the three-part test, a recent decision involving the Municipality of Bayham is instructive with respect to the IPC's interpretation of the discretionary exemption under subsection 6(1)(b) of the legislation. In that case, the municipality received a request for access to a copy of a "confidential staff report" dated August 3, 1999. The municipality denied access to the record, claiming the application of section 6 of the Act and suggesting that reports appropriately considered by the municipal council in closed session pursuant to the *Municipal Act* remained confidential. In reviewing the facts and law with respect to the interpretation of section 6, the adjudicator made the following observations:

> The appellant concedes that Parts 1 and 2 of the test set out above have been satisfied by the municipality. She takes issue, however, with the municipality's assertion that the disclosure of the record would reveal the substance of council's deliberations. She submits that:

---

23 *City of Kingston*, Order M-196 (October 1, 1993).
24 *Strathroy Public Utilities Commission*, Order MO-1230 (August 19, 1999).

> ... the representations of the municipality state that the tax clerk's report is a chronological account of financial transactions and exchanges concerning my property taxes and that "these are the facts on which the council actually deliberated." If that is so, I would respectfully ask the municipality why my husband and I attended the meeting at all. I submit that we requested and attended the meeting in order to inform council of our situation of financial hardship and disability and request relief, and that the actual substance of the council's deliberations was whether or not any relief was possible given our circumstances. Information regarding our current financial and medical problems was provided in person by myself and my husband, as well as in my written presentation, while the tax clerk's report dealt with "the actions of staff to deal with problems presented by the individuals." I therefore conclude that the disclosure of the report would not reveal the actual substance of council's deliberations regarding our request for relief. In addition, while the tax clerk's report provided the council with background information regarding payment of my taxes, and staff action to collect taxes, this information would not be revealed by disclosure of the report, as it was previously known to me and referred to in my presentation.
>
> In my view, based on the reading of the record, it contains information whose disclosure would reveal precisely the substance of council's deliberations. The record addresses the circumstances surrounding the appellant's tax arrears and the steps taken by the appellant and her husband to bring them up to date. The record also addresses specifically and in detail the appellant's request for relief and the position taken by the municipality in response. This is the substance of what council was being asked to decide upon, how the municipality ought to respond to the appellant's request for relief. In my view, the disclosure of the record would reveal the substance of council's deliberations and the record qualifies for exemption under clause 6 (1) (b).[25]

---

25 *Municipality of Bayham*, Order MO-1487 (November 20, 2001).

Chapter 13
PROTECTION OF PRIVACY

Where a municipality or local board has been successful in meeting all of the components of the three-part test under clause 6 (1) (b), it remains open to an appellant to prove that the mandatory exception in clause 6 (2) (b) applies to override this discretionary exemption. Thus, the appellant can introduce evidence to show that the "subject-matter of the deliberations" was considered at a meeting open to the public. For example, in a 1996 case, an adjudicator ruled as follows with respect to an appellant's lack of evidence in substantiating a claim under clause 6 (2) (b) of the Act:

> In its representations, the appellant acknowledges that at least one meeting on the subject was held by the committee of the whole council, but argues that other meetings between city officials and the fire chief may also have been held and that these meetings may not have been *in camera.*
>
> In my view, the appellant has provided no evidence to support this assertion, and it is, therefore, not sufficient to attract the exception in clause 6 (2) (b). Accordingly, I find that clause 6 (2) (b) does not apply.[26]

This same argument was set out in a similar fashion by the adjudicator in the Municipality of Bayham case cited above:

> With respect to the possible application of the exception in clause 6 (2) (b), the municipality states that:
>
>> The record in this case was, as noted above, not considered at a meeting open to the public. The meeting was not open to the public for the reasons outlined above.
>
> In its reply submissions, the municipality confirms that the appellant and her husband were not present at the *in camera* portion of the council meeting when council actually discussed the subject-matter of the record. The appellant and the municipality agree that the appellant and her husband were "excused" from this portion of the council meeting. As a result, I find that the part of the meeting at which the record at issue was discussed was not

---

26 *City of Orillia*, Interim Order M-806 (July 10, 1996).

"open to the public" and that the exception in clause 6 (2) (b) has no application in the present circumstances.[27]

In essence, a municipality's reliance on the discretionary exemption to withhold the substance of *in camera* deliberations (s. 6 (1) (b)) may be overridden if the subject-matter is subsequently considered at an open council meeting (s. 6 (2) (b)). However, this unique application begs the following important question. If a municipal council must exercise its powers by a resolution or by-law (usually passed during an open meeting), how does it adhere to this statutory requirement without triggering the disclosure override provision in clause 6 (2) (b) of the statute? In an investigation report involving the Peterborough County Board of Education, it was noted that when a local board puts forward a public resolution dealing with the recommendation of a committee that met in closed session, the resolution "need only refer to the recommendation of the committee (for example, by number and/or date), and need not contain any personal information." In a subsequent appeal involving this same board of education, a resolution entitled "Motion 7.1.3 Personnel Issue," which recommended "that the personnel issue considered in the committee of the whole board on Thursday, August 25, 1994 be approved," was challenged by an appellant who believed that there was no reason to "truncate the description of the motion in such an extreme fashion." When the board referred to the investigation report, the adjudicator stated:

> While the investigation report does indicate that a public resolution may refer to a committee resolution by number and date only, this represents only one of several approaches which a board can take to describe the subject-matter discussed in an *in camera* meeting. Moreover, there is nothing contained in this report which precludes an institution from describing the subject-matter of such a meeting in greater detail provided that personal information regarding an identifiable individual is not disclosed.
>
> In my view and consistent with the tenets of open government, it is desirable for public motions to contain as much information as possible without negating the legitimate and legislatively sanc-

---

[27] *Municipality of Bayham,* Order MO-1487 (November 20, 2001).

Chapter 13
PROTECTION OF PRIVACY

tioned reasons for considering certain matters in the absence of the public.[28]

A 1994 decision involving the City of North York provided further insight into overcoming such concerns:

> In his representations, the appellant states that the North York city council, in a public meeting held immediately following the *in camera* meeting of its committee of the whole on May 29, 1992, adopted the recommendations of the committee to approve the management agreement.
>
> In its representations, the city argues that the council simply adopted, without discussion, the recommendation of the committee of the whole. In Order M-241, I determined that the adoption without discussion by council at a public meeting of a report which was discussed at an earlier *in camera* meeting could not be characterized as the consideration of the subject-matter of the *in camera* deliberations. In the circumstances of this appeal, I similarly conclude that the subject-matter of the deliberations of the *in camera* meeting were not considered in the open council meeting within the meaning of clause 6 (2) (b). Accordingly, I find that the exception provided by this section has no application to the management agreement.[29]

Finally, at least one decision has determined that media coverage of a matter considered *in camera* does not necessarily trigger the clause 6 (2) (b) override:

> The appellant points out that the city's decision to retain outside consultants to investigate the possible leak of confidential documents was covered by the local media. The appellant submits that because this information is in the public arena, the exception to clause 6 (2) (b) applies and the investigation report should not be afforded the protection of clause 6 (1) (b). A copy of the newspaper article is included with the appellant's representations. In my view, the fact that this information was reported by the press has no bearing on the information contained in the investigation report. I find that there is no evidence that the subject-matter of the

---

28 *Peterborough County Board of Education*, Order M-481 (revised), (March 7, 1995).
29 *City of North York*, Order M-392 (September 30, 1994).

deliberations was considered at a council meeting open to the public. In my view, the exception in clause 6 (2) (b) does not apply in the circumstances of this appeal.[30]

These decisions seem to suggest a distinction between disclosure of the mere results of the *in camera* deliberations and the "subject-matter" of the closed session. In effect, the reporting of a particular decision made at a closed meeting does not necessarily equate to the deliberations of the subject-matter being considered in an open meeting.

Advice/Recommendations of Officer, Employee or Consultant – s. 7

Subsection 7 (1) of the legislation provides the head with the discretion to refuse access to a record if that disclosure "would reveal advice or recommendations of an officer or employee of an institution or a consultant retained by an institution." Pursuant to that provision, the interpretation often given to the words "officers" or "employees" include those persons who work for an institution or who perform duties under a contract of employment. However, the advice or recommendations of an officer or employee of another institution cannot be exempted under this provision, nor can those of a volunteer.

In addition, the assistant commissioner recently outlined the following definitions for the key terms, "advice" or "recommendations" in this exemption:

> A number of previous orders have established that advice or recommendations for the purpose of subsection 7 (1) must contain more than mere information. To qualify as "advice" or "recommendations," the information contained in a report must relate to a suggested course of action that will ultimately be accepted or rejected by its recipient during the deliberative process ... Information in records that would reveal the advice or recommendations is also exempt from disclosure under subsection 7 (1) of the Act.[31]

Despite this discretion, subsection 7 (2) prohibits a head from refusing to disclose a record under subsection 7 (1) that contains:

    (a) factual material;

---

30 *City of North York*, Order M-611 (October 13, 1995).
31 *Town of Amherstburg*, Order MO-1611 (February 12, 2003).

(b) a statistical survey;

(c) a report by a valuator;

(d) an environmental impact statement or similar record;

(e) a report or study on the performance or efficiency of an institution;

(f) a feasibility study or other technical study, including a cost estimate, relating to a policy or project of an institution;

(g) a report containing the results of field research undertaken before the formulation of a policy proposal;

(h) a final plan or proposal to change a program of an institution, or for the establishment of a new program, including a budgetary estimate for the program;

(i) a report of a committee or similar body within an institution, which has been established for the purpose of preparing a report on a particular topic;

(j) a report of a body which is attached to an institution and which has been established for the purpose of undertaking inquiries and making reports or recommendations to the institution;

(k) the reasons for a final decision, order or ruling of an officer or an employee of the institution made during or at the conclusion of the exercise of discretionary power conferred by or under an enactment or scheme administered by the institution.

In a recent decision involving the Town of Amherstburg, Assistant Commissioner Tom Mitchinson provided the following review with respect to the municipality's reliance on subsection 7 (1) of the Act to deny access to the request for a "visioning statement" prepared by the council in the spring of 2001:

> In Order 94, former Commissioner Sidney B. Linden commented on the purpose and scope of the subsection 13 (1) exemption in the provincial *Freedom of Information and Protection of Privacy Act*, which is equivalent to subsection 7 (1) in the municipal Act. He stated that it "... purports to protect the free flow of advice and

recommendations within the deliberative process of government decision-making and policy making." Put another way, the purpose of the exemption is to ensure that:

> Persons employed in the public service are able to advise and make recommendations freely and frankly, and to preserve the head's ability to take actions and make decisions without unfair pressure [Orders 24, P-1363 and P-1690].[32]

Furthermore, subsection 7 (3) states that a head "shall not refuse under subsection (1) to disclose a record if the record is more than twenty years old."

Law Enforcement – s. 8

Section 8 of the *Municipal Freedom of Information and Protection of Privacy Act* provides a discretionary exemption for those records relating to police and by-law enforcement investigations, as well as certain other investigative and protective functions. Section 2 of the legislation defines "law enforcement" to mean "policing," as well as "investigations or inspections that lead or could lead to proceedings in a court or tribunal if a penalty or sanction could be imposed in those proceedings, as well as the conduct of such proceedings." Pursuant to such a broad definition, it is likely that the enforcement of various municipal by-laws (eg. a property standards by-law or no-smoking by-law) would likely constitute a law enforcement activity under this definition. The structure to section 8 can be summarized as follows:

- provides an exemption where disclosure could reasonably be expected to interfere with law enforcement, as well as certain other activities;
- exempts certain types of law enforcement records;
- provides that a head may refuse to confirm or deny the existence of records in either subsection 8 (1) or subsection 8 (2); and
- sets out in subsections 8 (4) and 8 (5) various exceptions to the above-noted exemption.

---

32 *Town of Amherstburg*, Order MO-1611 (February 12, 2003).

In a recent case, the Gananoque Police Service denied access to a number of records in a particular request, including relying upon clause 8 (1) (a), whereby the disclosure could reasonably be expected to "interfere with a law enforcement matter." In addressing this exemption, Assistant Commissioner Tom Mitchenson provided the following comments concerning the "ongoing" nature of a "law enforcement matter" under this particular provision:

> In order for a record to meet the requirements of this section, the matter to which the record relates must first satisfy the definition of the term "law enforcement" found in subsection 2 (1) of the Act. This definition includes "policing," which I find was clearly the type of activity undertaken by the police in the context of creating the records at issue in this appeal.
>
> The purpose of the exemption contained in clause 8 (1) (a) is to provide an institution with the discretion to refuse access to records in circumstances where disclosure of the records could reasonably be expected to interfere with an ongoing law enforcement matter. The institution bears the onus of providing evidence to substantiate first, that a law enforcement matter is ongoing and second, that disclosure of the records could reasonably be expected to interfere with the matter.[33]

Reference may also be had to another discretionary exemption that is set out at clause 8 (1) (d) of the legislation, which provides that a head may refuse to disclose a record if it could reasonably be expected to "disclose the identity of a confidential source of information in respect of a law enforcement matter, or disclose information furnished only by the confidential source." This unique provision was the subject of an early appeal involving the Town of Whitby in 1993. In that case, the municipality had received a request under the legislation for information relating to complaints it had received about the requester's property. Ultimately, the town denied access to some of the information pursuant to clause 8 (1) (d) of the Act. Upon appeal, former Assistant Commissioner Irwin Glasberg described one of the two issues on appeal as follows: "whether the discretionary exemption provided by clause 8 (1) (d) of the Act applies to the name of the councillor, which was withheld by the town." After determining that the municipality's by-law enforcement process

---

33 *Gananoque Police Service*, Order MO-1561 (August 8, 2002).

qualified as "law enforcement" under the Act, the assistant commissioner provided the following outline of this particular discretionary exemption:

> I must determine whether a municipal councillor may be considered a confidential source of information for the purposes of clause 8 (1) (d) of the Act. In its representations, the town deals with this issue in the following fashion:
>
>> [It is important to provide] both members of council and their constituents with some measure of confidentiality to enable councillors to effectively perform their representative role. Almost every councillor has a caseload of citizen inquiries which require investigation and, where possible, resolution. Such inquiries can be screened and redirected to appropriate agencies, but most citizens want the personal attention of their elected representative and in many cases do not want their identity disclosed. To deal effectively with such inquiries, members of council must be able to act with the knowledge and assurance that they are not leaving themselves open to personal attack, criticism and complaint each and every time they act in good faith and [in] the public interest on behalf of a constituent ...
>
> Based on the wording of clause 8 (1) (d) of the Act, I accept that a confidential source of information could include a municipal councillor. Furthermore, on the facts of this case, I find that the councillor, although he received information from other individuals about the requester's property, was the actual source of the complaint provided to the town.[34]

Having made this determination, the assistant commissioner then went on to determine whether or not the release of the councillor's name would disclose the identity of a confidential source of information:

> In its presentations, the town has indicated that, since 1982, it has maintained a consistent policy of keeping the names of complainants, including members of council, confidential with respect to by-law enforcement matters.

---

34 *The Corporation of the Town of Whitby*, Order M-147 (June 17, 1993).

I have carefully reviewed the record and the representations provided by the parties. Based principally on the town's stated policy of protecting the names of complainants in by-law enforcement cases, I find that, when the councillor provided the information to town officials, there was a reasonable expectation that councillor's identity would be kept confidential. It follows, therefore, that the disclosure of the councillor's name would reveal a confidential source such that the town is entitled to rely on clause 8 (1) (d) of the Act as a basis for not releasing this information.

Economic and Other Interests – s. 11

Section 11 of the *Municipal Freedom of Information and Protection of Privacy Act* provides a discretionary exemption for certain proprietary information of institutions, as well as the premature disclosure of some plans or negotiating strategies. Briefly, clauses 11 (a) through (g) set out the types of information and specific circumstances covered by this exemption. A decision involving the City of Mississauga is useful in appreciating how the IPC interprets the various clauses found in section 11. In this particular case, the requester/appellant had sought access to information relating to whether the companies providing bus shelter advertising and bus advertising to the municipality had been allowed, by the city, to renegotiate the "guaranteed amount" in their contracts. In denying this request, the city relied upon clauses 11 (a), (c) and (d), which provide as follows:

11. A head may refuse to disclose a record that contains,

    (a)   trade secrets or financial, commercial, scientific or technical information that belongs to an institution and has monetary value or potential monetary value;

    ...

    (c)   information whose disclosure could reasonably be expected to prejudice the economic interests of an institution or the competitive position of an institution;

    (d)   information whose disclosure could reasonably be expected to be injurious to the financial interests of an institution.

After noting that clauses 11 (c) and (d) "take into consideration the consequences that would result to an institution if such a record were released," the adjudicator went on to note that these two provisions contrast with subsection 11 (a), "which is concerned with the type of record, rather than the consequences of disclosure."

In analyzing the exemption under subsection 11(a), the adjudicator found that the municipality must establish that the information:

1. is a trade secret or financial, commercial, scientific or technical information; and
2. belongs to an institution; and
3. has monetary value or potential monetary value.

Upon determining that the record in that case qualified as both financial and commercial information, the adjudicator found that the city had satisfied the first part of the tripartite test under clause 11 (a). Turning to the remaining two components of the test, the adjudicator commented as follows on the contractual nature of the record:

> In order for the city to meet Parts 2 and 3 of the test under clause 11 (a), the city needs to establish that the contract belongs to the city and has monetary value. Adjudicator Liang in Order MO-1462 recently addressed the application of clause 11 (a) to a contract. In that order, Adjudicator Liang was asked to decide whether a contract for land ambulance services between an institution and a successful bidder should be disclosed to the requester. In that case, Adjudicator Liang made the following finding in respect of the contract and Parts 2 and 3 of the test:
>
> > Applying the above principles to the facts of this appeal, I find that the information in Record 3 [the contract] does not qualify either as information "having monetary value," or the type of information which has been found to "belong to" an institution. The representations of the county described what it believes would be the harmful consequences of releasing this information, but do not establish that the information has inherent value, resulting for instance from the expenditure of money or the application of skill and effort to develop the information.
> >
> > I conclude, therefore, that Record 3 [the contract] does not qualify for exemption under clause 11 (a) of the Act.
>
> In my view, Adjudicator Liang's reasoning applies to the facts of this appeal. The city has failed to provide adequate evidence and

argument for me to conclude that the information contained in the record either belongs to it or qualifies as information that has monetary or potential monetary value. Accordingly, the city does not meet Part 2 of the test under section 11 (a) and I conclude that section 11 (a) has no application to the record.[35]

In addressing the city's reliance upon clauses 11 (c) and 11 (d), the adjudicator found that "the city must provide detailed and convincing evidence sufficient to establish a reasonable expectation of probable harm as described in these sections resulting from disclosure of the record." Ultimately, the adjudicator ruled that he was not satisfied that disclosure of the record in question could reasonably be expected to prejudice the municipality's economic interests or be injurious to its financial or economic interests. Therefore, he ruled that both clauses 11 (c) and 11 (d) did not apply in the circumstances of that appeal.

Solicitor-Client Privilege – s. 12

Section 12 of the legislation provides that a head "may refuse to disclose a record that is subject to solicitor-client privilege or that was prepared by or for counsel employed or retained by an institution for use in giving legal advice or in contemplation of or for use in litigation." Various IPC decisions have confirmed that this provision consists of two branches which provide an institution with the discretion to refuse to disclose:

1. A record that is subject to common law solicitor-client privilege; and

2. A record that was prepared by or for counsel employed or retained by an institution for use in giving legal advice or in contemplation of or for use in litigation.

In another case involving the City of London, the municipality received a request for a host of records relating to the requests for proposal (RFPs) for a particular infrastructure project. In relying on the solicitor-client privilege section to deny access to some records, the adjudicator described this particular privilege in the following fashion:

> Solicitor-client communication privilege protects direct communications of a confidential nature between a solicitor-client, or their agents or employees, made for the purpose of obtaining pro-

---

35 *City of Mississauga*, Order MO-1553 (June 28, 2002).

fessional legal advice. The rationale for this privilege is to ensure that a client may confide in his or her lawyer on a legal matter without reservation [Order P-1551].[36]

In upholding the city's decision on solicitor-client communication privilege, the adjudicator also noted that this privilege "has been found to apply to the legal advisor's working papers directly related to seeking, formulating or giving legal advice."

Recently, the Ontario Court of Appeal had an opportunity to review the provincial *Freedom of Information and Protection of Privacy Act* with respect to the "litigation privilege" found in the second branch of this discretionary exemption. In that instance, the requester had made an application under the provincial legislation for disclosure of materials that had originally been the subject of a prosecution and were, at that time, the subject of private litigation. The Act provided that one could refuse the disclosure of a record that was subject to solicitor-client privilege or was prepared by or for Crown counsel for use in giving legal advice or in contemplation of litigation. In light of the legislative history of this particular clause, the IPC held that common law rules for solicitor-client privilege applied to records prepared for, or by, provincial Crown counsel. At common law, the litigation privilege no longer protected documents collected for a solicitor's brief after the litigation has ended. In this case, the inquiry officer found that the prosecutor's file was no longer exempt after the end of the prosecution based on the litigation privilege. Upon review by the Divisional Court, it held that the inquiry officer's decision was "unreasonable," thereby rejecting the IPC's approach because the common law principles were not expressly incorporated into the branch of the exemption covering Crown counsel records. Upon further appeal to the Ontario Court of Appeal, the court unanimously upheld the decision of the Divisional Court and dismissed the appeal.[37]

Danger to Safety or Health – s. 13

Section 13 of the statute provides that a head may refuse to disclose a record "whose disclosure could reasonably be expected to seriously threaten the safety or health of an individual." The phrase "could rea-

---

36 *The Corporation of the City of London*, Order MO-1609 (January 31, 2003).
37 *Attorney General of Ontario v. Holly Big Canoe, Inquiry Officer; James Doe, Requester* (2002), 62 O.R. (3d) 167 (C.A.); affirming [2001] O.J. No. 4876 (Div. Ct.).

Chapter 13
PROTECTION OF PRIVACY

sonably be expected to" appears not only in section 13, but in several other exemptions under the *Municipal Freedom of Information and Protection of Privacy Act,* dealing with a wide variety of anticipated harms. In order to establish that the particular harm in question "could reasonably be expected to" result from the disclosure of a record, the party with the burden of proof must provide detailed and convincing evidence to establish a "reasonable expectation of probable harm." However, in a recent decision of the Ontario Court of Appeal, the court drew a distinction between the requirements for establishing "health or safety" harms under the provincial equivalents to clause 8 (1) (e) and section 13, and those harms under other exemptions in the legislation. The appellate court stated as follows:

> The expectation of harm must be reasonable, but it need not be probable. Section [8 (1) (e)] requires a determination of whether there is a reasonable basis for concluding that disclosure could be expected to endanger the life or physical safety of a person. In other words, the party resisting disclosure must demonstrate that the reason for resisting disclosure is not a frivolous or exaggerated expectation of endangerment to safety. Similarly, [section 13] calls for a demonstration that disclosure could reasonably be expected to seriously threaten the safety or health of an individual, as opposed to there being a groundless or exaggerated expectation of a threat to safety. Introducing the element of probability in this assessment is not appropriate, considering the interests that are at stake, particularly the very significant interest of bodily integrity. It is difficult, if not impossible, to establish as a matter or probabilities that a person's life or safety will be endangered by the release of a potentially inflammatory record. Where there is a reasonable basis for believing that a person's safety will be endangered by disclosing a record, the holder of that record properly invokes [sections 8 (1) (e) and 13] to refuse disclosure.[38]

Despite this decision, one adjudicator has subsequently reiterated that the party with the burden of proof under section 13 must still provide "detailed and convincing evidence" of a reasonable expectation of harm to discharge its burden. That adjudicator went on to note that this evidence "must demonstrate that there is a reasonable basis for believing

---

38 *Ontario (Minister of Labour) v. Big Canoe,* [1999] O.J. No. 4560 (C.A.), affirming (June 2, 1998), Toronto Doc. 28/98 (Div. Ct.), at p. 6.

that endangerment could be expected to result from disclosure or, in other words, that the reasons for resisting disclosure are not frivolous or exaggerated."[39]

In another decision involving the Metropolitan Toronto Police Services Board, a request by two reporters to access a list of all police officers was denied on the basis of section 13. The police admitted that there are various circumstances (eg. plain clothes duties involving members of the drug squad, intelligence or morality officers) where the disclosure of the names of such officers could reasonably be expected to seriously threaten the safety or health of an officer or his or her family. In light of this and other submissions, the inquiry officer was satisfied that the police had established that a serious threat to health or safety could reasonably be expected as a result of disclosing the records in question and, therefore, upheld the decision of the police.[40]

Information Soon to be Published – s. 15

Section 15 of the legislation provides that a head may refuse to disclose a record if:

(a) the record or the information contained in the record has been published or is currently available to the public; or

(b) the head believes on reasonable grounds that the record or the information contained in the record will be published by an institution within ninety days after the request is made, or within such further period of time as may be necessary for printing or translating the material for the purpose of printing it..

Where an institution invokes this particular exemption, it may wish to consider the convenience of the requester compared to the convenience of the institution under all of the circumstances. Furthermore, where an institution is dealing with a similar number of requests over a long period of time, and the institution will likely have to grant access to these records, it has been suggested that it may be advantageous for the institution to assemble a package of the information in question and have it available for a reasonable fee.

---

39 *Municipality of Clarington*, Order MO-1593 (November 28, 2002).
40 *Metropolitan Toronto Police Services Board*, Order M-913 (March 20, 1997).

Personal Privacy Exemption – s. 14

Section 14 of the *Municipal Freedom of Information and Protection of Privacy Act* establishes a mandatory exemption relating to the disclosure of "personal information" to a person other than the individual to whom the information relates, except in the circumstances specified in this provision. Recognized as one of the fundamental provisions of the legislation, section 14 balances the public's right of access to records with the individual's right of privacy respecting personal information. Subsection 2 (1) of the legislation states that "personal information" means recorded information about an identifiable individual including,

- information relating to the race, national or ethnic origin, colour, religion, age, sex, sexual orientation or marital or family status of the individual,

- information relating to the education or the medical, psychiatric, psychological, criminal or employment history of the individual or information relating to financial transactions in which the individual has been involved,

- any identifying number, symbol or other particular assigned to the individual,

- the address, telephone number, fingerprints or blood type of the individual,

- the personal opinions or views of the individual except if they relate to another individual,

- correspondence sent to an institution by the individual that is implicitly or explicitly of a private or confidential nature, and replies to that correspondence that would reveal the contents of the original correspondence,

- the views or opinions of another individual about the individual, and

- the individual's name if it appears with other personal information relating to the individual or where the disclosure of the name would reveal other personal information about the individual.

More specifically, the Act requires the head to refuse to disclose personal information, unless one of the circumstances listed in clauses 14 (1) (a) through (f) applies, which may be summarized as follows:

(a) consent;

(b) compelling circumstances affecting health or safety;

(c) records available to the general public;

(d) disclosure authorized by statute;

(e) research agreements; or

(f) disclosure does not constitute an unjustified invasion of personal privacy.

The remaining subsections under section 14 address various "invasion of privacy" matters, and can be summarized as follows:

- clause 14 (2) (a) lists circumstances that should be considered in determining whether a disclosure of personal information constitutes an unjustified invasion of personal privacy;

- subsection 14 (3) sets out circumstances where disclosure is presumed to be an unjustified invasion of personal privacy;

- subsection 14 (4) lists circumstances where disclosure does not constitute an unjustified invasion of personal privacy; and

- subsection 14 (5) of the legislation permits an institution to refuse to confirm or deny the existence of a record if disclosure would constitute an unjustified invasion of personal privacy.

Those interested in the interpretation of section 14 must also have reference to the public interest override provision found in section 16 of the legislation, as well as section 38 of the Act, the relevant provision when deciding the disclosure of personal information to the person to whom it pertains.

The number of IPC decisions concerning personal privacy are too numerous to mention. However, set out below are two cases concerning section 14 of the statute that specifically take place within the municipal context. The first concerns the subject of petitions to council, while the second addresses information about tax arrears.

The Township of Chatsworth received a request for access to a copy of a "complete petition against [a named association] that was presented to council" in 2001. Although the township granted partial access to the petition, including the covering memorandum as well as the body of the petition and a newspaper article that was attached to the last page, it denied access to all of the names, signatures, addresses and emergency telephone numbers on the basis that such a disclosure would be an "un-

Chapter 13
PROTECTION OF PRIVACY

justified invasion of personal privacy" under section 14 of the Act. The requester/appellant subsequently appealed the township's decision to the IPC.

In reviewing the relevant information contained in the records, it was not difficult for Assistant Commissioner Tom Mitchenson to determine that the information was "personal information" pursuant to subsection 2 (1) of the legislation. Conversely, the records did not contain any of the appellant's personal information.

With respect to interpreting the invasion of privacy provision, the decision noted that, where "a requester seeks personal information of other individuals, subsection 14 (1) of the Act prohibits an institution from disclosing this information unless one of the exceptions listed in subsection 14 (1) are present." In this case, the two exceptions that may have been applicable to the circumstances were found in clauses 14 (1) (a) and (f), which read as follows:

> 14 (1) A head shall refuse to disclose personal information to any person other than the individual to whom the information relates except,
>
> (a) upon the written request or consent of the individual, if the record is one to which the individual is entitled to have access;
>
> ...
>
> (f) if the disclosure does not constitute an unjustified invasion of personal privacy.

In reviewing previous IPC orders on whether or not personal information contained in a petition should be disclosed, the assistant commissioner reiterated the instructive comments with respect to the issue of implied consent by former Commissioner Sidney B. Linden in Order 154 – a provincial appeal, which dealt with a petition that was presented to the mayor and members of the city council:

> After reviewing [the relevant records at issue in that appeal] and taking into consideration the circumstances surrounding the creation of this information, it is my view that the author of the covering letters and the signatories of the petition can be found to have consented to the release of their personal information. While the consent of these individuals is not explicit it can, in my view, reasonably be implied in the circumstances of this case. It is signifi-

cant that the individuals who signed the petition voluntarily lent their support to a matter of public concern. Petitions as a general rule are not intended to be kept secret and it would appear from the face of this record that the personal information contained in the record has already been provided to a number of recipients including the mayor and members of the Scarborough city council. In my view, it is clear from the actions of those involved with the petition that they have consciously decided to forego some element of their personal privacy by taking a public stand on an issue of importance to them.[41]

The assistant commissioner then reviewed two other cases from former Adjudicator John McCamus, who had expanded on the original reasoning from Order 154 in subsequent decisions (Orders 171 and 172) as follows:

Petitions by their very nature are not documents that have an aura of confidentiality. The signatories to a petition do so voluntarily. By including their name on a petition, a signatory makes a public stand with respect to the issue being petitioned for. Petitioners are aware that they are revealing personal information about themselves when they add their names to a petition. They also realize that the petition will be circulated and used in whatever manner is necessary in order to further the cause which is the subject of the petition.

Further, petitions are usually collected in a fairly public manner. Proponents of a petition often seek additional signatories in shopping malls, in front of public buildings or in door-to-door campaigns. Individuals are approached to add their names to the petition and are given the opportunity to read the body of the petition. Upon doing so, the individual, who may or may not eventually become a signatory, will have the opportunity to see the names, addresses and signatories of those who have already lent their support to the petition.[42]

Adjudicator McCamus then followed the earlier ruling of Commissioner Linden and found that clause 21 (1) (a) of the provincial legisla-

---

41 *Ministry of Community and Social Services*, Order P-154 (March 7, 1990).
42 Cited in *Township of Chatsworth*, Order MO-1506 (February 5, 2002).

tion (which is identical to clause 14 (1) (a) of the municipal statute) applied, but also added that, even if it did not, he would have concluded that the release of the names of the petitioners in those appeals would not constitute an unjustified invasion of personal privacy.

In ordering the township to disclose all of the remaining portions of the petition, including the names, signatures, emergency numbers and mailing addresses on the document, the assistant commissioner drew the following conclusions with respect to the petition and section 14 of the legislation:

> I agree with the findings and reasoning of these previous orders, and find that they are equally applicable to the petition at issue in this appeal. I accept that the affected person who signed the petition did so voluntarily and lent their support to a matter of some public concern to them. However, there is nothing on the face of the record to indicate that it was intended to be a confidential document, nor is it reasonable to conclude any implied expectation of confidentiality in the circumstances. The petition is addressed to the "Township of Chatsworth" with a copy to the Director of Planning for Grey County, and was tabled for consideration at a meeting of the township council. Based on the information provided by the parties in the context of this appeal, I cannot determine with certainty that the petition is a public document, but unless the council meeting was a validly constituted *in camera* meeting under the *Municipal Act*, I can think of no reason why the petition would not be made available to residents of the township as a matter of routine business. In any event, it is clear that it was not a confidential document, and I find that in signing and providing their personal information to the petition, the affected person implicitly consented to this personal information being made available to others. Accordingly, the requirements of the clause 14 (1) (a) exception are present, and the personal information contained in the petition does not qualify for exemption under subsection 14 (1) of the Act and should be disclosed to the appellant.[43]

In a 1995 case involving the City of Ottawa, the municipality had received a request from a local newspaper reporter for access to a list of all properties whose municipal taxes were in arrears, the amounts owing,

---

43 *Ibid.*

the term, the property owner, and any other information about the arrears that would be recorded on title. In response, the city advised the requester that no tax arrears had been registered on title. Furthermore, it also identified one responsive record, but denied access to it based on a number of exemptions, including the invasion of personal privacy provision found in section 14 of the Act. Upon appeal, Assistant Commissioner Tom Mitchinson found that the names, property addresses and associated entries for those listings qualified as "personal information" for the purposes of section 2 of the legislation. Conversely, the assistant commissioner found that, where a listing indicated that the owner of the property was a sole proprietorship, partnership, unincorporated association or corporation and not a natural person, then the information contained in those listings did not qualify as personal information.

Having determined that at least part of the record in question contained personal information, subsection 14 (1) of the statute prohibits disclosure of such information to any person other than the individual to whom the information relates, except in the specific circumstances listed under that provision. In this instance, the assistant commissioner reviewed the circumstances found in respect of clause 14 (1) (c) regarding records available to the general public, 14 (1) (d) concerning disclosure authorized by a statute, and 14 (1) (f) the fact that the disclosure did not constitute an unjustified invasion of personal privacy. The decision sets out the municipality's arguments with respect to the first two provisions, as well as the assistant commissioner's conclusions in the following fashion:

> With reference to clauses 14 (1) (c) and (d), the city states that neither the *Municipal Tax Sales Act* (the MTSA) nor the *Municipal Act* require municipalities to create a record available to the general public which would list all properties on which tax arrears are owing. The city points out that it is authorized to provide a statement of arrears to potential purchasers of specific properties, but that this statement is only available to parties who have an interest or potential interest in a particular property. The city also submits that because the MTSA includes a provision for making tax arrears information available to the public through a tax arrears certificate registered on title, there is no public interest in an earlier release of unofficial information.

> Having reviewed the print-outs and the representations, in my view, clauses 14 (1) (c) and (d) do not apply in the circumstances

of this appeal. I find that the print-outs themselves were not created to be made available to the general public, nor does any "Act of Ontario or Canada" expressly authorize the disclosure of lists such as the ones at issue in this appeal.[44]

With respect to the final point in this appeal, the appellant argued that the information was available for individual properties as a matter of public record, and therefore should not be protected under the Act. In this regard, the assistant commissioner reviewed a previous ruling of the IPC, being Order 180, which quoted from an earlier decision in *United States Department of Justice v. Reporters' Committee for Freedom of the Press* (1989), 109 S.C.T.1468 where the Supreme Court of the United States considered the question of access to criminal identification records (rap sheets) that contained descriptive information, as well as a history of arrests, charges, convictions and incarcerations of individuals. In upholding the city's decision not to disclose the registered owners and property addresses for individually-owned properties that appear on the various print-outs, the assistant commissioner concluded:

> I am aware that the information about tax arrears owing on any particular property can be obtained upon request by members of the public, including the appellant. I also agree, as the appellant points out, that through diligence and investigation someone might be able to compile a list of properties on which tax arrears are owed. However, in my view, it does not necessarily follow that an easily retrievable computerized record of the names and addresses of all individuals with tax arrears owing should be disclosed.

> Having considered the representatives of both parties in this appeal, I find that the information contained in the listings for properties owned by individuals satisfies the requirements of a presumed unjustified invasion of the named individuals under clause 14 (3) (f) of the Act.

---

44 *City of Ottawa*, Order M-800 (July 4, 1996); but see the discussion below on the recent Divisional Court decision in *Phinjo Gombu v. Tom Mitchinson (Assistant Commissioner) and Toronto (City)*, [2002] O.J. No. 1776.

General Exceptions to Exemptions – ss. 5 and 16

Throughout the Act, and particularly with respect to the exemption from disclosure, specific criteria are mandated, and the manner in which the exemption may be weighed is set out in detail. Such criteria must be regarded in the context of the particular subject-matter and the circumstances of the request.

In two instances, exemptions from disclosure are specifically overridden by the Act.

Compelling public interest – An exemption from disclosure of a record under sections 7, 9, 10, 11, 13 and 14 does not apply if a compelling public interest in the disclosure of the record clearly outweighs the purpose of the exemption.[45]

Grave environmental health or safety hazard – Despite any other provisions of the Act, a head, having given notice to any party affected, and having heard any representations, shall as soon as practicable disclose the record if the head has "reasonable and probable grounds to believe that it is in the public interest to do so and that the record reveals a grave environmental, health or safety hazard to the public."[46]

A more detailed examination of these two issues can be found in Chapter 12, Freedom of Information.

Labour Relations Exemption – s. 52

In 1995, the Province of Ontario enacted Bill 7, being the *Labour Relations and Employment Statute Law Amendment Act*. This statute amended the *Municipal Freedom of Information and Protection of Privacy Act* to exclude most employment-related and labour relations information in which an institution has an interest. Specifically, subsections 52 (3) and (4) provide as follows:

> 52 (3) Subject to subsection (4), this Act does not apply to records collected, prepared, maintained or used by or on behalf of an institution in relation to any of the following:

---

45 *Municipal Freedom of Information and Protection of Privacy Act*, R.S.O. 1990, c. M.56, s. 16.

46 *Ibid.*, ss. 5 (1), (2), (3).

1. Proceedings or anticipated proceedings before a court, tribunal or other entity relating to labour relations or to the employment of a person by the institution.

2. Negotiations or anticipated negotiations relating to labour relations or to the employment of a person by the institution between the institution and a person, bargaining agent or party to a proceeding or an anticipated proceeding.

3. Meetings, consultations, discussions or communications about labour relations or employment-related matters in which the institution has an interest.

52 (4) This Act applies to the following records:

1. An agreement between an institution and a trade union.

2. An agreement between an institution and one or more employees which ends a proceeding before a court, tribunal or other entity relating to labour relations or to employment-related matters.

3. An agreement between an institution and one or more employees resulting from negotiations about employment-related matters between the institution and the employee or employees.

4. An expense account submitted by an employee of an institution to that institution for the purpose of seeking reimbursement for expenses incurred by the employee in his or her employment.

The labour relations exclusion found in the provincial *Freedom of Information and Protection of Privacy Act* was recently the subject of an Ontario Court of Appeal decision in *Ontario (Solicitor General) v. Ontario (Assistant Information and Privacy Commissioner)*.[47] Briefly, this appeal concerned three unrelated requests for access to information in the possession of various Ontario government ministries. In each instance, the provincial government relied, in varying degrees, on subsec-

---

47 [2001] O.J. No. 3223 (C.A.), reversing [2000] O.J. No. 1974, leave to appeal dismissed [2001] S.C.C.A. No. 509 (June 13, 2002).

tion 65 (6) of the provincial statute, which is largely identical to subsection 52 (3) of the *Municipal Freedom of Information and Protection of Privacy Act*, cited above, in order to deny access to certain relevant records.

Traditionally, the IPC had interpreted that this section of the legislation only applied to a record involving a matter in which an institution had a "current legal interest." This meant that the commissioner would only allow an institution to refuse access to a record where the disclosure could affect the institution's current legal rights or obligations. In the IPC's view, records about past matters, which had long since concluded, or could not otherwise affect a government's legitimate interest, should be subject to the normal access and privacy rules established under the Act by the various exemptions.

Although the Divisional Court agreed with this interpretation, the Ontario Court of Appeal overturned that ruling. In the appellate court's view, the words "in which an institution has an interest" simply refer to matters involving a government's own workforce. In effect, the court held that the interest in question does not have to be either legal in nature or a current interest, thus greatly expanding the meaning of this particular provision. On June 13, 2002, the Supreme Court of Canada dismissed the Information and Privacy Commissioner's application for leave to appeal, thereby upholding the Ontario Court of Appeal's decision on the interpretation to be placed on subsection 52 (3) of the *Municipal Freedom of Information and Protection of Privacy Act*.

Another appeal concerning the City of Hamilton is instructive with respect to examining the broad interpretation of the non-application of the legislation to such labour relations matters. The municipality received a four-part request under the *Municipal Freedom of Information and Protection of Privacy Act* for access to records relating to the proposed transfer of management of two health care facilities from the city to two other organizations. The City of Hamilton located the records responsive to the request, but denied access to them, claiming that they fell outside the ambit of the legislation due to the operation of subsection 52 (3) of the Act.

The records at issue in this particular appeal consisted of eight pages of notes taken during several meetings involving the city and various organizations concerning the proposed transfer of management of the two health care facilities. In denying access to these records, the city relied on subsection 52 (3), paragraph 3 of the legislation which provided that the Act did not apply to records collected, maintained or used by or on behalf of an institution in relation to any of the following:

> Meetings, consultations, discussions or communications about labour relations or employment-related matters in which the institution has an interest.

In order to fall within the scope of paragraph 3 of subsection 52 (3), the adjudicator determined that the municipality must establish the following:

1. the records were collected, prepared, maintained or used by the city or on its behalf; and

2. this collection, preparation, maintenance or usage was in relation to meetings, consultations, discussions or communications; and

3. these meetings, consultations, discussions or communications are about labour relations or employment-related matters in which the city has an interest.

After quickly determining that requirements 1 and 2 of this test had been satisfied, the adjudicator turned his attention to the component concerning the institution's "interest" in the matter. After reviewing the relevant jurisprudence, including the Ontario Court of Appeal's ruling in *Ontario (Solicitor General) v. Ontario (Assistant Information and Privacy Commissioner)*,[48] the adjudicator upheld the city's decision to deny access to the records pursuant to the following rationale:

> Based on my review of the records and the information provided to me by the city and the appellant, I am of the view that the city has the requisite degree of interest in the subject-matter of the records to meet the third part of the subsection 52 (3), par. 3 test. The interest of the city went well beyond the "mere curiosity or concern" referred to by the Court of Appeal in its decision in *Ontario (Solicitor General)*, as the records directly addressed potential labour relations issues surrounding the agreements under consideration. Similarly, the passage of time cannot operate to remove the records from the exclusion in subsection 52 (3), par. 3, as described in the decision in *Ontario (Solicitor General)*.

---

48 *Ibid.*

As I have found that the records were prepared, maintained and used by the city in relation to meetings, discussions, consultations or communications about labour relations or employment-related matters, the third requirement for subsection 52 (3), par. 3 has been satisfied.[49]

Privacy on the Defensive

An excellent, albeit early evaluation of the significant dilemma arising from the "erosion of privacy by the pressures of technology and the persistence of barriers against wider sharing of information with the public" was raised in the IPC's 1993 Annual Report. Citing the 1993 Supreme Court of Canada decision *R. v. Dersch*,[50] the commissioner reiterated Madam Justice L'Heureux-Dubé's observation that in:

> ... our modern informational society, where intimate details of one's life may be available through computerized information accessible to many more persons than those initially entrusted with the knowledge, the security that information will be kept in privacy may be even more significant than one could have historically imagined.

The commissioner, noting that we are witnessing a "steady erosion of privacy through the creep of technology," advocated that "we need a new privacy paradigm." Insisting that society should recognize existing privacy rights as inviolate, the commissioner argued that:

> Those who propose to alter existing privacy levels should be required to demonstrate that the benefits to be gained outweigh the privacy to be lost.

> In such a balancing process, we must ensure that the odds are not stacked against privacy by the tendency to overestimate the potential benefits of technology. Only if we take an objective view of what technology can actually deliver, can we actually determine if the privacy losses are acceptable.[51]

---

49 *City of Hamilton* (formerly City of Hamilton and Region of Hamilton-Wentworth), Order MO-1587 (November 15, 2002).

50 *R. v. Dersch*, [1993] 3 S.C.R. 768.

51 1993 Annual Report from the Information and Privacy Commissioner/Ontario (June 1994).

Chapter 13
PROTECTION OF PRIVACY

Almost a decade later, it appears little has changed. At the time of publication, Ontario still did not have a "Chief Privacy Officer," despite the plea of the IPC noted at the beginning of this chapter. Furthermore, two additional decisions seem to lend credence to the concerns about a "steady erosion of privacy through the creep of technology."

In the 2000 case involving the City of Toronto, the municipality received a request from a member of the media for access to an electronic list of donors who had made contributions to the campaigns of candidates in the 1997 municipal election. In its decision letter, the city denied access to these records pursuant to clause 15 (a) of the Act, which provides that the information "is currently available to the public." The letter concluded by noting that "hard copies of the records relating to campaign contributions are required to be filed with the city clerk and, in accordance with municipal elections legislation, are maintained as a public record of personal information." In addition, the municipality also advised the requester of the specific location he could attend to review the records in question. The city also acknowledged, in its correspondence, that it had an electronic copy of the requested information, which it maintained for administrative purposes only, and further indicated to the requester that this electronic record was not created nor maintained as a public record of personal information. The requester subsequently appealed the city's decision to deny access to an electronic version of the requested record.

In upholding the decision of the city not to release the responsive records in this instance, Assistant Commissioner Tom Mitchinson found that the appellant's arguments with respect to clauses 14 (1) (c), (d) and (f) did not apply to the circumstances in this case.[52] The IPC found that, because there was no mention of a database designed to administer the city's rebate program, therefore, disclosure of this personal information in bulk electronic form was not expressly authorized by the legislation. Furthermore, the assistant commissioner held that disclosure of the entire database would constitute an unjustified invasion of personal privacy.

In an interesting postscript to this decision, the assistant commissioner stated that "finding the appropriate balance between the right of access to government-held information and the right to personal privacy is sel-

---

52 *City of Toronto*, Order MO-1366 (November 23, 2000).

dom more complex than when faced with requests for publicly available personal information in electronic format." The assistant commissioner then reiterated the previous views of the IPC that were set out in a 1996 decision dealing with a request for electronic access to property assessment roll data:

> In Ontario, assessment information is publicly available by law. For years, anyone has been able to go to the office of the clerk of a municipality and view the assessment roll. However, the paper medium on which information was stored provided a built-in privacy protection. Also, it was possible to go into a municipality and copy out the information contained on the paper rolls. Using the appellant's situation as an example, in order to do so he would have to travel to 11 municipal offices and copy thousands of pages. The sheer enormity of this task made in unlikely that assessment information would be used other than for assessment-related purposes. Using the words of the U.S. Supreme Court, I have described this as privacy protection based on "practical obscurity."
>
> But, as these rolls are transferred to electronic format, it grows much easier to retrieve and manipulate the personal data they contain, and to use it for purposes other than those originally intended. Indeed, this ability to manipulate data as described by the ministry [of Finance] is one of the added benefits of having information in electronic format.
>
> In my 1994 Annual Report to the Legislative Assembly, I said that I believe the transition to electronic records requires that the whole question of what personal information truly belongs on the public record needs to be rethought.[53]

In his final words on the City of Toronto appeal in 2000, Assistant Commissioner Mitchinson provided the following insightful remarks:

> No such rethinking exercise has taken place, and we find ourselves several years down the road, with electronic technology transforming our world at an accelerated pace, and no closer to clarifying how best to address the inherent tension between the

---

53 Postscript to Order P-1316 (December 16, 1996).

right to know and the right to expect governments to preserve our privacy.

On May 10, 2002, the Divisional Court overturned the IPC's ruling and ordered the City of Toronto to disclose to the media requester the electronic database containing the names, addresses and other personal information of individuals who had made contributions to candidates in the 1997 municipal election.[54] The IPC's concern that disclosure of the electronic record could allow for mass invasion of personal privacy by permitting easy opportunities for distribution was rejected. In fact, the Divisional Court held that the list should be released and found that the added convenience of the reporter receiving the record in electronic form outweighed any privacy concerns. Although leave to appeal this decision was granted by the Ontario Court of Appeal on September 12, 2002, that appeal was subsequently abandoned by both the IPC and the city in the spring of 2003.

On April 29, 2003, Information and Privacy Commissioner Ann Cavoukian released her results on a privacy investigation entitled "The Toronto Police Service's Use of Mobile Licence Plate Recognition Technology to Find Stolen Vehicles."[55] In late January 2003, a newspaper reporter contacted the IPC office to seek the commissioner's views about a new technology being tested by the Toronto Police Service called the Mobile Licence Plate Recognition (MLPR) system. The three-month MLPR pilot project involved using a video camera system mounted on the top of a police car (the street sweeper) that scans the licence plate numbers of various parked cars and compares them to a "hot list" of stolen vehicles. Although the street sweeper was being used only to find stolen vehicles, the newspaper reported that the MLPR system could also be linked to a global positioning system (GPS) technology to enforce such things as municipal parking by-laws.

Commissioner Cavoukian subsequently launched a privacy investigation into police use of the MLPR technology after having received a complaint from a member of the public who expressed concerns about the arbitrary surveillance by the police and alleged that the technology

---

54 *Phinjo Gombu v. Tom Mitchinson (Assistant Commissioner) and Toronto (City)*, [2002] O.J. No. 1776.

55 "Privacy Investigation: The Toronto Police Service's Use of Mobile Licence Plate Recognition Technology to Find Stolen Vehicles," MC-030023-1 (April 29, 2003).

violated the unreasonable search and seizure section of the *Canadian Charter of Rights and Freedoms*. Although the commissioner concluded that the Toronto police's use of the MLPR technology to find stolen vehicles was in compliance with the legislation, the IPC made the following two recommendations with respect to the protection of privacy:

1. In any future technology projects that involve the collection of personal information, the Toronto police should sign a contract with any private-sector entity not subject to the Act to which they disclose this personal information. Such a contract would include strong privacy-protection clauses that prohibit the private-sector entity from misusing or inappropriately disclosing any personal information that it receives from the police. This would include a prohibition on matching the personal information with any other information about an individual that the private-sector entity has collected from other sources. In addition, a requirement that the private-sector entity's employees sign confidentiality agreements should be included.

2. If the Toronto police decide to test or implement the GPS-configured MLPR system at some point in the future, they should first consult with the IPC to discuss the privacy implications of using this technology. In addition, they should conduct a privacy impact assessment to determine whether this system meets basic privacy requirements.

The prolonged absence of a thorough review of "what personal information truly belongs on the public record" means that privacy rights in the electronic age will continue to unfold in a piecemeal fashion based on the latest IPC or court rulings.[56]

---

56 For example, see the decision of Alberta's Information and Privacy Commissioner Frank Work, Q.C. regarding the limited use of surveillance cameras by police in a shopping and entertainment district in Edmonton: Edmonton Police Service, Investigation Report F2003-IR-005 (August 6, 2003).

Chapter 14
ACCESS & PRIVACY OBLIGATIONS OF A MEMBER

> *In our view, councillors do not need the information of all constituents in order to discharge their responsibility to help those who request assistance with respect to a particular building permit, planning or other similar matter. It is our view that section 32 (d) [disclosure made to an officer or employee who needs the record in the performance of his or her duties] does not apply to the routine disclosure of or access to personal information of a large group of city residents where this disclosure does not directly relate to a particular land use or planning matter. We are also not persuaded that activities such as welcoming new residents to a ward are sufficiently connected to the city's service functions to fit within the scope of section 32 (d).*
>
> Tom Mitchinson, Assistant Commissioner
> October 28, 1998

Three fundamental questions frequently arise concerning the legal obligations of a member of council or a local board under the relevant municipal freedom of information and protection of privacy legislation that affects them and the records they possess. These questions may be summarized as follows.

Protection of privacy – Does the statute impose any obligations upon a member of a council or local board restricting access to, or protecting the privacy of, information obtained in confidential circumstances, such as at a closed meeting or in order to discharge their constituency responsibilities?

Records of member – Are the records created and/or maintained by a member of council or a local board subject to the same access rights or privacy provisions in the Act as those afforded to any other record of the municipality or local board?

Head of council - chair of local board – Are any additional obligations or limitations imposed upon the head of council in his or her capacity as chief executive officer of the municipality[1] or upon the chair of a local board?

Although firm opinions may be expressed on each of these questions, the ultimate answers are complex, being dependent upon a number of factual matters that may:

- vary depending upon the particular circumstances;
- differ depending upon the office held; and
- be affected by a relevant policy adopted by the council or local board.

They will also be subject to such considerations as:

- applicability of the specific access or privacy provisions of the Act;
- status of the record created or maintained by the member or his or her staff; and
- potential for the misuse of insider information, as discussed in detail in Chapter 10, Members' Code of Conduct.

Protection of Privacy

In Ontario, the *Municipal Freedom of Information and Protection of Privacy Act* fails to expressly address the status of any records obtained by members in confidential situations (eg. *in camera* meetings). Despite this omission, clause 6 (1) (b) is a discretionary exemption that allows the head to refuse to disclose a record "that reveals the substance of deliberations of a meeting of council, board, commission or other body or a committee of one of them if a statute authorizes holding that meeting in the absence of the public." Moreover, subsection 48 (1) of the statute does state, with absolute finality, that:

No person shall,

    (a)   wilfully disclose personal information in contravention of this Act;

---

1   *Municipal Act, 2001*, S.O. 2001, c. 25, s. 225.

(b) wilfully maintain a personal information bank that contravenes this Act.[2]

Personal information and personal information banks (PIBs) are considered to be separate, albeit related, entities under the Act. The legislation expressly recognizes the need for PIBs in the municipal context and specifically defines them to be "a collection of personal information that is organized and capable of being retrieved using an individual's name or an identifying number or particular assigned to the individual."[3] However, the institution must establish the need for the PIBs' existence and publish an annual list of the PIBs that it maintains. The statute further provides that every person who contravenes these provisions "is guilty of an offence and on conviction is liable to a fine not exceeding $5,000."[4]

This offence section should be carefully regarded by members of councils or local boards. Ironically, while the legislation emphatically prohibits the wilful disclosure of personal information, it is silent as to the disclosure of:

- third party information, afforded mandatory protection;[5] and
- economic and other interests, afforded permissive protection.[6]

Despite this omission, it is suggested that the disclosure of third party information can result in the appeal process being triggered. If the appeal is successful, the institution would be bound by the Commissioner's decision, or else face the penalties provided for in section 48. Furthermore, it is arguable that the disclosure of economic interests really harms only the institution itself, and that may be why there is no express prohibition with respect to it.

Disclosure of Personal Information

As noted at the beginning of this chapter, there is still some uncertainty concerning the ability of municipal councillors or local board members to receive and disclose "personal information" while carrying out the

---

2 *Municipal Freedom of Information and Protection of Privacy Act*, R.S.O. 1990, c. M.56, ss. 48 (1) (a), (b).

3 *Ibid.*, ss. 2 (1) 34 and 35.

4 *Ibid.*, s. 48 (2).

5 *Ibid.*, s. 10.

6 *Ibid.*, s. 11.

duties of their respective public offices. Briefly, section 32 of the *Municipal Freedom of Information and Protection of Privacy Act* prohibits an institution from disclosing personal information unless one of the dozen exceptions is applicable. For municipalities or local boards, this will often mean reliance on one of the following three exceptions set out in section 32 as follows:

(b) if the person to whom the information relates has identified that information in particular and consented to its disclosure;

(c) for the purpose for which it was obtained or compiled or for a consistent purpose; or

(d) if the disclosure is made to an officer or employee of the institution who needs the record in the performance of his or her duties and if the disclosure is necessary and proper in the discharge of the institution's functions.[7]

With respect to clause 32 (d), reference should also be had to subsection 3 (2) of Ontario Regulation 823 under the Act, which states that "every head shall ensure that only those individuals who need a record for the performance of their duties shall have access to it."[8]

One of the earliest cases to analyze clause 32 (d) was the 1992 court case of *H.(J.) v. Hastings (County)*.[9] In that instance, the applicants contended that the following municipal resolution passed by the county council should be declared null and void:

> Whereas the policy of the Ministry of Community and Social Services dealing with the release of the names of individuals on general welfare assistance requires a resolution from council as a whole,
>
> And whereas such a resolution provides for release only to council as a whole,
>
> And whereas members of council have previously expressed interest and concern in this matter,

---

7 *Ibid.*, ss. 32 (b), (c) and (d).
8 Ontario Regulation 823, R.R.O. 1990, "General," s. 3 (2).
9 *H. (J.) v. Hastings (County)*, (1992), 12 M.P.L.R. (2d) 40.

Be it therefore resolved that such a list of recipients be made available to council at the next regular meeting.

The applicants argued that the resolution was:

- prohibited by the *Municipal Freedom of Information and Protection of Privacy Act*;
- beyond the power of a municipal corporation;
- discriminatory; and
- in violation of the *Canadian Charter of Rights and Freedoms*, in particular sections 7, 8 and 15.[10]

The Honourable Mr. Justice R. G. Byers, having considered the relevant sections of the *Municipal Freedom of Information and Protection of Privacy Act*, noted that clause 32 (d) permitted disclosure of "personal information" to an "officer" or "employee" who "needs the record in the performance of his or her duties and if the disclosure is necessary and proper in the discharge of the institution's functions." With respect to this particular issue, the Trial Judge only commented that "the words officer or employee are not defined in the Act" and that "municipal councillors may well not be included in those words." Without further analysis, the judge then focused his examination on the *General Welfare Assistance Act*, as well as the "need and necessity" standard for disclosing information under clause 32 (d) of the freedom of information legislation. Byers J. observed that under the *General Welfare Assistance Act*:

> The province determines eligibility, and supplies most of the funds to municipalities which then pay out the benefits.
>
> Benefits are paid out by a welfare administrator, who wears two hats: first, as a municipal employee reporting to council, and secondly as a holder of a statutory position with independent duties and responsibilities under the Act.[11]

---

10 *Charter*: section 7 is "the right to life, liberty and security of the person;" section 8 is "the right to be secure against unreasonable search or seizure;" and section 15 is the "equality rights" provision.

11 *H. (J.) v. Hastings (County)*, (1992), 12 M.P.L.R. (2d) 40 at 44. See also the *General Welfare Assistance Act*, R.S.O. 1990, c. G.6.

Turning to the council resolution and the facts surrounding it, the Trial Judge established the "need and necessity" test under clause 32 (d) as follows:

> The resolution of September 5, 1990, is not particularly helpful as to why council wants the names of welfare recipients. It merely says that members of council have previously expressed interest and concern.
>
> But s. 32 (d) requires more than mere interest and concern on the part of councillors. It specifically requires that the information be needed and be necessary.
>
> In my view there is no evidence in this case of that need nor of that necessity.[12]

In conclusion, the judge determined that the municipality had failed to demonstrate a need for disclosing the names to the county council and was therefore prohibited by section 32 from receiving the personal information. In a rather candid aside, Mr. Justice Byers stated, "I would say this, however. I see no reason why, in a proper case, the warden of the county could not be entitled to see the names of welfare recipients." While the judge did not state the basis for this conclusion, it may have arisen from the fact that the warden is both head of council and chief executive officer of the corporation.

Curiously, the IPC drew the opposite conclusion of this same issue in its earlier investigative report, dated August 1, 1991:

> It is our view that the council has the ultimate responsibility for supervision and administration of the general welfare program within the county. The council, as officer(s) of the institution, has enunciated a need for the information and stated that the transfer is necessary and proper for the discharge of its supervisory function. Thus, in our view, the requirements of subsection 32 (d) of the Act are met. In the circumstances of this case, the social services department would be in compliance with the subsection if it transferred a list of general welfare recipients to its council.[13]

---

12 *Ibid.*
13 *Ibid.*, at 42.

Chapter 14
ACCESS & PRIVACY

In the years following the 1992 court decision concerning Hastings County, the IPC has had a number of other opportunities to review the rights of municipal councillors to receive "personal information" pursuant to section 32 of the legislation.

In 1995, the IPC investigated a complaint against a municipality based on the following allegations.[14] The municipality stated that one of its building inspectors had notified the complainant that he was using one of his properties in contravention of the zoning by-law. The municipality further alleged that the complainant called a departmental manager and requested that they defer issuing a compliance order as he was considering running for ward councillor in the 1994 municipal election and the order might jeopardize his chances. Although the complainant denied that such a call took place, the municipality acknowledged that the deferral request was discussed with various officials in the department, as well as the ward councillor. In addition, the municipality conceded that the councillor subsequently obtained further information about the complainant's property from the manager of the department. The complainant alleged that the councillor then used the personal information disclosed to him in his campaign literature and that this was a breach of the Act.

In responding to this complaint, the municipality submitted that the disclosure of the complainant's personal information was pursuant to clause 32 (c). This clause is an exemption to the prohibition on disclosing personal information if it is "for the purpose for which it was obtained or compiled or for a consistent purpose." In this case, the municipality provided personal information to the councillor "in order that the councillor could participate fully in discussions respecting the unusual request for a deferral of a work order on a property in his ward." In addition, the municipality submitted that it advised its elected representatives "of any special consideration either being granted or requested in respect of a property in his or her ward, in order that the ward councillor can properly deal with any inquiries he or she may receive respecting the request under consideration."

With respect to clause 32 (c), former Assistant Commissioner Ann Cavoukian (now commissioner) found that "the municipality would have obtained or compiled the fact that the complainant had allegedly

---

14 *A Municipality*, Investigation I94-079M (June 19, 1995).

requested the department to delay issuing an order to comply against his property, in order to decide whether or not to grant the request, for the ultimate purpose of administering its zoning by-law." In dismissing the municipality's argument regarding clause 32 (c), the assistant commissioner found as follows:

> The municipality has not provided us with any information demonstrating that the councillor played a role in deciding whether or not to grant a property owner's request to delay the issuance of an order to comply. Thus, it is our view that the municipality's disclosure of the complainant's personal information to assist the councillor in dealing with any enquiries he received regarding the complainant's request was not for the purpose for which it had obtained this information.[15]

In a similar complaint, the IPC initiated an investigation as a result of allegations that personal information had been disclosed to some members of council in violation of the legislation. On August 30, 1995, the complainant's solicitor had written to the town expressing concerns about power boat races and associated activities that were scheduled to occur the following month at a local park. At the town's administration and finance committee meeting on that same day, the committee agreed that the solicitor's correspondence should be read aloud during the open portion of the meeting.

Upon concluding that the information in question was personal information as defined in the Act, the compliance review officer then turned her attention to whether or not the personal information was disclosed in compliance with section 32 of the legislation. In responding to this question, the town submitted that the disclosure of the complainant's personal information at the open committee meeting was in compliance with clause 32 (a) and (d) of the statute. With respect to clause 32 (d), the compliance review officer found as follows:

> Clause 32 (d) of the Act applies only if a disclosure is made to an "officer" or "employee" of an institution. In this case, the complainant was concerned that the letter was disclosed at an open committee meeting to the press and public. Since members of the

---

15 *Ibid.*

press and public are not officers or employees of the town, it is our view that clause 32 (d) of the Act did not apply.[16]

Although the IPC ultimately concluded that the disclosure of the personal information in this instance was not in compliance with section 32 of the legislation, the compliance review officer did set out the following alternate approaches, which may have been acceptable to the commissioner in these types of cases:

> We accept that the committee members needed to be aware of the complainant's concerns about the boat races and, in our view, if the disclosure had been made during a closed session of the committee, it would not have been an infringement of the Act. It is also our view that these concerns could have been raised in the open session of the committee without identifying the complainant.

More recently, the IPC received a complaint that three cities had routinely provided incumbent members of council with access to citizens' names, addresses, amounts paid for their homes, amounts of downpayments and the names of vendors. The three cities were subsequently amalgamated and were referred to as "the city" for the purposes of the investigation report. In response to the inquiry as to whether or not the personal information disclosed to the councillors was in compliance with clause 32 (d) of the legislation, the city submitted that "many councillors believe that they have a responsibility and a duty to be fully knowledgeable about any planning or land use issue brought forward by or concerning their constituents."[17] In addition, the municipality argued that "councillors also wish to be in a position to welcome new residents to their wards and to create accurate mailing lists in order to communicate directly and by name with their constituents."

In concluding that the city's routine disclosure of various lists of personal information to members of council was not in accordance with section 32 of the legislation, Assistant Commissioner Tom Mitchinson, found as follows:

> In our view, councillors do not need the information of all constituents in order to discharge their responsibility to help those who request assistance with respect to a particular building permit,

---

16 *A Town*, Investigation I96-001M (April 29, 1996).

17 *A City*, Investigation MC-980018-1 (October 28, 1998).

planning or other similar matter. It is our view that clause 32 (d) does not apply to the routine disclosure of, or access to, personal information of a large group of city residents where this disclosure does not directly relate to a particular land use or planning matter. We are also not persuaded that activities such as welcoming new residents to a ward are sufficiently connected to the city's service functions to fit within the scope of clause 32 (d).

Despite this conclusion, the assistant commissioner did recognize that councillors may be able to access such information for constituency matters under certain conditions:

We accept that councillors should be able to respond to issues raised by constituents and to have access to information necessary to properly discharge their responsibilities. In circumstances where personal information of a constituent is required in order to meet this end, it should only be disclosed to the councillor in compliance with section 32 of the Act. This can be achieved, for example, under clause 32 (b), which permits the disclosure of personal information with the consent of the person to whom the information relates.[18]

In an effort to enhance the privacy protection for such records, it is recommended that a member treat all records with the same respect, regardless of the type of information in his or her possession. Ontario's Information and Privacy Commissioner has outlined the following practical ways in which elected or appointed representatives can help prevent the unauthorized disclosure of such confidential or "personal" records:

- do not leave a document containing personal information on your desk, in your car, in your home or other areas where others may have access to it;
- ensure that personal information on your computer screen is not visible to others;
- ensure that the files in your office are secure;
- do not discuss the personal information of others in open areas, such as reception areas and hallways; and

---

18 *Ibid.*

- do not disclose an individual's personal information during a public council meeting without the individual's written consent.[19]

Records of Member

In accordance with subsection 4 (1) of Ontario's *Municipal Freedom of Information and Protection of Privacy Act*, the access provisions apply to records that are "in the custody or under the control of an institution." The underlying criteria in establishing whether the records of a member of a council or a local board come within the ambit of the Act hinge upon the following:

- whether the information to which access is sought constitutes a record; and
- whether such record is in the custody or under the control of the institution.[20]

The definition of "record" provided by the legislation is extremely broad and, as noted earlier, appears to be all-encompassing. In fact, it is suggested that the statutory definition need not be confined to those "official" records produced on behalf of the council or local board, but will conceivably include "notations, sketches, and other handwritten notes which an alderman might make during the course of a council meeting."[21] Assuming this to be true, the next inquiry is whether or not the records are in the custody or under control of an institution.

---

19 Information and Privacy Commissioner/Ontario and the City of Ottawa, "Working with the Municipal Freedom of Information and Protection of Privacy Act: A Councillor's Guide" (November 2001).

20 *Municipal Freedom of Information and Protection of Privacy Act*, R.S.O. 1990, c. M.56, ss. 2 (1) and 4 (1).

21 In preparing this chapter, the author acknowledges the advice contained in the informed, widely circulated opinion on this crucial issue prepared by Michael Minkowski, Deputy City Solicitor, former City of Gloucester, dated September 14, 1990.

Custody and/or Control

The so-called "custody" and/or "control" question was first analyzed by the IPC in relation to the legislation applicable to the provincial government in 1989, although it was later considered in the context of the local government statute, as well. The phrase was the subject of close scrutiny in Interim Order P-120 made by former Commissioner Sidney B. Linden with respect to the Ministry of Government Services.[22] In that case, the commissioner stated that determination of the question of whether an institution has custody and/or control of particular records depended on the following 10 factors:

1. Was the record created by an officer or employee of the institution?

2. What use did the creator intend to make of the record?

3. Does the institution have possession of the record, either because it has been voluntarily provided by the creator or pursuant to a mandatory statutory or employment requirement?

4. If the institution does not have possession of the record, is it being held by an officer or employee of the institution for the purposes of his or her duties as an officer or employee?

5. Does the institution have a right to possession of the record?

6. Does the content of the record relate to the institution's mandate and functions?

7. Does the institution have the authority to regulate the record's use?

8. To what extent has the record been relied upon by the institution?

9. How closely is the record integrated with other records held by the institution?

10. Does the institution have the authority to dispose of the record?

Noting that these 10 questions "are by no means an exhaustive list of all factors which should be considered," the commissioner stated further

---

22 *Ministry of Government Services*, Interim Order P-120 (November 22, 1989).

that, in his opinion, "they reflect the kind of considerations which a head should apply in determining questions of custody or control in individual cases."

On February 27, 2001, Adjudicator Laurel Cropley issued a ruling with respect to the subsection 10 (1) of the *Freedom of Information and Protection of Privacy Act*,[23] which equates to subsection 4 (1) of the *Municipal Freedom of Information and Protection of Privacy Act*. In this recent case, the appellant had submitted a request to the Ministry of the Solicitor General for access to certain records from the Ontario Fire Marshal's Office relating to carbon monoxide detectors. In one of its decision letters on this matter, the ministry advised the appellant that any records maintained by the Fire Marshal's Public Fire Safety Council (the council) were not in its custody or under its control. Upon appeal, the ministry reiterated this position and also indicated that both it and the Underwriters' Laboratories of Canada (ULC) were disputing the appellant's position that certain records of the ULC were, in fact, under the control of the ministry. The adjudicator began by identifying the "list of indicia of custody and/or control" originally set out by Commissioner Linden and went on to establish additional criteria of her own, as well as those set out in subsequent jurisprudence:

> In the Notice of Inquiry, I asked the ministry, the council and ULC to provide representations in response to the following questions regarding subsection 10 (1). These questions expand upon a list of indicia of custody and/or control originally identified by former Commissioner Sidney Linden in Order 120. I also made reference to other authorities under each question, where appropriate.

1. Does the ministry have a statutory power or duty to carry out the activity which resulted in the creation of the record? [Order P-912, upheld in *Ontario (Criminal Code Review Board) v. Ontario (Information and Privacy Commissioner)* (March 7, 1997), Toronto Doc. 283/95 (Ont. Div. Ct.), affirmed (1999), 47 O.R. (3d) 201 (C.A.)].

2. Was any record created by an officer or employee of the institution?

---

23 *Freedom of Information and Protection of Privacy Act*, R.S.O. 1990, c. F.31.

3. Is the activity in question a "core," "central" or "basic" function of the ministry? [Order P-912].

4. Are there any provisions in any contracts between the ministry and the council/ULC in relation to the activity which resulted in the creation of the records, which expressly or by implication give the ministry the right to possess or otherwise control the records? [*Greater Vancouver Mental Health Service Society v. British Columbia (Information and Privacy Commissioner)*, [1999] B.C.J. No. 198 (S.C.)].

5. Was there an understanding or agreement between the ministry and the council/ULC or any other party that the records were not to be disclosed to the ministry? [Order M165].

6. Who paid for the creation of the records? [Order M506].

7. What use did the creator intend to make of the records?

8. Was the council/ULC an agent of the ministry for the purposes of the activity in question? If so, what was the scope of that agency, and did it carry with it a right of the ministry to possess or otherwise control the records? [*Walmsley v. Ontario (Attorney General)* (1997), 34 O.R. (3d) 611 (C.A.)].

9. What is the customary practice of the ministry in relation to possession or control of records of this nature, in similar circumstances?

10. Does the ministry have the authority to regulate the records' use?

11. Does the ministry have the authority to dispose of the records?

12. What is the customary practice of the council/ULC in a similar trade, calling or profession in relation to possession or control of records of this nature, in similar circumstances?

13. To what extent did the ministry use or rely or intend to use or rely on the records? [P-120]

14. Who owns the records? [Order M315]

15. Has the council/ULC refused to provide the ministry with a copy of the records and, if so, to what extent, if any, should this affect the determination of the control issue?

16. Who has physical possession of the records? Does the ministry have possession of the records, either because they have been voluntarily provided by the council/ULC or pursuant to a mandatory, statutory or employment requirement? Does the ministry have a right to possession of the records?

17. If the institution does not have possession of the record, is it being held by an officer or employee of the institution for the purposes of his or her duties as an officer or employee?

18. How closely is the record integrated with other records held by the institution?[24]

The "purposive" method in posing these types of questions was noted by Senior Adjudicator David Goodis in an appeal involving the Township of King in 1999:

> These questions reflect a purposive approach to the "control" question under subsection 4 (1). A similar approach has been adopted in Ontario and other access to information regimes. In *Ontario (Criminal Code Review Board) v. Ontario (Information and Privacy Commissioner)*, [1999] O.J. No. 4072, the Court of Appeal for Ontario (at p. 6, par. 34) adopted the following passage from the Federal Court of Appeal judgment in *Canada Post Corp. v. Canada (Minister of Public Works)* (1995), 30 Admin. L.R. (2d) 242 at 244-245:
>
>> The notion of control referred to in subsection 4 (1) of the *Access to Information Act* ... is left undefined and unlimited. Parliament did not see fit to distinguish between ultimate and immediate, full and partial, transient and lasting, or "*de jure* and *de facto*" control. Had parliament intended to qualify and restrict the notion of control to the power to dispose of the information, as suggested by the appellant, it could certainly have done so by limiting the citizen's right of access only to those documents that the government can dispose of or which are under the lasting or ultimate control of the government.[25]

---

24 *Ministry of the Solicitor General*, Order PO-1873 (February 27, 2001).

25 *Township of King*, Order MO-1251 (November 16, 1999).

Officer or Employee

In the context of the records of a member, another significant issue to be determined is whether or not such a person can be considered to be an officer or employee of the municipal corporation or local board. If so, it is possible that any records that the member creates could be subject to the constraints imposed by the Act.

Almost a century ago, the common law stated that members of council were generally not employees of the municipal corporation. In the early case of *Davies v. The Sovereign Bank*, the Ontario Supreme Court drew this conclusion:

> While aldermen, as members of the municipal council are in one sense officers of the corporation, I do not think the framers of the rule intended to include them in the expression "officer or servant of such corporation." They are merely legislative officers of the corporation and, with the exception of the mayor or other head, who is, by ... the *Municipal Act* ... the "chief executive officer of the corporation" no individual executive or ministerial duties are imposed upon them. They are not employed by, nor are they in any way under the control of the corporation while in office. They have no authority to act for the corporation, except in conjunction with other persons constituting a quorum.
>
> The *Municipal Act* itself draws a sharp distinction between members of council and officers of the corporation ...
>
> From the association and the rule of the words "officer or servant" I think the inference is against the word "officer" being intended to extend to persons who are merely legislative officers, and that the true intention was to embrace only such persons as officers of a municipal corporation who are such in the usual sense of that word, namely, persons under the control of the corporation and entrusted or employed to administer its affairs, or a person whose duty it is to execute the will of its legislative body.[26]

As noted earlier in this chapter, Mr. Justice Byers gave little judicial consideration to the issue of whether or not members of a county council were officers or employees under the Act. However, in light of that decision, the IPC unsuccessfully petitioned the provincial legislature in

---

26 *Davies v. The Sovereign Bank* (1906), 12 O.L.R. 557 at 558.

1994 to amend the legislation to include a specific definition for the term "officer" in clause 32 (d).[27]

In a 1996 case involving the City of Toronto, a councillor read part of a letter aloud during the course of an open meeting of council. When a request was subsequently received seeking a copy of this correspondence (as well as other records), the city denied access on the basis that these records were "not within its custody or under its control." Upon appeal, the inquiry officer set out the following matters to be addressed:

> In my view, in the circumstances of this appeal, there are two situations in which the records may be subject to an access request under the Act. In the first case if the councillor were found to be an "officer" of the city, he would be considered to be a part of the institution, and records maintained by him in conjunction with this position would thus be subject to the Act. Such a finding would end the analysis and it would not be necessary to go on and consider the second situation. A contrary finding, however, would not automatically remove records from the application of the Act. Rather, it would then be necessary to consider the second situation.
>
> In the second case, even if the councillor were found not to fall within the purview of the Act, records held by him personally may still be subject to the Act if it is determined that they are also within the custody or under the control of the city (Order P-239).[28]

In seeking to determine whether or not a councillor is an "officer" of an "institution" for the purposes of the legislation, the inquiry officer drew the following general conclusions:

> In my view, the authorities referred to above all indicate that, except in unusual circumstances, a member of a municipal council is generally not considered to be an "officer" of a municipal corporation. An example of an unusual circumstance would be where a municipal councillor of a small municipality has been appointed a commissioner, superintendent or overseer of any work pursuant

---

27 "Suggested Changes to the Municipal Freedom of Information and Protection of Privacy Act: Submission to the Standing Committee on the Legislative Assembly" (January 1994).

28 *City of Toronto*, Order M-813 (July 31, 1996).

to section 256 of the [former] *Municipal Act*. In this regard, the authorities indicate that this would be an extremely unusual situation, and where it occurs, the councillor would be considered an "officer" only for the purposes of the specific duties he or she undertakes in this capacity. In these cases, a determination that a municipal councillor is functioning as an "officer" must be based on the specific factual circumstances.[29]

Therefore, it appears clear that, subject to the qualifications concerning the role of the chief executive officer (discussed below in greater detail), the records of a "member" are not likely to be considered the records of an "officer or employee of the municipal corporation" for the purposes of applying the factors set out above.

Personal/Constituency Records

Another related issue of whether or not a member's records may be subject to the legislation, by virtue of being in the custody or under the control of the municipality or local board, addresses a member's personal or constituency records. In a 1996 appeal to the IPC, the City of North York denied a request for numerous records of a councillor that the municipality argued were "not in its custody or control." After determining that the councillor was not an "officer" of the institution, the inquiry officer upheld the city's decision to deny access to the councillor's records for the following reasons:

> With respect to the remaining criteria listed in Order 120, based on a careful review of the records, the representations of the parties and the particular circumstances of this case, I find that the councillor's records are the councillor's personal records held by her in her capacity as the elected representative of her constituents and relate to her mandate and functions. I find that the city does not have these records in its possession, nor does it have any right to possess them. I have no evidence before me that these particular records have been relied upon by the city. I also find that the records are not integrated with other records of the city and the city has no authority to regulate the records or to dispose of or other-

---

29 *Ibid*; see also s. 256 of Ontario's former *Municipal Act*, R.S.O. 1990, c. M.45, which stated that a "member of the council of a village or township having a population of 3,000 or less may be appointed commissioner, superintendent or overseer of any work, other than a highway."

wise deal with them. Accordingly, I find that the records are not in the custody or under the control of the city.[30]

Members of a council or local board, therefore, must recognize that the records they create and maintain generally fall into two distinct categories:

- records that are "in the custody or under the control" of the municipality or local board (and therefore generally subject to the access provisions and protection of privacy requirements of the Act); and

- personal records (which usually fall outside the ambit of the legislation).

Physical Location of Records

A related question has been raised concerning the storage of a member's personal records or constituency information and whether there is a greater risk of its release in response to an access request if it is integrated within the municipality's records management system. In effect, the question remains whether or not the storage of a member's records in the municipality's record management system can be deemed to bring such records, including "constituency" or "personal" information under the "custody" or "control" of the municipality to a greater degree than if they are stored somewhere else. The significance of the physical location of any records subject to an access request has been discussed in previous IPC orders. In Interim Order P-120, former Commissioner Linden made the following general observations with respect to the physical location of such records:

> In my view, although mere possession of a record by an institution may not constitute custody or control in all circumstances, physical possession of a record is the best evidence of custody, and only in rare cases could it successfully be argued that an institution did not have custody of a record in its actual possession.[31]

This general viewpoint has been discussed in other IPC decisions dealing with the physical storage of records for MPPs and municipal councillors. In a provincial access request, the office of the premier was

---

30 *City of North York*, Order M-846 (October 10, 1996).
31 *Ministry of Government Services*, Order P-120 (November 22, 1989).

asked to provide copies of records seized by the Ontario Provincial Police from the office of a former employee of the premier. The assistant commissioner drew the following conclusions with regard to the physical possession and location of the records in question:

> It is clear from the representations of the secondary affected person that the scope of his duties while employed with the institution encompassed Liberal Party of Ontario matters. The records at issue in this appeal are directly related to this Liberal Party of Ontario role. However, in my view, these records have been integrated into the operations of the institution in a manner which constitutes custody under the Act. A secondary affected person has acknowledged that no special steps were taken to separate the storage and maintenance of these records from other records relating to his employment with the institution, and it would appear that these records were integrated with other files held by the institution. In my view, the secondary affected person assumed responsibility for the care of these records, and had control over their use.[32]

In 1996, the commissioner had an opportunity to address a similar question with regard to the "constituency records" of a councillor for the City of Toronto. As previously noted, the city councillor received a letter, which was then read aloud at a council meeting on November 7, 1995 without identifying its author. This record was subsequently the subject of an access request, along with a host of other documents. The city denied access to the requested records and maintained that they were not within its custody or under its control. In upholding the city's decision, the inquiry officer drew the following observations with regard to the records in question:

> The city does not have custody of the requested records. I find that they are the constituency records of the councillor regardless of the fact that they may have been received by the councillor at an office at city hall as opposed to his constituency office. Further, I am satisfied that these records have not been provided to council or integrated with records held by the city.[33]

---

32 *Office of the Premier*, Order P-267 (February 4, 1992).
33 *City of Toronto*, Order M-813 (July 31, 1996).

Chapter 14
ACCESS & PRIVACY

In another appeal based on the provincial legislation, a requester sought access to a variety of documents originating from or received by the tourism minister during a two-year period. In responding to this request, the ministry argued that some of the records in question did not relate to the portfolio of responsibility of the minister of tourism. Rather, they related "to the minister's constituency matters dealing with municipal restructuring which are unrelated to tourism or the powers or duties of the ministry." In light of this observation, it was argued that records generated in the minister's capacity as a member of the provincial legislature were not subject to or identified as records required to be retained by the ministry. After reviewing Order M813 with respect to the constituency records of a municipal councillor, the adjudicator agreed with the ministry submission:

> On a consideration of the factors as a whole, I am satisfied that they support a conclusion that the records in dispute are not "in the custody or under the control" of the ministry. They were not created by its employees or officers in respect of matters within the mandate of the ministry, or to be used by the ministry. Although the ministry has possession of the records, in the sense that the records were stored on its premises, they have not been kept in separate files and have not been integrated with other ministry records. Further, the ministry's records retention policies do not require the ministry to take responsibility for the retention or disposal of these records. While it is possible that none of these facts would be determinative on its own, taken together, they support the position of the ministry in relation to the issue of "care and control."[34]

Despite the indication from these appeals that a document created and held by a municipal councillor (or other elected official) that is a constituency or personal record may be exempt from the statutory access process, it is also important to note that a record so described can also be linked to the corporate business of the council and, therefore, may not be exempt regardless of where the record is physically stored. For example, in a case involving the City of Mississauga, the requester was seeking access to a host of information, especially records regarding grants-in-lieu of taxes levied and received with respect to the Toronto Lester B. Pearson International Airport. With respect to the peculiar fil-

---

34 *Ministry of Citizenship*, Order PO-1947-F (September 13, 2001).

ing of these documents, the adjudicator observed that "records dealing with this subject could reasonably be expected, for the most part, to contain information about the work of city council pertaining to issues beyond the constituency level, and could therefore not be excluded on the basis that they are constituency records." The adjudicator then went on to suggest what may happen if the councillor's personal records were integrated within the municipality's records management system:

> If the councillor's personal papers were integrated into the city's operations, it might be argued that they, too, would be in the custody or under the control of the city, notwithstanding the records policy. However, the city submits that the "personal papers" are maintained by the councillors in "storage areas that are not accessible to employees of the city," which in my view indicates that their personal or constituency papers are not integrated into the operations of the city and cannot be made subject to the Act on that basis.

Finally, the adjudicator went on to make the following finding with regard to this unique situation:

> Accordingly, responsive records in the possession of a councillor may fall within the custody or control of the city, regardless of where they may physically be located in city hall. I will order the city to obtain, from city councillors, the responsive records in their possession that are in the city's custody or control, based on the foregoing analysis, and to prepare a decision letter with respect to access to these records by the appellant.

In November 2001, the IPC, in conjunction with the City of Ottawa, issued a brochure entitled "Working with the Municipal Freedom of Information and Protection of Privacy Act: A Councillor's Guide." In response to the question of whether or not a councillor's own records are accessible under the Act, the guide provides the following qualified answer:

> Councillors' records are considered "personal" records that are not subject to the Act where they are not related to the discharge of the councillor's responsibilities as [a] member of council or to some other aspect of ... council's mandate, and they are not in the custody or control of the [municipality]. A careful analysis of all relevant factors is required.

In discussing the more specific issue of a record's "custody" and/or "control," the guide provides the following words of caution:

> There are no hard and fast rules to decide whether a record is under the "custody or control" of the [municipality or local board] and therefore subject to the Act. Even records relating to constituency matters may be accessible if a consideration of the factors leads to the conclusion that they are in the custody or control of the institution.[35]

Head of Council – Chair of Local Board

In the 1976 case of *Re Simpson and Henderson*,[36] the court clearly stated that where a person holds more than one statutory office, the offices and the records held or developed pursuant to that statutory function do not merge. Each office, and the records of that office, must be regarded as a separate entity despite the fact that the functions are performed by the same person. For example, in Ontario, section 225 of the *Municipal Act, 2001*[37] does reiterate that it is the statutory role of the "head of council" to "act as chief executive officer of the municipality." Unfortunately, as a result of what is perceived as a legislative drafting oversight over a century ago, no specific duties were conferred upon the office of chief executive officer.[38] Thus, there is no clear separation between the functions of:

- municipal council (the perceived responsibility of the office of the head of council); and

- municipal corporation (the perceived responsibility of the office of chief executive officer).[39]

While in normal corporate circumstances such responsibilities would clearly be those of the chief executive officer (and originally were, before 1897), they are now conferred upon the office of head of council.

---

35 Information and Privacy Commissioner/Ontario and the City of Ottawa, "Working with the Municipal Freedom of Information and Protection of Privacy Act: A Councillor's Guide" (November 2001).

36 *Re Simpson and Henderson* (1976), 13 O.R. (2d) 322; 71 D.L.R. (3d) 24; *Municipal World*, August 1976, p. 206.

37 S.O. 2001, c. 25, s. 225.

38 S.O. 1897, c. 223, s. 279.

39 For a discussion on this point, see the *Municipal World* publication *Head of Council*, by M.J. Smither and C.P. Stobo, 20 Question Series, p. 11.

Numerous other statutory references also confer specific responsibilities upon that same office.[40]

The head of council must therefore contend with records that fall into the following three categories:

- personal records (which usually fall outside the ambit of the legislation);
- records that are "in the custody or under the control" of the municipality or local board; and
- records developed and maintained in his or her capacity as head of council and/or chief executive officer of the municipality.

Whether or not the record-holdings of a mayor are different from other members of council was the subject of the appeal previously discussed involving the City of Mississauga. With regard to this particular question, the adjudicator made the following poignant observations in light of the mayor's statutory role:

> Part VI of the [former] *Municipal Act* deals with "officers of the municipal corporation." It begins with section 69 [now clause 225 (a) of the *Municipal Act, 2001*], which describes a mayor as the "head of council and the chief executive officer of the corporation." This in itself indicates that the mayor is an "officer" of the municipality. The inclusion of the term "head of council," which includes a mayor in the description of statutory rights and duties of a municipality's "officers," provides a further indication that, for the purposes of the *Municipal Act*, the mayor of a municipality is to be considered an "officer." Further support for this view is found in section 70 (b), which leads me to the conclusion that a mayor of a municipality is to be considered an "officer."
>
> The city's "Elected Officials' Records Policy," discussed in the preceding section, indicates that it applies to councillors and the mayor. This policy, adopted by council in 1986, predated the Act. In my view, the positions of councillors and the mayor under the Act are different because the mayor is an officer of the municipal corporation, while councillors are not. I find that, because she is an officer of the municipal corporation, the mayor's record-hold-

---

40 For example, see *Municipal Act, 2001*, S.O. 2001, c. 25, ss. 241, 242 and 249.

ings in relation to her duties as mayor form part of the city's records for the purposes of the Act. By contrast, in some circumstances, records of the mayor that do not relate to mayoral duties, and are maintained separately as constituency or personal papers, may not be subject to the Act (see Order P-267).[41]

Therefore, with the exception of personal or constituency records developed in one's capacity as a "member," most other records of the head of council/chief executive officer will likely be subject to the access provisions and protection of privacy requirements of the freedom of information statute.

Policy of the Institution

A records management policy developed by a municipality or local board cannot override any provisions of a provincial statute like the *Municipal Freedom of Information and Protection of Privacy Act*. However, such a document, when carefully prepared, can provide both legal insight and practical guidance to the members of a council or local board on these complex issues.

An excellent example of such a policy, as discussed in Order MO-1403, was that adopted by the City of Mississauga, which is set out in Appendix A to this chapter.[42]

Custody and Control Case Law

While not directly germane to the issue of the obligations of a member, the question of custody and control of other records has been addressed under Ontario's *Municipal Freedom of Information and Protection of Privacy Act*. In many instances, the seminal comments of former Commissioner Sidney B. Linden in Interim Order P-120, cited earlier in this chapter, were regarded.

The following appeal cases provide both practical examples and useful guidance, which may ultimately affect a determination with respect to the issue of whether or not the records of a member, or indeed an institution, should be disclosed pursuant to a freedom of information request.

---

41 *City of Mississauga*, Order MO-1403 (March 1, 2001).

42 Appreciation is extended to Terence L. Julian (former city clerk), City of Mississauga for providing a copy of this policy, which was recommended by former Information and Privacy Commissioner Tom Wright.

Audit records – The Halton Board of Education received a request "for access to all auditor's working papers ... concerning the audit of certain courses offered by the board." Access was denied and the sole issue in this appeal was whether the papers were "records" that were in the custody or under the control of the board.

Having referred to Interim Order P-120, the inquiry officer made reference to the "Generally Accepted Auditing Standards" set out in the *Handbook of the Canadian Institute of Chartered Accountants*. The officer noted that paragraphs 5145.06 and 5145.07 stated:

> The auditor should document matters which in his or her professional opinion are important in providing evidence to support the content of his or her report.
>
> Audit working papers are the property of the auditor.

Submissions were also considered concerning judicial decisions from appellate courts in Canada and the United Kingdom. Many of these held that working papers and other documents brought into existence by chartered accountants in the preparation of a final audit of the client's books are the property of the accountant and not the client. Furthermore, the facts showed that the records sought were in the physical possession of the auditor. Finally, the Institute of Chartered Accountants also submitted that:

> Not only would the auditor be restricted from disclosing information contained in the working papers to third parties, he or she is also responsible for insuring that the client or the client's staff are prevented from obtaining access to these files. The working papers may contain information about auditing procedures, payroll records and independent confirmations that should not be made available to the client or members of the client's staff.

The inquiry officer upheld the board's decision not to release the records.[43]

Psychological report re: suitability for promotion – The Regional Municipality of Halton Police Services Board received a request for access to all rough notes, tests, and any other recorded information used by a psychologist (affected person) to draft a psychological report about the

---

43 *Halton Board of Education*, Order M-152 (June 25, 1993).

suitability of the requester for promotion. The board denied access to the records claiming that they were not in its custody or under its control.

Having regard to the indicia listed in Interim Order P-120, the inquiry officer reviewed the other evidence, which indicated that the affected person administered a number of tests to the candidates and that he also took some notes to serve as an "aide-memoire" to recollect the conversations and interaction that took place during the assessment. The affected person indicated that the records are in his personal possession, located in his office files, and are not integrated with other police records at all. Furthermore, the records did not fall under the police records retention schedule. The board had no legal obligation to be responsible for the creation, storage, maintenance, form or style of the records, nor did it have any legal control over the disposition of the records. The board stated further that they had not relied on the records at all.

The inquiry officer found that the records were neither in the custody, nor under the control of the board.[44]

Private correspondence – Medical Officer of Health – The Simcoe County District Health Unit received a request for all records of the requester's complaint to the College of Physicians and Surgeons of Ontario regarding the testing of drinking water at a particular location. The health unit responded that "the records do not exist in our files." The health unit also indicated that the applicant had already obtained the records from another source.

The applicant confirmed he had already been notified by another source, but the letters received did not contain the enclosures referred to in the relevant correspondence. The assistant commissioner, having weighed the circumstances surrounding the appeal and the relationship between the applicant and the health unit, found them to be somewhat unique. First, the two parties had been involved in a number of appeals involving records similar to the ones at issue in this case. Second, he accepted that, in order for an individual to request that his or her personal information be corrected under the Act, the institution to whom this application is directed must acknowledge that it has custody of the document in question.

---

44 *Regional Municipality of Halton Police Services Board*, Order M-165 (June 21, 1993).

Having referred to the findings in Interim Order P-120 and the duty of a doctor and the health unit to report to the college, the assistant commissioner noted, in particular, that the letters were written on health unit stationery and that the medial officer of health signed them in his official capacity. The contents of the two letters were also evaluated. The assistant commissioner concluded:

> Based on my review of the letters, I am also satisfied that their contents are linked to an important mandate of the health unit under section 11 of the *Health Protection and Promotion Act*, which is to investigate complaints about potential environmental hazards. In short, I find that the nexus which exists between the contents of the letters and the functions of the health unit suggest that these records pertain primarily to the activities of the institution and only secondarily to the MOH in his personal or professional capacity.[45]

Having considered also the grammatical style of the correspondence, the assistant commissioner ordered the health unit to obtain copies of the letters in question and to provide the applicant with a decision letter regarding access to the letters and to the enclosures, which the health unit already had within its custody.

Solicitor's records – The Village of Wellington received a request for access to certain records in the possession of a named solicitor for the municipality concerning a particular corporation, its solicitors or engineers, up to December 31, 1992. The village ultimately took the position that it did not have custody or control of records in the possession of the solicitor.

The inquiry officer observed that, in the circumstances of this appeal, "where the village does not have the actual custody of the records held by the solicitor, the relevant question is whether any responsive records in the custody of the solicitor are under the control of the village." Having referred to Interim Order P-120 in general, and specifically questions 5 and 10, which he considered particularly relevant, the officer stated:

> In my view, records in the custody of the solicitor which are the property of a client may be said to be under the client's control for the purposes of the Act.

---

45 *Simcoe County District Health Unit*, Order M-271 (February 21, 1994).

In this regard, he cited the *Solicitors Act*,[46] the case of *Aggio v. Rosenberg*[47] and then quoted from the text entitled *The Law Relating to Solicitors*[48] to the following effect:

> Documents in existence before the retainer commences and sent to the solicitor by the client or by a third party during the currency of the retainer present no difficulty since their ownership must be readily apparent. The solicitor holds them as agent for and on behalf of the client or third party, and on the termination of the retainer must dispose of them (subject to any lien he may have for unpaid costs ...) as the client or third party may direct.
>
> Documents which only come into existence during the currency of the retainer and for the purpose of business transacted by the solicitor pursuant to the retainer, fall into four broad categories:
>
> > (i) documents prepared by the solicitor for the benefit of the client and which may be said to have been paid for [by] the client, belong to the client;
> >
> > (ii) documents prepared by the solicitor for his own benefit or protection, the preparation of which is not regarded as an item chargeable against the client, belong to the solicitor;
> >
> > (iii) documents sent by the client to the solicitor during the course of the retainer, the property in which was intended at the date of dispatch to pass from the client to the solicitor, eg. letters, belong to the solicitor;
> >
> > (iv) documents prepared by a third party during the course of the retainer and sent to the solicitor (other than at the solicitor's expense), eg. letters, belong to the client.

The inquiry officer found that, based on the evidence presented, the principles enunciated in the *Aggio* case prevailed over the "policy" formulated by the solicitor's firm, in order to determine ownership of the records physically within the solicitor's custody. Ultimately, the officer ordered the village to arrange for a review of the responsive records in

---

46 *Solicitors Act*, R.S.O. 1990, c. S.15, s. 6 (6).

47 *Aggio v. Rosenberg (1981)*, 24 C.P.C. 7.

48 *The Law Relating to Solicitors* (6th edition) by Corderley.

the solicitor's custody to determine which records are under its control, based on the criteria set out in the order.[49]

Cellular phone invoices – The Town of Whitby had received a request for records detailing the cost of the cellular phone used by the town's administrator for the years 1992 and 1993. The municipality provided access to that part of the invoice that showed the total amount billed, but indicated that it did not have custody or control of the detailed listing of the chargeable calls. Applying the approach as set out in Interim Order P-120, the inquiry officer found that the sole issue on appeal was "whether the town [had] custody and control of the records at issue pursuant to subsection 4 (1) of the Act."

In asserting that it never had a right to the records, the town submitted that it considered the detailed listing of chargeable calls to be the personal information of the administrator. As such, the municipal council passed a resolution which provided that the administrator was not required to submit this information to the town. In rejecting this unique argument, the inquiry officer emphasized the voluntary nature of this resolution:

> The resolution passed by the town council is not something the town council was legally required to do, nor is it sufficient to bring information within the definition of personal information for the purposes of the Act, nor is it dispositive of the issue of whether the town has custody or control of the requested records. The town council is able, at any time, to pass another resolution altering or replacing its previous resolution, and is in complete control of whether it chooses to exercise its right to possess the records. Further, I have confirmed that, as the account is in the name of the town, the cellular company would, at the request of the town, provide the town with copies of all invoices previously issued, including the detailed list of chargeable calls. Accordingly, the town's claims that it had no right to possess the records and that the records do not exist are, in my view, without basis in fact.

The officer subsequently found that the municipality had the necessary control over the cell phone records as follows:

---

49 *Village of Wellington*, Order M-371 (August 10, 1994).

The responsible administration of public funds is central to the mandate and function of every public institution and the town has an obligation to properly manage its record holdings in accordance with the intent of the Act. The only limits on the town's custody or control of the requested records have been imposed by the town itself and, accordingly, I find the town does have the requisite degree of control over the records within the meaning of section 4 of the Act.[50]

---

50 *Town of Whitby*, Order M-452 (January 30, 1995).

Appendix A

CITY OF MISSISSAUGA
ELECTED OFFICIALS RECORDS POLICY

The City of Mississauga differentiates between the official civic records of the mayor and councillor and their personal papers. Each type of record will be identified and dealt with as follows:

Official civic records consist of administrative records generated by the mayor's and councillors' offices and as such are to be inventoried and scheduled for disposal according to the records retention by-law. These records include:

- records regarding assignment of office space;
- the provision of supplies, equipment and services;
- the hiring of staff;
- records used in determining organization charts and policy statements;
- records used in explaining operating procedures or functions such as procedures manuals;
- reports prepared for inclusion in committee meeting files.

Personal papers are not considered official records and as such may be dealt with by each individual as she/he so desires. These records include:

- constituency and subject files;
- their own records on any committee or board.

While in office, if the elected official so desires, she/he may store personal records in the Municipal Inactive Records Storage Facility but the retention and disposition of these records will not be legislated.

Appendix A

Upon leaving office, personal records qualify for consideration for federal tax credits through the *Income Tax Act* if the elected official chooses to donate their records to the Region of Peel Archives. The intent to donate personal records to the Region of Peel Archives should be made known to the records manager, who will review the records, and arrange for an appraisal by the regional archivist. The regional archivist will then make arrangements for the tax credits based upon the value of the records. In the event that a second appraisal is required, all costs incurred for the appraisal will be the responsibility of the elected official.

City of Mississauga Recommendation 202-86, Administration and Finance Committee, adopted by council on February 10, 1986.

Chapter 15
PUBLIC ACCOUNTABILITY PUZZLE

> *Accountability, in its simplest terms, is the obligation to answer for a responsibility that has been conferred.*
>
> Report of the Independent Review Committee on
> The Office of the Auditor General of Canada (1975)

To describe the current plight of local government in Canada as being in a continuous state of change is not exactly making an observation of earth-shattering proportions. For most of those familiar with the municipal scene, it is merely stating the obvious. During the course of the last two decades, municipalities and local boards have been subjected to a host of alterations, modifications and innovations.

These have included vast mergers and amalgamations; significant provincial downloading (often alleged to be "revenue-neutral"); increased demands for various services; and new, modern enabling legislation with some novel approaches as to how local governments may now operate.

Putting the Pieces Together

All of these changes and challenges have occurred amidst the lament for more "open local government" – the broad theme of this book. But, precisely which key pieces to the public accountability puzzle is that phrase meant to encompass, and how can municipalities and local boards across Canada hope to identify and then meet such expectations?

As expressed succinctly in the quotation that opened this chapter, "accountability" in local government vernacular can simply be defined as "the obligation to answer for a responsibility that has been conferred" either on a municipal council or a local board. In essence, public accountability is a concept fundamental to our democratic system of local government. In its most rudimentary state, "accountability" requires municipal councils and local boards to publicly step forward and assume responsibility for the decisions that they have made.

It is arguable that such public accountability is capable of producing several positive results, including:

- ensuring that local government bodies and officials are answerable to the public for their policies, actions and expenditures; and
- promoting increased public awareness and involvement in the local government decision-making process.

Having said that, it is important to recognize that the underlying intent of such eloquent observations can be effectively captured in the age-old axiom: "Public business is the public's business!" But, are these issues concerning openness and accountability really relevant to local governments in Canada today? Perhaps a review from a non-governmental point of view would help put such matters in context.

Toronto Board of Trade Report

In September 2003, the Toronto Board of Trade released its Final Report of the City Governance Task Force entitled "Responsible and Representative: Better Governance for Toronto."[1] Among the six guiding principles that the board identified as necessary in order to "build the foundation for good municipal government" in Toronto were the concepts of "transparency" and "accountability." The report's comments with respect to transparency were as follows:

> As a matter of course, all formal matters of this municipality are handled in an open and transparent manner. The only exceptions are based on respect for the right of privacy for individuals and business in matters of labour relations/personnel, litigation, security of municipal property and real estate. The city's processes, procedures and behaviours support information sharing, open communication and easy interaction among all stakeholders. The decision-making processes contribute to transparency and trust by engaging citizens early, and by supporting a sharing of accurate and sufficient information.
>
> For example, this means:

---

1 Toronto Board of Trade, "Responsible and Representative: Better Governance for Toronto," Final Report of the City Governance Task Force (September 2003).

- Citizens readily access information on the decision-making process, on the issues being considered and on how they can participate.
- The decision-making process and final conclusions are subject to public scrutiny.
- There are processes to facilitate efficient, timely decision making.

In a similar fashion, the board's practical analysis of "accountability" as a key principle of municipal governance is also worth repeating:

> Elected officials are publicly accountable for decisions made and actions taken. Similarly, city administrative staff are responsible for executing those decisions and fulfilling their duties. Elected officials and staff work in partnership to achieve the city's strategic vision. There is an adherence to a set of objectives that reflect the strategic vision.
>
> Elected officials and staff commit to high ethical standards as well as professional and personal integrity. Performance of both elected officials and staff on meeting the goals of the strategic plan is measured. Decisions are reached through the appropriate procedures, and in accordance with set rules and regulations.

For example, this means:

- Elected officials meet standards set for accountability.
- Elected officials execute decisions in a timely, cost-effective and responsible manner.
- Once decisions are made, there are consequences for inaction.
- There is an appropriate delegation of responsibilities between elected officials and staff.
- There is regular and transparent reporting on the performance of elected officials and staff in meeting the objectives of the strategic plan.

- There is adherence to the objectives set out in that strategic plan.
- There is a public record of decisions made by elected officials.
- There are measures to assess service delivery.
- Agencies, boards and commissions are accountable to elected officials.
- A code of conduct exists for both elected officials and staff.
- There are consequences for unethical behaviour.[2]

The report's analysis not only acknowledged that the principles identified are "interconnected and reinforce one another," but also observed, rather ominously, that "a weakness in one will undermine the success of all." It should come as no surprise that one-third of the Toronto Board of Trade's formula to foster responsible and respectable decision making in Canada's largest municipality encompasses the principles of openness (i.e. transparency) and accountability.

However, many municipalities and local boards have embraced these fundamental concepts in order to complete the public accountability puzzle. A review of three key pieces to the public accountability puzzle is appropriate. These are principles that members of local government in Canada should be familiar with, either by provincial statutes or their own policies.

Open vs. Closed Meetings

One of the cornerstones of the ideological foundation for accountable local government is the important concept of "transparency." As discussed in Chapter 2, Open vs. Closed Meetings, the rights of a person to attend a municipal council meeting were interpreted in a restricted fashion at common law such that no legal rights would exist, save and except those set out in the legislation. In effect, constituents or members of the media had no legal right to attend and listen to the deliberations of a municipal council or local board. Therefore, the public was often deprived

---

2   *Ibid.*, at p. 20; along with transparency and accountability, the other four principles identified were: leadership; city-wide focus; civic engagement; and citizen-focused, sound management.

of an essential component of the local government decision-making process.

It was not until 1984, with the publication of the "Provincial/Municipal Working Committee's Report on Open Meetings and Access to Information," that things began to change in Ontario. The committee noted that some municipal councils often met at *in camera* meetings, thereby shielding the public from their various discussions and debates. While recognizing that this approach met the "letter of the *Municipal Act*" at that time, the committee went on to indicate that this practice was "not in accord with the growing demand for public knowledge of and input into municipal decisions."

The desire for increased access to the local government decision-making process was also an issue addressed in the courts from time to time. For example, recall the judicial comments on the decision with respect to the 1988 "workshop" held in Hamilton-Wentworth and in the case concerning a council "retreat" at a ski lodge outside of Ottawa in 1991. In light of this background, significant amendments were made to Ontario's *Municipal Act*. Effective January 1, 1995, the legislation stipulated that all meetings, including any regular, special, committee or other meeting of a council or local board shall be open to the public. In addition, the Act established one mandatory and seven discretionary exceptions to the general rule for open meetings. Each of these statutory exemptions is based on the particular subject-matter being considered by the local government body.

However, anecdotal evidence would suggest that these statutory changes have not been consistently applied by municipal councils and local boards across Ontario. While most local government bodies adhere to the open and closed meeting provisions of the *Municipal Act*, various newspaper stories and some case law indicate that a trend in favour of *in camera* meetings persists in some areas.[3] To that end, various options have been contemplated with respect to making the open meeting provisions even more effective. For example, on December 15, 1999, Mr. Brad Clark, MPP for Stoney Creek, rose in the provincial leg-

---

3 See for example Joanne Peach, "Has Democracy Been Hung Out to Dry? How much is too much when politicians take their meetings behind closed doors?" *Woolwich Observer*, July 27, 2002, p. 12.

islature and provided the following comments with respect to the *Fewer Municipal Politicians Act, 1999:*

> If we want to talk about accountability, I have some suggestions on how we put accountability back into municipal government. How about doing like the State of Michigan and enacting an open meetings rule, an Act for open meetings, whereby if any public body, any municipal council, does not adhere to the *in camera* rules and closes the doors to the public on any issue illegally, each individual councillor who participated can be fined? In Michigan, it's a $1,000 fine for the first offence; second offence, $2,000 and/or 12 months in jail. They don't have problems with *in camera*, illegal meetings. Why don't we do that to bring in accountability?[4]

This same issue found its way into the 2002 Annual Report of Ontario's Information and Privacy Commissioner, Ann Cavoukian. One of the two major issues highlighted in the press release was the commissioner's call for a new "open meetings law" for local government in Ontario. After observing that the *Municipal Act* established a series of rules by which municipal governments would conduct business, aimed at "the policy objective of open and transparent decision making," the IPC Annual Report goes on to state, "we have some concerns that they may not go far enough in addressing public expectations."[5] Drawing on various examples from the U.S., the report emphasized that "open meetings laws and FOI laws are often seen as complementary components of the broader system of public accountability." Briefly, the IPC set out four basic elements that a comprehensive and effective open meetings law should have. In effect, such a statute must:

- impose obligations on public bodies to ensure that meetings are open to the public and that people are given proper and adequate advance notice;

- provide members of the public with a right to complain if they feel that open meetings rules have not been followed;

---

[4] Legislative Assembly of Ontario, *Official Report of Debates (Hansard)*, December 15, 1999.

[5] IPC Annual Report 2002 (June 2003) at p. 5.

- establish an efficient and accessible oversight body that can investigate complaints and resolve disputes; and

- provide remedies and penalties if the law has been breached.

With respect to the "efficient and accessible oversight body" to investigate complaints under such a piece of legislation, the commissioner eschews lengthy and costly court proceedings, and points out that "in U.S. jurisdictions that have a Freedom of Information Commission, that body is given oversight responsibility for both FOI and open meetings laws. That's a model that may make sense here in Ontario, as well."

Less than a week after the 2002 IPC Annual Report was issued, a private member's bill on the subject of open meetings was introduced into the Ontario Legislature. On June 17, 2003, Bill 106 – the *Transparency in Public Matters Act, 2003* – was brought forward by Carolyne DiCocco, MPP for Sarnia-Lambton. Upon introducing this draft legislation, DiCocco referenced the IPC's 2002 Annual Report:

> I introduced this same bill in 2001 and 2002. This open meeting Act is needed, according to the latest report of the Privacy Commissioner. The bill requires specific provincial and municipal councils, boards, commissions and other public bodies to hold meetings which are open to the public. The public can only be excluded from meetings of the body when certain specified types of matters are going to be discussed. Minutes of the meeting open to the public have to be made available to the public in a timely fashion and must contain sufficient detail. Section 8 imposes a penalty for failure to comply with the requirements for notice, minutes and rules.[6]

Finally, in October 2003, the IPC issued a follow-up report to its earlier open meetings recommendations, entitled "Making Municipal Government More Accountable: The Need for an Open Meetings Law in Ontario." The report urges the Ontario Government to introduce "a comprehensive open meetings law" that would apply to municipal governments:

> Ontario needs a tough new municipal open meetings law to ensure government actions are open and transparent. The *Municipal Act*

---

6 Legislative Assembly of Ontario, *Official Report of Debates (Hansard)*, June 17, 2003.

does not go far enough. It does require, with limited exceptions, that councils and boards conduct their business at open meetings where the public can attend and observe the debate. However, accessible, transparent government goes far beyond opening the doors to a meeting.

The broader objective of transparency is to ensure that citizens understand how decisions are made and have an opportunity to participate in the decision-making process. To be truly effective, we need a law that will encourage integrity in our municipal governments and help ensure that elected and appointed municipal officials are operating in the public interest.[7]

Obviously, this renewed concern for increased transparency in the decision-making process of local governments is an ongoing issue in Ontario, and likely elsewhere in Canada.

Members' Conduct

If one accepts the veracity of the old expression that "perception is reality in politics," then members of municipal councils and local boards are likely to be viewed in a suspicious manner, much like Caesar's wife. In essence, they must not only conduct themselves in an open and ethical fashion, but they must also "appear" to be doing so.

Many readers of the first edition of this book will recall that its publication in 1995 coincided with the implementation of many substantive changes to the former *Municipal Act*, as well as the proposed introduction of the *Local Government Disclosure of Interest Act* in Ontario. In April 2000, the Ontario Legislature narrowly passed a motion requesting that the government proclaim the latter Act in force. That statute – which was never proclaimed in effect – was based primarily on the principles found in the provincial *Members' Integrity Act,* and was subsequently repealed effective January 1, 2003, leaving only the *Municipal Conflict of Interest Act, 1983* as the fundamental code of conduct for local government officials in Ontario.

In addition to this legislated code of conduct, elected or appointed members of councils or local boards are also obligated at common law to "keep an open mind" when considering any matters before them. Fur-

---

7 Ann Cavoukian and Tom Mitchinson, "Making Municipal Government More Accountable: The Need for an Open Meetings Law in Ontario" (October 2003).

thermore, they should be well acquainted with and adhere to the relevant provisions of the Criminal Code of Canada, including the municipal corruption and breach of trust sections. Local government entities may also be interested in developing their own codes of conduct for members, in order to better ensure that their actions satisfactorily reflect both the legal requirements and the public's perception that they are performing their duties in an open and accountable manner.

As with the potential for new open meeting legislation, there have been efforts on the part of the provincial legislature to resurrect, from time to time, concerns about an apparent lack of accountability in the arena of local government. These concerns often harken back to the fact that MPPs in Ontario have seemingly stricter guidelines with respect to integrity and accountability issues.

Most recently, on June 5, 2003, David Christopherson, MPP for Hamilton West, moved a motion that "in the opinion of this House, the Government of Ontario should support the principle of greater accountability for politicians at the municipal level and consult with the Association of Municipalities of Ontario and municipalities on how municipal politicians can be subject to the similar legislated requirements of public disclosure, accountability, and independent investigation with which all members of the Legislative Assembly and executive council currently comply." After 10 other MPPs spoke in support of this motion, it was unanimously passed by the provincial legislature.[8] Taken in conjunction with the City of Toronto's efforts to establish an "arms-length integrity commissioner," as well as the testimony from the judicial inquiries involving MFP Financial Services, it is not difficult to foresee change in this particular area.

FOI vs. Privacy

Not surprisingly, the third main theme of this book with respect to achieving a more open and accountable local government has focused on the balancing act between providing greater access to information held by local governments, versus their responsibility to protect individual privacy with regard to such information. Upon introducing the *Freedom of Information and Protection of Privacy Act* into the provincial legislature, former Attorney General Ian Scott made the following

---

8   Legislative Assembly of Ontario, *Official Report of Debates (Hansard)*, June 5, 2003.

comments with respect to this legislation being an important component of the public accountability puzzle:

> When there is true openness in government, we will have a society that is trustful of its government, not fearful of it. We will have a society that is enlightened by information and able to make thoughtful choices as to the future shape of our society.[9]

Described as an "interesting balancing routine," the purpose of the *Municipal Freedom of Information and Protection of Privacy Act* has clearly been to balance the public's right to know and access various information held by local governments with an individual person's right to have their privacy protected with respect to such requests. As well-known figures who consider and debate public policy issues in an open forum, members of municipal councils and local boards often also deal with issues raised by individual constituents in their community. Therefore, councillors and local board members must be vigilant of the ramifications of handling and maintaining all forms of information that come within their purview.

Some Final Thoughts

Whether in the midst of a heated election campaign, or merely seated at a late night meeting, many councillors or local board members want to be featured by the media in order to show to their constituents that they are hard at work. Ironically, one of the easiest ways to guarantee local and occasionally national media exposure is for a councillor or a local board member to demonstrate, by their daily actions, that they are not accountable to the public and that they do not favour increased transparency in local government.

The purpose of this final section, offered in a rather tongue-in-cheek fashion, is to identify the top four ways that councillors and board members can attain such notoriety:

1. Whenever possible, forego any orientation opportunities with regard to such issues as open/closed meetings, conflicts of interest or FOI matters.

    This "know-it-all" approach will not only free up valuable time for councillors and members of local boards, it

---

9 Legislative Assembly of Ontario, *Official Report of Debates (Hansard)*, July 12, 1985.

will also provide them with the opportunity to repeat the following phrase with a feigned look of puzzlement on their face: "Really? I did not know that." Furthermore, isn't it time that some brave and litigious soul took another try at overturning that ancient, legal maxim, "Ignorance of the law is no excuse"?

2. Ignore any and all concerns (by either the media, community groups or even individual members of the public) that allege your local government body is not sufficiently open or accountable.

Simply put, if you don't recognize a potential problem, you don't have to expend any efforts to either investigate or respond to it. After all, who is going to remember such insignificant allegations when the next municipal election rolls around? Remember, hear no evil, see no evil.

3. Never bother to seek a professional opinion or assistance from either your senior staff or those outside your local government (i.e. lawyer, auditor, FOI Coordinator, the Provincial Integrity Commissioner or the Information and Privacy Commissioner, etc.) regarding those pesky "grey" areas in any provincial laws concerning accountability.

As anyone associated with local governments in Canada will tell you, seeking the opinion of a lawyer, or any other professional, will likely cost money that your municipality or local board does not have. In any event, if you do seek such professional advice, there is the possibility that another member may wish to follow it, and that leads down the dangerous path of knowledge being a bad thing as expressed in No. 1 above.

4. Refuse to consider the consequences that could result in the face of an unresolved accountability issue, including allegations about an improperly closed meeting, a potential conflict of interest/bias situation or a possible violation of the respective freedom of information legislation.

Why even consider such trivial matters unless someone is challenging your local government, either before a quasi-judicial board or in the courts? We already know

> that no lawyer wants to take on a defendant with pockets as deep as a local government entity – or do they?

Obviously, the comments above are meant to bring a wry, knowing grin as you complete this book. Hopefully, as you resume your duties with either your municipality, local board or other public sector entity, you'll have a chance to share with your colleagues some new insights on your own, open local government.

About the Author

A graduate of the University of Ottawa, Faculty of Law (1987), Rick O'Connor became a solicitor with the former Region of Ottawa-Carleton where he practiced in the areas of municipal, labour and employment law, as well as administrative litigation, since his 1989 call to the Bar in Ontario. With the amalgamation of the City of Ottawa in 2001, he was appointed Deputy City Clerk while retaining the title of Legal Counsel.

As a community volunteer, he was previously Vice-Chair of a Committee of Adjustment, Chair of a Property Standards Committee and Secretary Treasurer of the Ottawa Children's Aid Society's Board of Directors. In addition, he has been a member of various municipal and provincial task forces on local government, including the Association of Municipalities of Ontario's Fiscal and Labour Policy Committee (1996-1997) and the Legislative Committee for the Association of Municipal Managers, Clerks and Treasurers of Ontario (2002-2004).

The author of numerous legal articles, as well as being a regular speaker to various municipal organizations, Rick co-authored *Conduct Handbook for Municipal Employees and Officials* (2nd ed., 2003) and is Editor-in-Chief of the bi-monthly national newsletter, *Municipal Liability Risk Management*.

Other publications from Municipal World

For further information, or to order any of the following Municipal World publications, contact us at: mwadmin@municipalworld.com, or telephone 519-633-0031 (toll free 1-888-368-6125).

Advice to Ratepayers (Smither) – Item 0030

By-law and Question Voting Law – Item 1288

Candidates and Electors – Item 1219

Deputy Returning Officers Handbook – Item 1280

Electing Better Politicians: A Citizen's Guide (Bens) – Item 0068

How to Campaign for Municipal Elected Office (Smither/Bolton) – Item 1284

Making a Difference: Cuff's Guide for Municipal Leaders (Cuff) – Item 0059

Measuring Up: An Evaluation Toolkit for Local Governments (Bens) – Item 0061

Media and Local Government (Smither) – Item 0040

Municipal Election Law – Item 1278

Ontario's Municipal Act - codified consolidation – Item 0010

Public Sector Performance Measurement: Successful Strategies and Tools (Bens) – Item 0060

Run and Win in Local Government (Clarke) – Item 0020